About Access Archaeology

Access Archaeology offers a different publishing model for specialist academic material that might traditionally prove commercially unviable, perhaps due to its sheer extent or volume of colour content, or simply due to its relatively niche field of interest. This could apply, for example, to a PhD dissertation or a catalogue of archaeological data.

All *Access Archaeology* publications are available in open-access e-pdf format and in print format. The open-access model supports dissemination in areas of the world where budgets are more severely limited, and also allows individual academics from all over the world the opportunity to access the material privately, rather than relying solely on their university or public library. Print copies, nevertheless, remain available to individuals and institutions who need or prefer them.

The material is refereed and/or peer reviewed. Copy-editing takes place prior to submission of the work for publication and is the responsibility of the author. Academics who are able to supply print-ready material are not charged any fee to publish (including making the material available in open-access). In some instances the material is type-set in-house and in these cases a small charge is passed on for layout work.

Our principal effort goes into promoting the material, both in open-access and print, where *Access Archaeology* books get the same level of attention as all of our publications which are marketed through e-alerts, print catalogues, displays at academic conferences, and are supported by professional distribution worldwide.

Open-access allows for greater dissemination of academic work than traditional print models could ever hope to support. It is common for an open-access e-pdf to be downloaded hundreds or sometimes thousands of times when it first appears on our website. Print sales of such specialist material would take years to match this figure, if indeed they ever would.

This model may well evolve over time, but its ambition will always remain to publish archaeological material that would prove commercially unviable in traditional publishing models, without passing the expense on to the academic (author or reader).

Digital Imaging of Artefacts: Developments in Methods and Aims

edited by

Kate Kelley and Rachel K. L. Wood

Access Archaeology

ARCHAEOPRESS PUBLISHING LTD
Summertown Pavilion
18-24 Middle Way
Summertown
Oxford OX2 7LG

www.archaeopress.com

ISBN 978-1-78969-025-5
ISBN 978-1-78969-026-2 (e-Pdf)

Cover image courtesy of Alison Pollard and Artas Media.

This book is available direct from Archaeopress or from our website www.archaeopress.com

Foreword

Jacob L. Dahl

In a recent article in *Scientific American*, David Pogue discusses the fight against 'file format rot' (D. Pogue, 'How to Fight Format Rot', *Scientific American*, November 1, 2017). Pogue begins his article with a story about how his own digital sheet-music files had fallen victim to file format rot and bases the remainder of the article around a discussion with staff from the Library of Congress, an institution where file format rot could have more serious consequences than for most of us. Unsurprisingly, the Library of Congress has been a leader in digitisation of collections for two decades. Somewhat offhandedly, Pogue mentions the dramatic increase in capture resolution over the past two decades. Consequently, the digitisation of the Library of Congress collections is never finished: the files have to be continuously re-formatted to prevent format rot, and the original documents have to be continuously re-imaged with new and improved technology. Although one of the ultimate goals of digitising heritage collections is to reduce handling, we should therefore not expect that one round of digitisation will ever be enough—rather we should expect to produce generations of images, documenting the objects in increasingly better quality, but also any change over time.

My own knowledge of cultural heritage imaging comes from years of imaging cuneiform tablets and cylinder seals, and the observations of this introduction are almost entirely derived from my work in this area over the past two decades, and from my association with the Cuneiform Digital Library Initiative (CDLI, https://cdli.ucla.edu). The CDLI is without question the world's leading online project for cuneiform studies, serving a catalogue with more than 330,000 records and large amounts of meta-data such as well-structured transcriptions of more than 100,000 of these ancient texts, as well as various generations and types of visual documentation. Like the Library of Congress, we have also experienced an almost exponential growth in the possible capture resolution concurrently with a reduced cost of storage, yet we have resisted the temptation to increase our general capture resolution (600 ppi, serving only 300 ppi images online). There are two particular reasons for this. Obviously, cuneiform studies are not as well funded as an institution such as Library of Congress and never will be: increasing capture resolution leads to an increase in capture time and costs. But more importantly, perhaps, all of our objects originate from countries in the Middle East where access to the Internet is still lagging behind that which can be expected on campuses in other parts of the world, and increased file size will therefore lead to reduced access to these objects in the countries of origin.

But there is another, more crucial, reason for continuing to image everything first with simple techniques and at a relatively low resolution. In order to get an overview of a cuneiform tablet collection (and some are very large, such as the British Museum with more than 100,000 tablets), speed is of the essence. Capturing most collections at the same resolution also makes data management an easier task. Consider having to recover data after any emergency if your core data consists of thousands of tiny JPEGs used to deliver a non-static image in tiles (the standard delivery method for Reflectance Transformation Imaging data, e.g. https://cdli.ucla.edu/?q=rti-images). An overview of collections also enables us to answer different research questions and to fully integrate the study of text and artefact. And in the end, any image is better than no image. We need only remind ourselves of the most recent destruction of cultural heritage in the Middle East to conclude that whatever can be done to capture the form and content of cuneiform tablets and other artefacts should be done.

Insisting on such simple standards does not mean that we have neglected any investigation or use of other novel capture technologies. About 10 years ago, I enthusiastically joined an Oxford-Southampton collaborative project led by Graeme Earl to build and test several camera dome systems for Reflectance Transformation Imaging (RTI) and to increase use and awareness of these systems in Oxford, Southampton, and beyond. Following some initial difficulties, especially how to share the results of dome captures online, we eventually co-opted this technology to target specific objects within a given collection. We therefore decided on a pragmatic approach to capturing these endangered collections. We insist on initially imaging all collections with the same technique (flatbed scanners) and the same resolution to gain an overview of the collection and to be able to quickly present collections online. We then use this overview to identify those objects that we deem important to capture with specialist equipment. This choice is made on a number of criteria. Is the object unique? Is it a high-impact object? Is the text deciphered? Is the text difficult to read and/or the object deteriorating? Is the object sealed? Usually, about one-fifth of a collection needs special attention, whereas the other four fifths can be imaged using standard equipment.

Whereas we had thus overcome the problems of imaging seal impressions by using RTI, the physical seals themselves remained very difficult to digitize. The most common Mesopotamian seal found impressed on cuneiform tablets, and therefore of particular interest to us, is the cylinder seal. These tiny cylindrical seals, engraved in intaglio on stones with a great variety of visual grain, are notoriously difficult to image. In modern publications, they are traditionally rolled in plasticine or a similar product and a black-and-white photo of the impression is reproduced. The paper by Dahl et al. (pp. 47-72) describes in detail the work we have undertaken to capture a fuller representation of cylinder seals. This work has the potential to revolutionise the study of cylinder seals, and with it the study of ancient Near Eastern art and iconography, and of ancient Near Eastern administration. To date, no unifying catalogue of cylinder seals exists, and no-one knows how many seals there are in collections worldwide. Instead, individual collections, often with very idiosyncratic collecting histories, have been published with little regard to the implications for wider study of cylinder seals. Being in its infancy, imaging cylinder seals will therefore surely lead to generations of images, and the constant need to update formats to avert format rot. But that is not a problem, as we must expect technology to progress and new research questions to be asked.

Drs Kelley and Wood assembled an exciting group of scholars for what was first thought of as an informal gathering, but which quickly developed into an important, albeit brief, workshop on current trends in imaging of ancient artefacts. A healthy mix of historians, engineers, and curators contributed to the success of the workshop. It is my view that it is exactly when we are able to bring together specialists from different disciplines that we make progress in the digital humanities, as well as in traditional humanities disciplines. It is a testimony to this that all of the papers here engage with humanities research questions, while exploring new methods to answer them.

Acknowledgements

The workshop that forms the basis of this volume would not have been possible without the financial support of Wolfson College's Academic Research Fund and Digital Research Cluster. We are particularly indebted to Prof. David Robey of the Digital Research Cluster for his enthusiasm in the formative stages of the project. The editors also wish to thank the funding bodies whose support gave them the opportunity to organize the event and the time to work on the preparation and editing of the volume: the John Fell Fund made possible the work of *Seals and their Impressions in the Ancient Near East* research project (2016–2017) at the University of Oxford, and the Leverhulme Trust sponsored the British Museum and University of Oxford research project *Empires of Faith* (2013–2018).

Our warmest thanks go to all the contributors to the workshop and the volume for their dedication and energy in engaging in this venture and sharing their work and experiences, and to all those who came to the workshop and participated in the discussion, especially Elena Draghici-Vasilescu and Jamie Cameron.

We would like to extend special thanks for the encouragement and support of the principal investigators of *SIANE* and *Empires of Faith*, Profs Jacob Dahl and Jaś Elsner, respectively, as well as that of our colleagues at the British Museum and the University of Oxford. We are also grateful to the participation of Wolfson College's Ancient World Research Cluster in the workshop, and for their continuing fellowship and community. Particular thanks are due to Louise Gordon and the Wolfson College Events Office for facilitating such a productive event, and for being extremely flexible when faced with an ever-expanding number of participants.

We are grateful to David Davison and Ben Heaney at Archaeopress for the production of this book, and to all those who granted permission for images, which are crucial for a subject such as this. We would also like to thank J. D. Hill and the British Museum for their support in the publication of this volume. Finally, we would like to make an additional thank you to all the host institutions of the artefacts under study for supporting and making welcome the various projects represented in the following pages.

Kate Kelley & Rachel Wood, October 2018.

Contributors

Editors

Dr Kate Kelley received her Doctorate of Philosophy in Assyriology from the University of Oxford in 2018 and is a specialist in the socio-economic history of early Mesopotamia. She is a Postdoctoral Fellow at the University of British Columbia (2018–19), and formerly a Research Associate at the Oriental Institute, Oxford for the project Seals and Their Impressions in the Ancient Near East (2016–17). Kate has been working for the Cuneiform Digital Library Initiative since 2012, including digitizing cuneiform tablets in the Louvre, the National Museum of Scotland, and the Yale Babylonian Collection.

Dr Rachel K. L. Wood is Lecturer in Classical Archaeology at Corpus Christi College, Oxford and a Junior Research Fellow at Wolfson College, Oxford, specialising in the art and archaeology of ancient Iran. In her previous position as a postdoctoral researcher with the British Museum and University of Oxford project *Empires of Faith,* she was an assistant curator of the Ashmolean Museum's exhibition *Imagining the Divine: art and the rise of world religions* (October 2017–February 2018).

Contributors

Juan Aguilar received a BA in Assyriology and Religious Studies from Heidelberg University and a Master's degree in Anthropology of the Americas at the University of Bonn. During his training as an archaeologist, he has excavated in Germany, Syria and Iraq, and later specialised in excavation photography, photogrammetry and drone mapping, working for projects in Iraq, Mexico, and Nicaragua. In addition to his studies, he has been active as an independent filmmaker and has completed two feature-length documentary film projects, *A Better Road* on Tibetan nomad people, and *Scanning The End* on laser scanning an ancient Maya city, together with one fictional short film entitled *Override.* He is currently working on the 'Rock Art of Iraqi Kurdistan Project' by Heidelberg University.

Professor Jacob Dahl is a specialist of the pre-Classical cultures and languages of the Near East at Oxford University. He has written on early Babylonian socio-economic history, early Near Eastern writing systems, and Sumerian literature. He works on the decipherment of proto-Elamite, the last undeciphered writing system from the ancient Near East with a substantial number of sources (more than 1600 tablets divided between the Louvre Museum and the National Museum of Iran). As a co-PI of the Cuneiform Digital Library Initiative, Dahl seeks to document and safeguard Mesopotamia's contribution to our shared world history by making the ancient records available freely online.

Steven Dey founded ThinkSee3D Ltd, a professional 3D studio near Oxford specialising in applying 3D technologies to natural and cultural heritage projects for museums and university researchers. Steven has produced hundreds of 3D digital models (using photogrammetry, structured light scanning and CT) and replica 3D physical objects (using colour and high resolution 3D printing) for clients including the British Museum, National Museum Scotland, Birmingham Museums Trust, UCL and the Universities of Oxford, Birmingham, York and Cambridge. A physics graduate from the University of Warwick, Steven went on to invent a collaborative decision software tool (AWARD) that is a UK government standard and was used in the procurement of major venues at the 2012 Olympics.

Dr Alexander Geurds is Associate Professor and Senior Researcher in the School of Archaeology at the University of Oxford and Associate Professor in the Faculty of Archaeology at Leiden University. He also holds a position as Assistant Professor Adjunct at the University of Colorado (Boulder) and served as Academic Director of the Netherlands Research School for Archaeology ARCHON between 2015 and 2018. He has carried out fieldwork in the Netherlands, the Antilles, Mexico and Nicaragua. He is the founding editor of the book series 'The Early Americas: History and Culture'(Brill). He primarily works on the prehistory of Middle and South America, with broader research interests in monumental sculpture, technology, archaeological theory, the contemporary conditions of archaeological fieldwork and the history of archaeology.

Professor Haris Procopiou is Professor of Aegean Archaeology at the University of Paris 1, Panthéon-Sorbonne. She is attached to the National Centre of Scientific Research (CNRS) Laboratory "Archéologie et Sciences de l'Antiquité" (ArScAn, UMR 7041). A specialist in ground stone tools, prehistoric agricultural techniques, and lapidary technologies, she applies use wear and residues analysis. Her recent studies and publications focus on tactile and visual perception of archaeological surfaces and on the role of senses and emotions during craft production. She participates in several archaeological fields in Greece and the Near East and in ethnographic studies in Morocco and Tunisia. She has directed two projects on lapidary crafts and technological transfers in the eastern Mediterranean supported by the French National Agency of Research (ANR). She has directed ethnoarchaeological field studies in Greece and India as also campaigns of experimental archaeology.

Hendrik Hameeuw is a Researcher at the Royal Museums of Art and History in Brussels and a faculty member at the University of Leuven (KU Leuven). He specializes in the application of imaging methods for Ancient Near Eastern artefacts, such as multi-light reflectance, SfM (Structure from Motion) photogrammetry and multispectral imaging.

Dr Jonathon S. Hare is a lecturer in Computer Science at the University of Southampton. He holds a BEng degree in Aerospace Engineering and Ph.D. in Computer Science. His research interests lie in the area of multimedia data mining, analysis and retrieval, with a particular focus on large-scale multimodal approaches. This research area is at the convergence of machine learning and computer vision, but also encompasses other modalities of data. The long-term goal of his research is to innovate techniques that can allow machines to understand the information conveyed by multimedia data and use that information for fulfil the information needs of humans.

David Howell is Head of Heritage Science at Bodleian Libraries. His current research applies imaging and analytical techniques to heritage objects. After a position as Head of Conservation Research for Royal Historic Palaces, he moved to the Bodleian to take up a role as Head of Conservation and Collection Care from 2005 until 2012. In his current role he oversaw the financing and conservation of the Gough Map of Great Britain and the Selden Map of China. David is a Trustee of Icon and The National Heritage Science Forum, and is an accredited conservator.

Professor Jeremy Johns is Director of the Khalili Research Centre and Professor of the Art & Archaeology of the Islamic Mediterranean at the University of Oxford. He is principally interested in the relationship between Islam and Christianity in the medieval Mediterranean as it is manifested in material and visual culture. His research has focused upon the archaeology of the transition from late antiquity to early Islam in the Levant and, especially, upon the archaeology, history, and art history of Sicily under Islamic and Norman rule, from the Muslims' conquest of the island in the 9th century to the destruction of the Islamic community of Sicily by Frederick II in the 13th century. He is also the co-investigator in a project on the reconstruction of the early Islamic rock crystal, 9-12th century AD (supported by Ranros Universal SA).

Professor Kirk Martinez is a specialist in Electronics and Computer Science at the University of Southampton. His imaging and image processing research includes the VASARI and MARC projects on high resolution colorimetric imaging. In the EU Viseum project a new system was designed to allow web browsers to view high resolution images (which became IIPimage). He founded the VIPS image processing library and has developed ten RTI imaging systems. He is also active in wireless environmental sensor networks.

Fiona McKendrick received a BA in Archaeology and Anthropology from the University of Oxford and now works at the Ashmolean Museum, Oxford, managing and distributing images and 3D models of museum objects, and integrating the technology into digital collections online, education, and public engagement. Previously, she served as the Education and Outreach Officer for the Institute for Digital Archaeology and has carried out fieldwork in the UK, Italy, and Canada. Her research interests include museum technology, digital archaeology, digitization, and heritage visualisation as an interpretive lens.

Dr Elise Morero is a postdoctoral researcher at the Khalili Research Centre for the Art and Material Culture of the Middle East (University of Oxford). As an archaeologist, specialising in the analysis and reconstruction of ancient manufacturing techniques, her research focuses on lapidary craftsmanship, using a multidisciplinary approach (archaeological and ethnoarchaeological data, experimental reconstruction of ancient techniques, traceological and tribological analyses). Her work integrates diverse periods and regions from the stone vase industry in the eastern Mediterranean world during the Bronze Age (3rd - 2nd millenniums BC) to to the Mughal jade industry (17-18th century AD). She is co-investigator of the project on the reconstruction of the early Islamic rock crystal vessel production, 9-12th centuries AD (supported by Ranros Universal SA), and for a research program on the reuse of hard-stone spolia in Sicily under the Norman and Hohenstaufen rulers, 12-13th century AD (supported by the Gerda Henkel Stiftung and the John Fell Fund).

Dr Alison Pollard is the Principal Investigator of a multispectral imaging and 3D scanning project on the Greek and Roman sculptures and inscriptions of the Arundel Collection in the Ashmolean Museum in Oxford. She was Project Curator for the redevelopment of the Arundel Collection and Randolph Sculpture Gallery, and is now Assistant Curator in the Department of Antiquities at the Ashmolean. Alison is Lecturer in Classical Archaeology at St John's College, Oxford, specialising in the art and archaeology of ancient Greece and Rome.

Dr Roberto Vargiolu is a researcher in tribology at the Laboratoire de Tribologie et de Dynamique des Systèmes of the École Centrale de Lyon (University of Lyon, CNRS). Specialising in methods of wear process analysis applied to humanities, especially archaeology and the history of technology, he is co-investigator of many international multidisciplinary projects in collaboration with archaeologists, historians, and museums such as the British Museum and the Louvre. He is also committed to the development of educational projects inspired by his scientific research projects. He has thus produced comic books and public performances for children explaining the multidisciplinary of scientific research, the role of tribology and ancient technology.

Dr David Young completed his PhD in geophysics at Cambridge University. As Research Associate at Edinburgh University (1980-85), he worked on human visual perception and motor control. At Sussex University (1985-2010), he taught many areas of computer science, while researching computer vision and artificial intelligence, concentrating on image motion and retinal image representations. He has continued working on digital image analysis at Southampton University, looking at time-lapse imagery of rivers for flow monitoring and deep learning applied to aerial imagery.

Professor Hassan Zahouani teaches mechanics and tribology of surfaces at the École National d'Ingénieurs in Saint-Étienne. He is director of the Centre of Bioengineering and the research team Mechanics of Materials and Processes at the Laboratoire de Tribologie et de Dynamique des Systèmes of the École Centrale de Lyon (University of Lyon, CNRS). He is also President of the French Society of Bioengineering and Imaging. Beside bioengineering, his research has mainly focused on analyses of use-wear mechanisms and the development of new methods of surface analysis, employed in several international multi-partners and multidisciplinary projects in co-direction with archaeologists and museums. He is at the originator of eight patents concerning the engineering of human skin and is President of the humanitarian association *Treatment of the Eyes and Skin* for the rural population in Morocco.

Contents

Introduction

Kate Kelley and Rachel K. L. Wood

This volume brings together new lines of research across a range of disciplines from participants in a workshop held at Wolfson College, Oxford, on 23rd May 2017. In light of rapid technological developments in digital imaging, the aim in gathering these contributions together is to inform specialist and general readers about some of the ways in which imaging technologies are transforming the study and presentation of archaeological and cultural artefacts. The periods, materials, geography, and research questions under discussion therefore are varied, but the contributions are united in shared interests concerning how technological development can encourage new types of research and public engagement.

Over eight chapters, various imaging methods are introduced and their capabilities explored. A key feature of this volume is the diversity of specialists involved, including archaeologists, art historians, conservators, curators, computer scientists, imaging technicians, and heritage outreach specialists. It aims to offer an exchange of ideas between groups working across the sciences and humanities, and joins the ranks of other volumes, conferences, and special journal editions that recognise the 'urgency of providing a common ground, where technology may meet humanities' (Stanco, Battiato, and Gallo 2011). Bridging these gaps is perhaps easier said than done, but we hope this collection will contribute fresh and up-to-date perspectives to a growing inter-disciplinary dialogue.

The aims of cultural heritage imaging projects can generally be divided into three groups: outreach, preservation/conservation, and historical or archaeological research—each of which is touched upon in this volume. A particular focus is put on research: digital imaging of material culture is a key component of the digital humanities, which broadens the scope and nature of 'traditional' humanities research questions by applying digital information technologies to the presentation, organisation, and mining of data. This includes both textually encoded data and, increasingly, visual data. In some ways, the study of uninscribed artefacts with imaging technologies has lagged behind that of archaeological landscapes and inscribed objects, although interest in artefact imaging is quickly growing in momentum.[1]

Not only 'how?', but 'why?' is an important question when it comes to the digital imaging of cultural heritage. When we have the ability to use new imaging techniques, in what situations should they be used? What are the aims and intentions in using particular imaging technologies? Popular and academic debate about, for example, 3D reconstructions of the arch of Palmyra, have emerged, often focusing on ethical and political issues (Clammer 2016; Harrowell 2016; Munawar 2017; Newhard 2015). Consequently, there are growing efforts to present applications of technology with more explicit comment on their significance and theoretical implications (Hermann 2016; Huggett 2015; Warwick, Terras, and Nyhan 2012), themes that are also brought out in this volume.

The following chapters explore applications of developing technologies in artefact imaging and the impact of those technologies upon the study and presentation of material culture. Technologies include photogrammetry, hyperspectral and multispectral imaging, reflectance transformation imaging (polynomial texture mapping), structured light scanning, portable light microscope, and 3D

---

[1] At least two other important recent conferences have presented a broader focus on imaging of cultural heritage, from objects to landscapes: '3D Imaging in Cultural Heritage' (The British Museum, 9–10th November 2017) and 'Digital Cultural Heritage' (The Final Conference of the Marie Skłodowska-Curie Initial Training Network for Digital Cultural Heritage, Olimje, Slovenia, 23rd– 25th May 2017). Both events demonstrate the interest, relevance, and advances made in recent work on the digital imaging of artefacts.

printing, among others. In the first chapter, Steven Dey provides perspectives from a 3D digital professional, describing various 3D imaging technologies and strategies in relation to artefacts, including photogrammetry, structured light scanning, CT and micro-CT scanning, and the potential applications of these methods for research and especially in public engagement and museum contexts. David Howell uses hyperspectral imaging to discover colour and lost polychromy on different types of artefacts and reflects on the future potential for new applications of these methods.

Three contributions to this volume discuss imaging of small objects including ancient seals, engraved gems, and coins. The contribution from the *Seals and their Impressions in the Ancient Near East* research team (Jacob Dahl, Jonathon Hare, Kate Kelley, Kirk Martinez, and David Young) discusses their project to develop and test a new system capable of imaging large numbers of ancient Near Eastern cylinder seals. Their work diverges from the majority of 3D imaging efforts by aiming to capture an entire corpus (of c. 50,000 objects) rather than select items. Elise Morero, Hara Procopiou, Jeremy Johns, Roberto Vargiolu, and Hassan Zahouani use a digital microscope and interferometry to identify tool traces that can assist in the study of lapidary craftsmanship, presenting aspects of their work on early Islamic rock crystal vessels and Mughal hard stone production. Hendrik Hameeuw explores technical difficulties in reconstructing the surface shape and appearance of stone seals and metal coins using photometric stereo (PS), challenging researchers to produce the most accurate images possible for each unique cultural heritage object.

Moving from the miniature to the monumental, a series of free-standing sculptures are discussed by Alexander Geurds, Juan Aguilar, and Fiona McKendrick, who take us to a small family-run museum in Nicaragua. They use photogrammetry as a means to create digital immersive virtual environments and augmented reality for understanding prehistoric statuary in its original landscape and assisting in its presentation to the contemporary public. In Oxford's Ashmolean Museum, Alison Pollard uses multi-spectral imaging on Roman marble sculpture from the Arundel collection to investigate polychromy, ancient and modern restorations, the carving process, and ancient and modern display, demonstrating how digital imaging can contribute to object biographies and the history of museum collections. In the final chapter, Rachel Wood documents the process of 3D imaging and printing of a high-impact, but materially challenging, object within the time constraints of planning a temporary exhibition, providing the viewpoint of a classical archaeologist making their first engagement with digital imaging.

References

Averett, E.W., D. B. Counts & J. M. Gordon (eds) 2016. *Mobilizing the Past for a Digital Future.* University of North Dakota: The Digital Press.

Bukreeva, I. (et al) 2016. Virtual unrolling and deciphering of Herculaneum papyri by X-ray phase-contrast tomography. *Scientific Reports* 6.27227, accessed 23/08/18: https://www.nature.com/articles/srep27227.pdf

Cameron, F. and S. Kenderdine (eds) 2007. *Theorizing Digital Cultural Heritage: A Critical Discourse.* MIT Scholarship Press Online.

Clammer, P. 2016. Erasing ISIS. How 3D technology now lets us copy and rebuild entire cities. *The Guardian*, 27 May 2016.

Harrowell, E. 2016. Looking for the future in the rubble of Palmyra: Destruction, reconstruction and identity. *Geoforum* 69: 81–3.

Hermann, J. 2016. Digital 3D models for Science Outreach. *Center for American Archaeology.* https://www.caa-archeology.org/digital-3d-model-koster-dog/

Hess, M. and S. Robson 2012. 3D imaging for museum artefacts: A portable test object for heritage and museum documentation of small objects. Paper delivered at *The XXII Congress of the International Society for Photogrammetry and Remote Sensing, 25 August – 1 September, Melbourne, Australia.*

Howell, D. forthcoming. *Conservation Research in Libraries.* Current Topics in Library and Information Practice. De Gruyter.

Huggett, J. 2015. Challenging digital archaeology. *Open Archaeology* 2015/1: 79–85. De Gruyter.

Macdonald, L. (ed.) 2006. *Digital Heritage: Applying Digital Imaging to Cultural Heritage.* Burlington, MA: Elsevier.

Munawer, N. A. 2017. Reconstructing Cultural Heritage in Conflict Zones: Should Palmyra Be Rebuilt? *Ex Novo Journal of Archaeology* 2017/2: 33–48.

Newhard, J. 2015. 3D imaging in Mediterranean archaeology. What are we doing, anyway? in B. R. Olson & W. R. Caraher (eds), *Visions of Substance. 3D Imaging in Mediterranean Archaeology:* 9–16. University of North Dakota: The Digital Press.

Roosevelt, C. H., P. Cobb, E. Moss, B. R. Olsen, S. Ünlüsoy 2015. Excavation is ~~destruction~~ digitization: Advances in archaeological practice. *Journal of Field Archaeology* 40/3 : 325–46.

Stanco, F., S. Battiato, and G. Gallo 2011. *Digital Imaging for Cultural Heritage Preservation. Analysis, Restoration, and Reconstruction of Ancient Artworks.*

Scopigno, R. (ed.) 2008– *Journal on Computing and Cultural Heritage.* New York: Association for Computing Machinery (ACM).

Warwick, C., M. Terras, J. Nyhan (eds) 2012. *Digital Humanities in Practice.* London: Facet Publishing.

Potential and limitations of 3D digital methods applied to ancient cultural heritage: insights from a professional 3D practitioner

Steven Dey

Abstract

This is a 3D practitioner's view of digital 3D heritage covering how 3D artefacts can be represented as digital data; the practicalities of using and manipulating this data; how the data can be captured; and what useful outputs and applications can be achieved using it, including a discussion of digital to physical replication and its many possible applications. The discussion is based on experiences in over 100 heritage projects undertaken over the last five years for numerous museums and universities in the UK and worldwide. The outcomes, issues, and insights gained in this practice are recorded with the hope of fuelling further discussion and research in this emerging field.

Introduction

This is a review of five years of research, development, and insight gained in the practice of providing 3D digital capture, 3D printed replication, and other 3D services to over one hundred heritage, educational, and research projects. A description of some basic digital 3D concepts is given, followed by an overview of some commonly used 3D scanning methods employed by ThinkSee3D. The chapter then discusses observed and potential heritage applications for digital 3D models and their physical world representations—3D prints—and offers some general conclusions. The hope is to provide some practical content and general insights to heritage practitioners, to record some lessons learnt and to further discussion on this topic. Experienced 3D technologists might find interest in the diversity of applications in perhaps less usual contexts. The services described were delivered by ThinkSee3D Ltd, an Oxford-based small private enterprise founded by the author in 2014. ThinkSee3D utilise a wide range of digital methods including 3D printing but also some traditional arts and crafts techniques to create replica natural and cultural heritage objects. ThinkSee3D has grown out of the global phenomena called the maker movement and is one of a small band of consultants and start-ups engaging with digital 3D technology in heritage.

Digital 3D basic concepts

Digital three-dimensional (3D) methods are the use of digital (computer based) tools which enable physical objects to be captured and represented as digital entities in a virtual digital 3D space so that they can be examined, measured, manipulated, and rendered. These entities are described here as '3D models' or 'digital 3D models'.

There are two common approaches to representing 3D models in computer software. Typically in heritage work, 3D 'mesh modelling' tools (Figure 1), rather than 3D 'vector' or 'curve' modelling tools, (Figure 2) are deployed because of the often complex nature of the objects represented and because the former currently has a larger set of applicable functionality. Further reasons to use mesh modelling tools are that 3D scanning tools create vertex clouds (a collection of unconnected 3D points defining a 3D surface) and meshes (described below) rather than vector models. Also, 3D printers universally use mesh models as input data.

The difference in these digital 3D representations is mostly in the method of storing and representing the 3D geometry. In the case of mesh models, a model is approximated as a series of defined points (called vertices or verts) connected along edges with the spaces between filled with faces (also called quads, triangles, or polygons/polys). Vertices can also contain and render colour information called vertex colours. In vector or curve models, lines are defined as directed vectors between points where the parameters of curves are stored rather than individual vertices. A simple example would be to imagine drawing a circle on a piece of paper: all you need to describe this circle as a vector is a centre point, a curve angle, and a curve radius. As a mesh, you would need to describe every point on the circle forming an array of connected Cartesian x,y points; but for a true circle this would be an infinite array, so in practice this means meshes can only be an approximation. Also important is that vector representations are not changed by alterations in viewing scale, whereas reducing the scale (zooming in) sufficiently on a mesh model makes apparent the connecting points, lines, and faces that approximate the surface. In practice, if a large object is scanned and then reduced in scale for, say, 3D printing, the mesh will likely not become apparent, but scanning smaller objects and scaling them up can often make the approximating mesh visible (as can choosing to model or scan with insufficient polys).

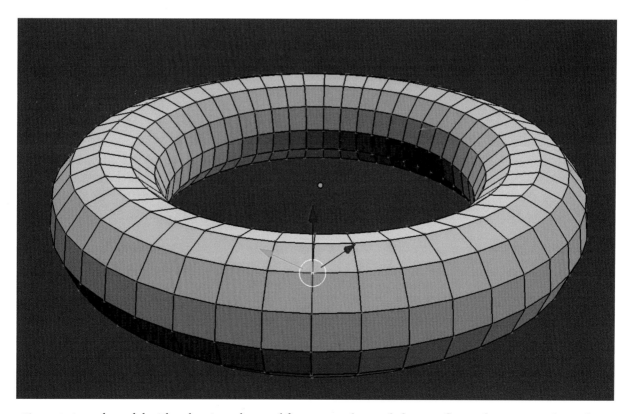

Figure 1. A mesh model with a showing edges and faces. Note that each face is a flat surface. Image: the author.

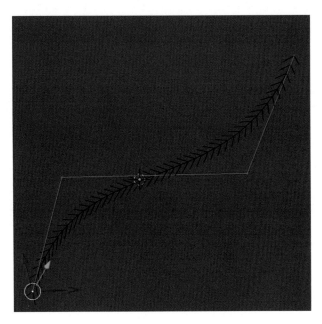

Figure 2. Vector representation of a curved line in black, defined by 4 points and the angled lines in orange.
Image: the author.

Vector 3D representations are used in CAD (Computer Aided Design) tools typically found in engineering and product design departments where precise representation of curved surfaces is important. Mesh modelling tools have developed largely out of the needs of the gaming, animation, and film industries, where the additions of photographic overlays, performance enhancements, and complex rendering allows for realistic (and fantastical) representations of virtual objects and worlds.

A final point on representing objects as digital models is that in most heritage work, mesh models of objects are only shells representing the outer surface of the object (for example, see Figure 3), and no representation of the internal matter is necessary because it is concealed. There are, however, applications where solid models that show the internal densities of matter in the object are essential. Solutions to this latter situation have developed out of medical scanning needs, such as the outputs of X-ray CT (Computed Tomography) scanners, which are becoming increasingly used in digital heritage. This will be discussed below in the section on 3D modelling from CT scans.

Figure 3. Monochrome mesh model of a Roman marble portrait of Antinous, c. AD 130–140, from a 3D photogrammetry scan of BM1805,0703.97 by Daniel Pett. Image: the author.

Digital 3D representations of heritage objects

The first thing to consider when thinking about digital 3D modelling in heritage is that mesh modelling tools can only ever approximate the surface of an object. This is generally not a problem as long as the mesh has sufficient density to represent the smallest feature in the target object (i.e. the mesh faces are smaller than the smallest features being represented)—but here follows an important trade-off: the more vertices, edges, and faces (referred to as the 3D geometry) that are used to represent an object, the more computational resources are consumed in the process of storing, rendering, and manipulating its digital representation.

A detailed model of a human skull derived from a CT scan, for example, could generate a mesh model with many millions of vertices, edges, and faces. Without consideration of the available computing resources, the result might be a model too large to view. A large and detailed model when stored as a file will consume many megabytes or even gigabytes of hard disk space and, if there is more than one such model, then problems of storing large collections of heritage data become evident.

A further point is that scanning large objects containing significant and particularly fine details are difficult to represent accurately in the 3D geometry in typical computing hardware—at least, not without dividing the digital model into manageable sections. A relevant case to highlight this issue is the 3D scanning of Assyrian wall panels undertaken by this author in 2016. The sculptural decoration on the panels is mostly in raised relief but with inscribed fine lines that are only apparent on close inspection. The British Museum houses some exceptionally fine examples of reliefs from Ashurbanipal's Nineveh palace, some of which are several metres long and high with sub-millimetre lines and details (Figure 4–5).

Figure 4. 3D scan of wall panel relief, banquet scene of the Assyrian king Ashurbanipal and his queen, c.645–35 BC, Nineveh, Iraq, BM1856,0909.53. Image: the author.

Figure 5. Detail of the Assyrian wall panel scan in Figure 4, showing fine raised-relief and incised details. Image: the author.

Attempting to store and utilise a model of this nature would result in a very large 3D model that would quickly overrun the resources of commonly-owned computer hardware. Large models become difficult to view and near impossible to manipulate. There are, however, some methods to deal with this situation, although each is a compromise.

The growth of the 3D computer games industry has driven the development of several useful technical solutions to 3D performance issues. Clearly in 3D computer games, the rendering of scenes must run at real-time speeds in order for the game to be functional. There are three solutions worth highlighting for heritage work, each having its advantages and limitations:

- Graphic Processing Units (GPUs)

- Texture or UV mapping

- Normal mapping and displacement maps

In the following discussion, these 3D technologies and their usefulness for solving the performance issues will be assessed.

3D Technologies

GPUs

While adding more memory and a faster processor will certainly improve the 3D processing performance of a computing device, the biggest improvement can be gained by specifically increasing the graphics processing power of the computer. This is done with a specialist processing unit known as a graphics processing unit or GPU. GPUs are the result of decades of computer graphics research and development. They contain large numbers of processing cores (each core being a tiny computer) that work in parallel to rapidly solve the millions of calculations necessary to render complex 3D models in real-time. To a large extent, GPUs were developed to satisfy the needs of the 3D video games industry, but higher performance GPUs from companies such as NVIDIA are particularly useful in heritage 3D work. In 3D photogrammetry scanning, for example, a GPU can be utilised to compute the huge numbers of calculations needed to generate 3D models from 2D photos (more on this below). It should be noted, however, that GPUs can be costly for individuals and smaller teams.

Texture or UV mapping

Instead of relying on 3D geometry alone to represent the surface of a scanned object, with its associated potential for performance issues, the UV mapping (or texture mapping) method wraps a 2D photographic image over a 3D object, effectively painting it with the colours of the surface details. The UV map itself is a photographic projection of the surface of the scanned object unwrapped and flattened into a 2D image. This is not unlike the more familiar 2D projections found in atlases of the spherical earth. Normally UV maps are derived from digital photographs of the object taken during the 3D scanning process. It is called a map because vertices and faces on the digital 3D model are mapped to elements on the UV image. UV refers to the U and V of a 2D axis in the 2D map, in contrast to the 3D axis which is typically represented as X, Y and Z.

This mapping method improves performance by allowing the practitioner to reduce the amount of geometry needed to give a fair representation of the object. Importantly, it also adds to information about an object by capturing more surface colour information in comparison to the point-based vertex colouring (Figure 6). Texture or UV mapping also allows low quality scans where geometry is missing or even noisy to still provide a passable-looking output, albeit for on-screen work only. Texture or UV mapping is used increasingly in digital heritage 3D work because it makes smaller and more manageable 3D models that can be used in many on-screen applications. In an example of a UV textured object, ThinkSee3D transferred some of the texture from the UV map back onto the 3D geometry to improve a 3D print (see Wood, this volume). Typical file formats used to store and transfer 3D models such as OBJ files (a format first developed by Wavefront Technologies) have built-in facilities to connect the UV or texture map to the 3D geometry. Many scanning methods (such as photogrammetry) generate files of this sort. The texture map itself is stored in a regular photographic image file format such as a JPG or PNG.

Figure 6. UV map of a bronze Isis lactans figurine in the British Museum; low poly models with and without texture wrap. Model data by Daniel Pett. Image: the author.

For online and on-screen work, this kind of representation can be very useful because detailed 3D models can be created and displayed on average computing hardware and over typical internet bandwidths. This explains the extensive use of UV mapping in online 3D repositories where catalogues of 3D models are available to view. An example of such an online 3D model repository is Sketchfab.com where many museums such as the British Museum have digital collections.

Problems only arise with UV mapping if fine topographical details need to be accurately rendered or measured or if a model is to be 3D printed at actual size, since the missing geometry will likely become manifest. 2D renders in high detail may also show the missing 3D details or they may look unnatural if examined closely.

Even if the number of polygons is not reduced in a 3D model, it is still worth undertaking a UV (texture) mapping process because of the valuable, detailed colour surface information gained. The need for scientific accuracy in this colour information demands that the photography or scan method applied must be properly colour calibrated. Ambient and added lighting, shadows, object materials, and highlighting should all be carefully considered. Projects should beware of some commercial industrial 3D scanners where the capture of texture is not particularly accurate or of high enough resolution (they were probably designed for industrial uses where colour information is less important than it is in heritage work).

Normal mapping and displacement maps

Normal mapping is a refinement of UV mapping created in order to further improve the realism of 2D projections on 3D surfaces. In this mapping method, a detailed normal map is created that records the direction light would bounce off the object across its surface. A normal can be thought of as a line or arrow projecting from the surface of a face or poly highlighting to the digital modelling software which surface is the outer surface, and therefore indicating to the software how to deal with incident virtual light (Figure 7). Colour in a normal map is used to show the direction of the normals (Figure 8).

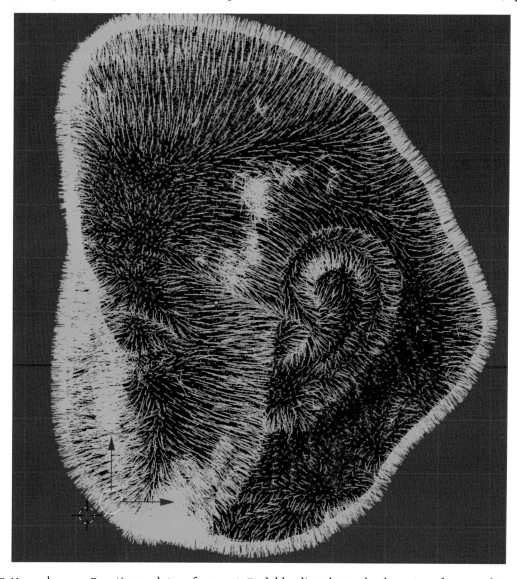

Figure 7. Normals on an Egyptian sculpture fragment. Each blue line shows the direction of a normal. Image: the author.

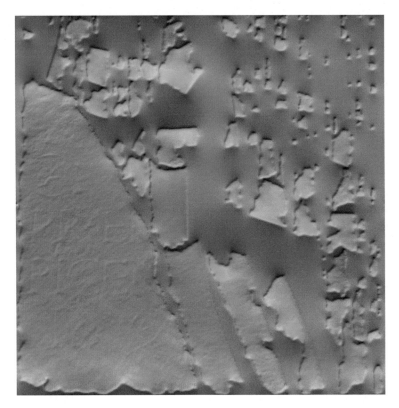

Figure 8. Colour represents direction in this 2D normal map of a Roman inscription. Image: the author.

Normal mapping means that the low geometry (or low poly) models can have surface textures that, on screen at least, behave more realistically than UV maps alone because more information on how light should interact with the model is given. At the same time, a normal map is only an improvement for on-screen work—for fine measurement and for 3D printing there is no improvement from using a normal map.

Some practitioners capture very fine surface details on heritage objects such as Mesopotamian tablets or reliefs using a useful scanning method known as Reflectance Transformation Imaging (RTI) or polynomial texture mapping. The outputs of these scans can be normal maps. RTI generates these maps by observing the shadows created on the surface of an object by obliquely placed lights in different orientations and positions around the object.

UV and normal maps have been described above, but there are in fact numerous types of 2D to 3D mapping methods that can be used to control online renders of 3D models including Ambient Occlusion, Specularity, Bent Normal, Height and many more, all of which are beyond the scope of this paper. One other map derived from normal mapping that is worth describing, however, is the displacement map. Displacement maps show how details in a 3D surface should offset that surface either projecting up or down from the surface. When applied, they recreate surface detail by actually displacing the 3D geometry of the model rather than just simulating this in the UV and normal texture. Displacement mapping typically requires an increase in the density of the 3D geometry, but to keep this extra geometry at a minimum the method can be applied selectively. In this way, detailed areas can have denser meshes, and less detailed areas can have less dense geometry.

This method of selective displacement mapping gives one possible solution to the problems of complexity at different scales, such as arose for the Assyrian reliefs mentioned previously. A 3D digital model of an Egyptian statuette of Isis rendered as a 3D print (Figure 9) had this displacement method applied selectively to create fine details such as the incised lines and dots that describe the wig. Interestingly, in this case these very fine details were not captured in the original 3D scan but were instead added later, using the 'normal' map as a guide to creating a displacement map.

Figure 9. A selective displacement map was used to create the detail of this Egyptian statuette's wig. Model data by Daniel Pett. Image: the author.

3D Scanning Methods

There are numerous 3D scanning methods, but this chapter is concerned with the methods frequently used in heritage projects by ThinkSee3D. The following descriptions of these methods focus on their practical application, rather than offering a detailed explanation of their technology or theoretical basis.[1] All 3D scanning methods rely on digital technology that converts photons of light (from X-rays in CT scanning, to infrared light in structured light scanning) into data representing 3D surfaces in the subject. Described here are a few observations and insights relating to these methods, including the advantages and disadvantages of the three main methods used.

---

[1] There is a wealth of published research on these various scanning methods stretching back decades. Some useful background can be found in Pavlidis et al. 2006, Remondino 2011, and Remondino et al. 2012, and regarding microCT in heritage see Abel et al. 2010.

Structure from Motion (3D photogrammetry)

Many digital heritage 3D practitioners make use of the first method to be discussed here, known as Structure from Motion (SfM) or 3D photogrammetry. It is a method of reconstructing 3D digital models from a series of digital photographic images (or frames from a digital video) taken with ordinary digital photographic equipment but processed in specialist photogrammetry software. The outputs of the method can be highly accurate digital 3D models with sub-millimetre feature accuracy overlaid with high-resolution photographic UV textures. These models can be as good as or better than those generated by many expensive scanning technologies for the relative low price of a digital camera and some SfM processing software. Satisfactory models are relatively easy to produce, but to achieve the best possible results there are many factors to consider: from the object texture and materiality, to the scene lighting and photographic method, and the various photogrammetry processing parameters.

To start, the subject should be lit with diffuse white light, minimising shadows. Bright sunlight should be avoided. Photographs are taken from as many angles as possible and to assist in this process a turntable is often used. Sometimes multiple cameras also are used on a rig to increase capture efficiency and reduce camera shake. The photos must be overlapping photographs of the target object taken from different viewpoints in focus across the whole object. The final output is a digital 3D reconstruction of the object and the reconstructed camera positions and parameters of the images. Typically, SfM software works in 5 stages:

1. Feature detection, feature matching, and camera position estimation (resulting in a sparse point cloud model and camera positions).

2. Dense point cloud reconstruction (resulting in a fully described model but only as points/vertices) Meshed surface reconstruction (resulting in a mesh 3D model needed for the UV mapping).

3. Photographic surface texture reconstruction – UV mapping (resulting in a photographic overlay describing the colours of the surfaces).

4. Hole filling and smoothing (close holes in the mesh usually due to missing geometry and smoothing to reduce noise).

The first stage identifies common surface features between the input digital photographs and uses those features' shifting position between the images to estimate camera positions in 3D space around the object. Usefully, no camera parameters or set camera positions are mandatory in order to undertake this process. If the parameters of the camera sensor and lens (including distortion parameters) are known, then they can be input into the software, otherwise most photogrammetry applications will estimate these parameters. In addition, if the digital photographs contain EXIF information describing the configuration of the image, such as exposure, f-number, size of image, and so on, then the software will typically use this information to assist in accurately positioning the cameras. Figure 10 shows the output of a camera alignment and sparse cloud generation for a scanned sculpture.

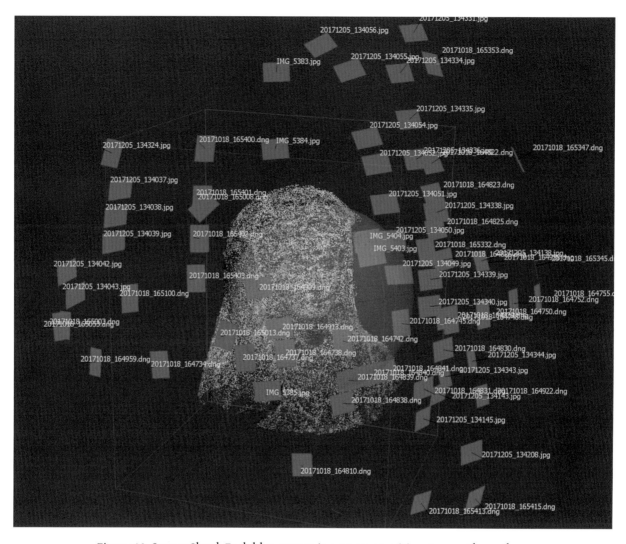

Figure 10. Sparse Cloud. Each blue square is a camera position. Image: the author.

The surface is then reconstructed as a dense cloud of points (or vertices) that can also have colour information (vertex colours).

Figure 11. Dense point cloud of a limestone funerary portrait relief from Palmyra, Syria. The surface is only constructed with vertices or points. Image: the author.

The dense point cloud reconstruction works by looking at the displacement of texture between the multiple images, using it to calculate the depth and position of points in digital 3D space. Note these points in 3D space can also record the local colour information (known as vertex colours). Figure 11 is a screenshot of a dense point cloud generation process, showing the coloured vertex points located on the surface of the sculpture.

The density of this point cloud is an important configurable option. The denser the cloud, the more surface is modelled (ideally). It is possible to construct a cloud denser than the resolution of the input photos, but that creates unnecessary data points and files larger than are needed to represent the object. Point cloud densities should, therefore, be carefully considered. Ultimately, the maximum resolution of the point cloud is determined by the resolution of the 2D imaging sensor in the camera and by the average distance of the camera from the subject. It is useful to imagine pixels from the camera sensor being projected out from the camera through the lens and onto the surface of the object. The intended application must also be considered when thinking about the density of the point cloud. For example, if the only application of the scan is to replicate an object with a 3D printer, then there is no point resolving a dense cloud finer than the resolution of the 3D printer.

Once the dense point cloud is constructed, a mesh modelling algorithm such as 'marching cubes' (Guennebaud et al. 2007) or 'Possion reconstruction' (Kazhdan and Hoppe 2013) is applied that connects the points in the cloud and fills in the faces, rejecting some erroneous noise in the process. The resulting model is referred to as a mesh. 'Noise' in this context refers to erroneous points that are off the true surface of the model (see Figure 12). Noise can be caused by a number of issues in the scanning process: poor focus or motion blur in the input images, poor lighting, shadows, specularity, and sometimes a lack of texture on the surface of the object. Smoothing algorithms can be applied to the mesh to remove possible noise but only with care, since these can remove detail as well as noise. Depending on the object, it is possible to apply the smoothing selectively, leaving good parts of the scan untouched.

Figure 12: Meshed image of a limestone funerary portrait relief from Palmyra, Syria. UV colour (left) and no colour (right), showing the effect of shadows on photogrammetry. Notice the noise and loss of accuracy in the geometry in the shaded region under the chin). Image: the author.

The final step is to utilise the photos that were used to create the dense 3D point cloud to create a texture or UV map (as described in earlier). Sometimes a subset of the images will be used and an appropriate resolution of texture map created. Although colour details can be captured earlier in the process, this method significantly increases the resolution of colour details on the surface.

The main advantages of 3D photogrammetry are that it is an effective and relatively easy method to use, even outdoors. It can be used to scan many types of objects, it is cheap to undertake (unlike other methods that require costly 3D scanners), it is relatively easy to learn, and it can be done at any scale—from miniature objects to entire landscapes (see Figure 13 and 14).

Figure 13. Large site photogrammetry scan from drone video, Giza, Egypt. Image: the author.

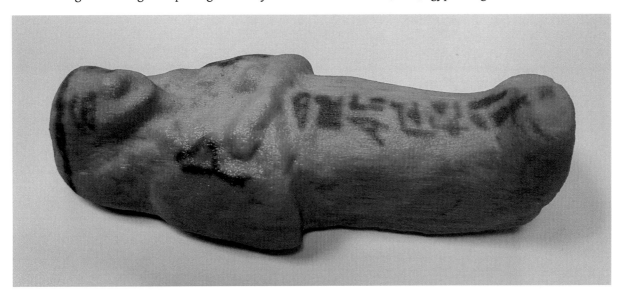

Figure 14. Small-scale photogrammetry of an Egyptian shabti in the Petrie Museum, UCL, scanned by the MicroPasts project (UCL and British Museum) and 3D-printed by the author. Image: the author.

The limitations of photogrammetry mean that certain objects are difficult or even impossible to scan. These include objects with high surface reflectance, transparency, or that are plain-coloured. This is because the method relies on seeing the same texture on the object surface between several photos. Specular lights in objects or transparent objects clearly lack this consistent texture (although there are some strategies to overcome these limitations). Specular lights can be minimised using polarized lighting; transparent objects can be modelled by physically applying a temporary textured surface, although not always ideal for ancient artefacts (see Wood, this volume); and to scan plain coloured objects, a complex patterned texture can be projected onto the object using a video projector giving the photogrammetry software recognisable patterns between photos.

Photogrammetry can also be used underwater to capture details of underwater environments or objects in a sunken settlement or wreck. The author, working with members of the University of Oxford Zoology department, undertook some 3D surveys of coral reefs in Honduras using photogrammetry (Figure 15) (Young et al. 2017).

Figure 15. Underwater photogrammetry of coral reef, Honduras, from diver transit videos created by Prof. Alex Rogers and his team at the University of Oxford, modelled by the author. Image: the author.

Scans can also be undertaken using different spectra of incident light (not just white light), which can be a useful method in restoration. Restoration work on objects will often become apparent when imaging, for example, in ultraviolet or infrared light; by using photogrammetry, a 3D model of this restoration can be created, helping restorers plan further restoration (Ueni et al. 2017).

Key to success with photogrammetry is good photography of the object and reasonable lighting conditions (diffuse daylight lighting with minimum highlights and shadows), but even less than perfect conditions can still result in a useable 3D model. The recommended camera for photogrammetry is a digital SLR with a 50 mm lens, but even contemporary mobile phone cameras can produce outstanding results (and in some cases better than a high-end SLR camera). Since nearly everyone has a mobile phone it means that with just a little training, anyone can undertake scientifically useful 3D scans (see Larkin and Dey 2017a). The photogrammetry software required to convert photographs into 3D models is readily available and, although some tools are costly, there are useful low-cost and even free equivalents available. Two examples commonly used are PhotoScan and RealityCapture—both have low cost or educational variants.

To produce detailed digital models, high numbers of input photographs are needed. Typically 100–350 input photos will give a detailed result, dependent on the object scale and detail. Consideration has to be given to processing time, however, which will be very dependent on the number and size of the images and the processing power of the computing device used. Photogrammetry is extremely processor-intensive, typically several billion calculations are needed to convert the digital photos into a digital 3D model. Processing time can easily run into hours or even days but, fortunately, most current photogrammetry software can utilise the parallel processing power of GPUs to significantly reduce this processing time. The resolution of the output model is also configurable, so sometimes it is prudent to only build to the resolution needed by the application. If a large number of objects need to be processed then it is worth considering the overall 3D modelling productivity.

Despite some limitations, photogrammetry or SfM is a remarkably useful tool in digital archaeology because of its low-cost and relative ease of use. It can easily compete with much more expensive methods of 3D scanning if used correctly. A final interesting point is that it is possible to apply this technique retrospectively to existing photograph or video collections. Models can and have been created from tourist photography or video of lost or remote sites or objects, even though the photographer(s) had no intention of 3D modelling a site or object. For example, ThinkSee3D, along with a team at the British Museum, used tourist photos to create 3D models and 3D prints of several pieces of African rock art (Figure 16). These 3D prints were created for use in events for blind and partially-sighted visitors (see below).

Figure 16. A photogrammetry model of ancient South African rock art. Model created from tourist photos using the displacement method for the indented carved animals. Image: the author, for the African Rock Art project at the British Museum.

3D models from X-ray CT scans

The output of a CT (Computed Tomography) scan of an object or person is a set of cross-sectional X-ray images showing the different density of materials inside the object. By X-raying in slices through the object, a 3D representation of target elements in the object or the objects surface can be created. The densities of elements are represented, usually, as different shades of grey. Different blocks of similar density (and therefore shade) can be highlighted and isolated (known as labelling) for study. Labelled items can then be converted into 3D surface models. CT scanners have slices of different resolutions from a few 10s of microns (Micro CT) up to several millimetres (Medical CT). Micro CT scanners tend to have smaller scan volumes as they are often used in material science or physics applications. Medical CT scanners can potentially scan objects several metres in length. There are also super high-resolution X-ray scanners associated with synchrotrons (Nano CT).

CT scanners are extremely useful in heritage applications because they allow 3D scanning not only of the outer surfaces of an object but also hidden internal structures. A fascinating example is the clay-covered Jericho Skull in the British Museum: the underlying human skull was revealed by a detailed CT scan at Imperial College and then 3D printed by ThinkSee3D. This model of the skull was then used by a facial reconstruction team to rebuild the owner's face (Fletcher 2014).

The potential of this method is also demonstrated by a collaboration between ThinkSee3D, Dr David Shlugman (a medical practitioner) with his supervisor Dr Andrew Shortland Cranfield University, the Ashmolean Museum, and Dr Stephanie Dalley (University of Oxford): an envelope-clad Sumerian tablet was digitally unwrapped using MicroCT at Cranfield University (Figure 17 and 18). After isolating the central region, the tablet was revealed and rendered by ThinkSee3D firstly as a high resolution digital model and then as a high resolution SLA (Stereolithographic) 3D print in acrylic (with 25 micron layers); then it was silicon moulded and cast into a more suitable terracotta composite material (Figure 19). This model of the tablet was then translated by Stephanie Dalley, who identified it as from the third dynasty of Ur (2112–2004 BC) and was an order from one official to another for the ingredients of that ancient staple, beer.

 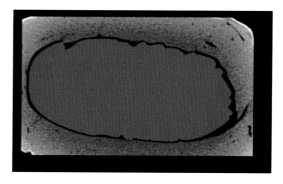

Figure 17 (left). CT surface model of a clay envelope containing a hidden cuneiform tablet. Image: the author.

Figure 18 (right). CT cross-sectional image of the tablet in its envelope. The air gap was caused by a modern attempt to preserve the tablet by baking it. Image: the author.

Figure 19. The CT-extracted 'beer tablet' revealed after 4000 years, rendered as a 3D print and then moulded and cast in terracotta composite.

ThinkSee3D have utilised this method on many other projects, including extracting mummy amulets from unwrapped Egyptian mummies and building a very detailed Chinese oracle bone model with inscribed text. The technique is a unique method for extracting hidden and intricate objects without damaging them, but it has also proven itself invaluable for modelling visible texts on the surfaces of objects such as Mesopotamian tablets, cylinder seals, or Chinese oracle bones, because line of sight methods such as laser scanning or photogrammetry struggle to 'see' all the sub-mm surfaces in the many inscribed marks on these artefacts. Even RTI methods might not be able to image slight overhangs caused by a stylus digging into a clay tablet. A CT scan, particularly a MicroCT scan, captures every surface since it is an X-ray technique and no surface is obscured. The only limiting factor is the space between the slices—hence MicroCT (a few 10s of microns) and not medical CT scanners are more appropriate for fine inscribed texts. There are also very high resolution X-ray scanners (associated with synchrotrons) that may be able to create even finer levels of detail on these tablets. The author has investigated the use of the Diamond Light Source synchrotron for this application.

One disadvantage of CT scanners is that they are big devices, so this scanning method is not portable: objects have to be brought to the scanner, which can be difficult for delicate or valuable museum objects. Fortunately, some major museums are investing in CT technology and most large universities have access to microCT scanners. It is also possible to rent time on hospital CT scanners for larger scans. Another consideration is that CT does not provide surface colours. There is no way to produce a UV map directly from this technology. However, it is possible to create the geometry with CT and to use photogrammetry for the UV surface and then combine this later, allowing CT scans to be coloured (although only for surface models). Another consideration is heat: objects may get warm when exposed to x-rays for prolonged periods of time. Finally, objects containing iron are difficult to scan because iron will scatter the x-rays and create star-burst effects in the cross-sectional images.

Structured light scanning

Structured light scanners use specialist hardware to project a light pattern (in infrared) onto an object that is then recorded by an infrared camera on the scanner. By observing how that projected pattern is transformed by the object's surfaces, the scanner calculates feature depths (see Dahl et al., this volume).

One advantage of these scanners is that they scan using specialist hardware, and so the time from scanning to model is typically much quicker than photogrammetry, which requires longer post-scan processing. Structured light scanners can often generate 3D models in real time, so errors in scans can be spotted immediately. The scanners are often calibrated too, so that the emerging 3D models are automatically scaled (most photogrammetry models need to be manually scaled). The disadvantages are that the scanners are relatively low resolution, typically 1–5 mm (apart from very expensive variants). They also do not offer the same level of surface detail compared with photogrammetry because, usually, a separate camera on the scanner will capture colours and this camera is not usually as high resolution as a typical digital camera or even recent phone cameras. Volumes that can be scanned are often limited due to the high processing and computing resources needed to create 3D models on the fly.

ThinkSee3D use this type of scanning for quick low resolution scanning, often where many objects are needed at a low level of detail (such as in planning exhibition spaces), for quick 3D measurement of objects (usually for natural history specimens), or even to scan living people.

Laser scanning

Laser scanning (not utilised by ThinkSee3D but described briefly here) is typically used for scanning landscapes and architectural scenes. By timing how long it takes a laser pulse to travel from the device to an object and back, the laser scanner calculates depth. The output of laser scanners are typically very large point clouds. The level of detail for this type of scanner does not normally go below a few millimetres, as is fitting for the type of subject. The big disadvantage of these scanners is that they are very costly, although they can be rented. Photogrammetry can perform similar architectural scans, although the time to process the point cloud will be considerably longer.

Rendering digital 3D models

Once an object is captured in the digital 3D realm, it can be rendered out of this realm into other digital or physical forms. Rendering essentially means interpreting and outputting the model from its internal 3D digital form into a form that is useful in research or appropriate for sharing or publication. This can be as simple as rendering a 2D representation of a 3D model for a publication or as sophisticated as rendering the object in physical space using methods such as 3D printing. There is not scope to fully explore the full possibilities of rendering in this paper but a few examples are shown below to hint at the potential of 2D and 3D rendering.

Realistic 2D scenes can be created using virtual lighting to create virtual highlights and shadows. This can help to reveal shallow markings on surfaces, for example. UV mapping and normal maps are applied to create a believable, almost photographic, view (Figures 20-21).

Figure 20. Fragment of a Latin inscription rendered in full photographic colour with UV and normal maps using a ray trace render engine. Image: the author.

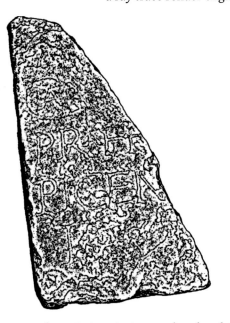

Figure 21. Fragment of a Latin inscription rendered as: left, a) a line drawing using edge and contour recognition algorithms and, right, b) in a monochrome false colour – note the clarity of the text in this render. Image: the author.

3D rendering of an object can be achieved with 3D printing or computer controlled cutting tools. This allows for the creation of replica objects. Experiences of this subject are too wide to cover in the scope of this paper but some of the applications are described below. Other new advances include rendering objects or environments for virtual reality (VR) headsets or rendering in a viewing application as an overlay on physical reality known as Augmented Reality (AR). ThinkSee3D are experimenting with rendering animated AR scenes onto 3D printed statues as a public engagement device, so that the statue can explain its own context.

Modifying 3D digital models from 3D scans

There are a number of reasons to modify data from a 3D scan. Firstly, it could be to repair obvious errors in the model caused by errors in the scanning process. Whether this is acceptable and to what degree depends largely on the application in mind. For example, contrast a model being used for a research question or to record a site versus creating a believable handling model for an educational experience. In the first cases, accuracy of data is key whereas in the latter case making the model fit for handling might be key. Other reasons for digital manipulation might be to replace a missing component in a reconstruction. ThinkSee3D have mirrored (and physically replicated) missing components of natural history specimens, for example (Larkin and Dey 2017b).

Over the last few years, some trials of reconstructing Assyrian palatial reliefs have been undertaken by the author. This concerns the digital assembly of existing dispersed components into a larger model, rather than manipulation of individual model geometry. The possibility of digitally restoring broken elements based on repeating formulaic designs seen in the extant reliefs is an interesting possibility. In this case, scholarly research and interpretation as much as digital skills would be required to drive the reconstruction decisions. An example of this is given below in the Applications section.

Another possible aspect of model manipulation is to change the scale of objects too large or too small for replicating physically, so that their dimensions can be manipulated to make scale models of archaeological sites or 3D print microscopic features scaled up 10s or 100s of times. Also, false colours can be used to highlight features or surface marks; this was carried out for a digital model created for the British Library where there was need to highlight some text on an ancient Chinese oracle bone.

The philosophy that the author adopts is to achieve as much authenticity as the input data, budget, and application will allow, but also to recognize that digital 3D models are still models: they contain approximations and errors even with the highest resolution 3D scan. At the same time, the models can be more than accurate enough for most applications, and the levels of error can be less than from those incurred by hand drawn images or even photographs of artefacts. An apposite anecdote on photographic accuracy is that even the great Flinders Petrie was forced to build his own pin-hole camera to better capture ancient Egyptian reliefs because he was dissatisfied with lens errors produced by commercial camera lenses of the time.

3D data preservation

There are many lost artefacts and art objects in the world that are only known from historical replicas (photos or drawings) and in some cases the replicas are better preserved than the original object. An example of this latter case is Trajan's Column, from which casts were taken in 1864 and stored indoors at the V&A Museum, while the original has been further damaged after being exposed to another 153 years of weathering and pollution. With the advent of 3D scanning and storage of digital objects, future lost or damaged objects will at least have a 3D record for study and possible replication. It might be the case that eventually the digital model could be the only record of the object, and so how and what data is stored, where it is stored, and how it is future-proofed needs to be carefully considered (see Dahl, this volume). Given that one 3D file representing an artefact could easily be a gigabyte or more, and an entire collection could be many terabytes, there are technological, economic, and longer-term data conservation questions to consider before embarking on any large-scale 3D digitisation project.

At least some of the key data to retain is the raw scan data (in photogrammetry, the digital photos) and some semblance of the model (perhaps the dense point cloud) so that the repository can easily be examined. Details of the equipment and software used, and a record of any physical replicas that were produced, and their location would also be recommended. With current technology, the monetary and time cost of scanning entire collections would be high (although this may change with future technological developments), so there is a need for selectivity in the choice of objects to be digitally preserved. Another data preservation question is that of what happens to the 3D data if a digital 3D repository ceases to operate? Many repositories are privately-run enterprises or are stored in institutions. Funding issues or providers ceasing to trade could threaten the preservation of this data.

Some applications of digital 3D in heritage

This is an introduction to some of the applications possible once an object is 3D digitised. There is not space to give a full account of all the applications but most of those listed have been applied to heritage projects by the author.

Measurement using digital 3D models

Physical objects that are delicate, inaccessible, or complex can be very difficult to measure accurately, but, once digitised and carefully scaled, all aspects of a model can be measured with relative ease. Length, angles, structure, and volume are all easily measured, but it is also possible to create measurement scripts that might look at variations in normal angles, for example, or calculate other morphometric parameters (Figure 22).

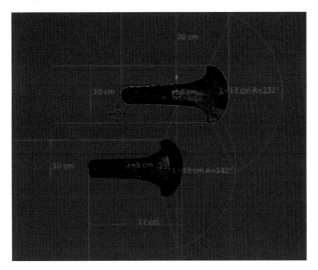

Figure 22. Measuring angles and lengths on Bronze Age axe heads as part of the Micropasts project (UCL and British Museum). Image: the author.

In another example, a tourist drone video of the Giza pyramids was turned into a measurable 3D model of the pyramids using photogrammetry by extracting frames from the video (Figure 13). The model was scaled based on the known height of one of the pyramids and from this now scaled model all possible distances and heights could be easily extracted (Figure 23). Indeed, the original use of photogrammetry—going back almost as far as photography itself—was for site surveying and this is where the name 'photogrammetry' derives.

27

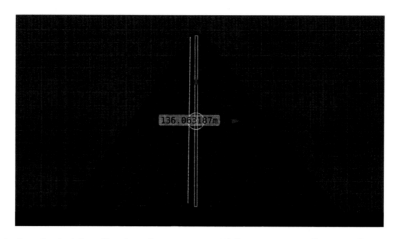

Figure 23. Calculating the height of a Giza plateau pyramid from a tourist drone video. Image: the author.

3D reconstruction

An interesting use of both digital 3D methods—3D rendering and 3D printing—is in historical object restoration and reconstructions. It is essential that this be undertaken with proper levels of scholarly research to back up restoration decisions but 3D digital reconstruction is a powerful tool in reconstructing sites and objects from the past.

Below is an example restoration project undertaken by the author as a trial of restoration techniques. The objective was to reconstruct a single figure from a large Ashurbanipal raised relief scene in the British Museum. The starting point for the project was a 3D scan of an extant element of a figure of a servant (Figure 24a), and a 19th-century drawing of the scene created on-site at the North Palace in Nineveh before the original was broken up and dispersed (Figure 24b). There are fragments of this scene in at least three museums across the world. The 3D model (from a photogrammetry scan) of the extant fragment was first digitally overlaid onto a digitised version of the 19th-century drawing (Figure 24c). The initial observation was that the alignment of 3D model and the drawing were close, indicating that the drawing was an accurate record of the original. Other parts of the drawings examined also seemed reasonably accurate compared with scanned models of extant fragments, apart from some evidence of the creation of perspective in the drawing.

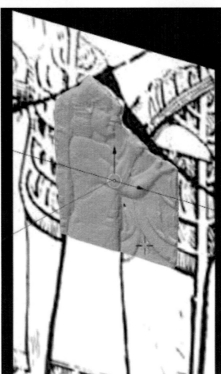

Figure 24. 24a (above left). 3D scan of extant fragment of the Nineveh relief under restoration; and 24b (above right) a 19th-century drawing of the Nineveh relief. Below, 24c: extant scanned fragment superimposed onto the 19th-century drawing.

Next, other scanned fragments were examined to find a suitable 'donor' area to digitally sample to replace the missing skirt and feet (Figure 25). The sample area was then digitally 3D sampled and pasted onto the broken fragment. Digital sculpting tools were used minimally to align the pasted skirt in-line with the drawing, and some simple blending was done at the join to make the new element match the extant (Figure 26).

Figure 25 (left). Another figure from an existing fragment with a similar skirt. Image: the author.

Figure 26 (right). The restored test figure, not complete (there is a vase to be removed). Image: the author.

The conclusion from the above restoration trial is that it was possible to restore missing elements digitally using this sample, paste, and blend method. The need to manipulate the missing element to the drawing was minimal in this case, a lot less than expected and, interestingly, may suggest the use of templates in the originals construction. Other trials suggested are to experiment with colour as some fragments have small flecks of paint left on them and this could have been reapplied in both 2D and 3D renders. The future ambition is to reconstruct the whole scene digitally and then 3D print the relief.

Public engagement

The use of 3D models, particularly 3D printed models, in public engagement is becoming increasingly common in museums. ThinkSee3D specialise in this field and have seen the impact of this drive to create believable handling replicas. The direct contact experience, even by proxy, is a powerful engagement tool (Di Giuseppantonio Di Franco et al. 2015); it appears to stimulate a greater interest compared with a viewing-only experience. Interestingly, ThinkSee3D's experience has shown that members of the public often respond to replicas as if they were real; seemingly treating them with the respect they would give to real historical objects.

An interesting case study of the use of handling models for a particular group was undertaken by ThinkSee3D and a team at the British Museum led by Elizabeth Galvin and Jennifer Wexler. Workshops with handling models were provided for blind and partially sighted people interested in African rock art. ThinkSee3D provided a series of 3D models relating to different rock faces and created projected 3D models of some of the animals represented in the incised and raised relief art. The reaction was very positive: remote and inaccessible art (and animals) were made accessible, delighting the participants and organisers.

For younger people, the impact of handling an ancient artefact (even if it is a proxy) seems to make the overall heritage experience more memorable and educational. Replicas that can be handled also make great props for historical storytelling in educational or museum contexts. The story of the object is of course key to creating enjoyable story-telling experiences with the replica, and the story immediately has many layers since there is the original context, the archaeological context (how it was found), the museum context (why is it important), and finally how technology replicated the original.

The observation that handling realistic 3D printed objects (with context explained) can illicit emotional responses in some people is fascinating, especially when compared with on-screen data or even when viewing objects in cases. This phenomenon, which is worthy of further study, is due perhaps to touch being a direct sensory experience.

The importance of creating realistic replicas should also be raised. It has been found that low cost plastic 3D printed replica objects do not elicit the same responses as realistic colour replicas. It seems that the make-believe has to be convincing to elicit some emotional response in the handler. Although no detailed survey has been undertaken, it has been noted that discussion of a plastic print tends to focus on the 3D printing process, whereas a realistic 3D colour printed replica seems to generate discussion about the origins of the original object. The 3D printing is forgotten in this latter case. Where the print material does not match the original material specification (type, weight, surface finish, or colour) closely enough, it is recommended to mould and cast in a suitable material from a print (see Figure 19).

Other technologies worthy of mention and becoming increasingly common in public engagement included Augmented Reality (AR) and Virtual Reality (VR) applications (see Geurds et al., this volume). These create immersive 3D content using digital models that can be viewed with specialised 3D viewing headsets or mobile devices (Figure 27). There is not scope within this discussion to expand on this further, although it has been trialled by ThinkSee3D for use in heritage and science engagement projects.

Figure 27. Augmented Reality (AR) application showing a digital 3D model overlaid on the real world (viewed from a mobile phone screen). Image: the author.

Animation and simulation

One interesting application of digital 3D models is in animating or in simulation to show the function of an object or even an environment around a site. Physics, particle, and fluid simulators are present in most 3D technology modelling, game engine, and animation applications, and these can be utilised for public engagement and also in research. In addition, game engine platforms that support first person game creation can be utilised to create 3D and virtual reality digital environments that can be explored by the user. For example, ThinkSee3D created a simple digital simulation using some basic physics and animation to simulate and confirm the suspected operation of the mechanism of an ancient Chinese cross-bow trigger. Another example being explored by the author relates to the direction of sunlight at different times of day and year and how this illuminates ancient cave and wall art. This can easily be simulated and explored in a virtual environment once a 3D model of the cave and its surroundings are digitised.

Cultural 3D data preservation and cultural heritage monitoring

The ability to capture objects by digital 3D means seems like an improvement over traditional methods of visually recording an object or site. On deeper examination, however, various factors including scanning limitations, the time needed, and the need to store large amounts of data mean that digital 3D models currently complement rather than replace other visual capture methods.

There are important data questions to answer such as the why, where, and how of preserving the data. Specifically, why, or for what purpose, should an object be 3D digitised, where will the data be stored (and preserved), and how will the object be scanned and stored? The significance of current captured data might not be apparent now but might prove significant to future generations especially if there is some unforeseen loss or damage to the original object. It is important, therefore, to treat this data thoughtfully. Consider the many 19th-century sculptural plaster casts in existence, many of which better preserve the details of the original creation than the often weathered, damaged, or (worst-case) lost originals. Just as these casts are proving useful research tools to contemporary researchers, so might the same be true of current digital scans to future researchers.

A possible 'when' question could be added: specifically, when should an object be scanned, or rather, how often? 3D scanning to monitor changes, especially in a more delicate item or site, is another useful application of 3D digital scanning. A comparative scanning process at set intervals enables a survey of changes over time and might help in the planning of restorations.

3D collections for comparative studies

The ability to form a digital or even 3D printed collection of objects from diverse sources opens up new lines of possible research. Once objects are 3D digitised they can be compared with similar objects from museums around the world and being in 3D this represents at a finer level of detail than previously. The University of York commissioned ThinkSee3D to create just such a collection of Star Carr Mesolithic headdress replicas as 3D prints that were located in 4 different museums for just such a comparative study, all of them scanned with photogrammetry.

Conclusions

There is clearly a broad, and advancing, selection of promising 3D technologies and applications becoming available to researchers and heritage professionals, opening up many new lines of research and development. The importance of keeping up with these advances and making informed decisions particularly when it comes to 3D scanning and storage of 3D heritage data is clear.

The ability of digital 3D to democratise museum collections in an unprecedented way, including objects not normally on display, provides enormous scope for new educational experiences and research opportunities. By making objects visible and active tools via an exciting delivery technology, they will hopefully reinvigorate interest in ancient cultures and help expand our knowledge and enjoyment of our collective past. The ability to recreate digital objects as physical objects using 3D printing allows for further types of experiences and increases access to collections, especially for younger people and the visually impaired.

This technology opens up interesting questions of digital rights and across the world different museums have taken widely different stances on this point. The danger of being too restrictive, it is contended, is that it may reduce a museum's relevance in this digital world, especially for the young. Allowing organisations and individuals to be inspired by and even derive new work from the past is actually a great opportunity for cultural organisation. Museums can become a driving force behind future culture by allowing a new generation of makers digital access to the works of celebrated makers of the past. Cultural museums are, after all, mostly a collection of 3D objects made by artists and craftsman who themselves were inspired by previous makers. 3D technology, and the internet, enables access on an unprecedented scale whilst not compromising the need for conservation (in fact, it helps in conservation and interpretation too).

It is important to state that all aspects of 3D have a cost, both monetary and in energy, despite being lower than in previous years. 3D printing can be expensive, 3D scanning is time consuming, and 3D data has to be stored. This leads to the conclusion that new types of curatorial choices are needed to decide what should be 3D digitised or 3D restored, and what should be replicated. If a major 3D project is undertaken it can become a complex archaeological, cultural, and political decision and one that can cause controversy, as happened recently with the recreation of the Palmyra Arch.[2]

Overall, these various 3D tools give new and as yet not well explored ways to view, measure, and even touch the remnants of the past, making this an exciting time to be involved in 3D digital cultural heritage. The continual development of 3D technology promises further useful tools for heritage professionals going forward and the development of more 3D tools specifically designed for heritage will no doubt follow.

Finally, it is hoped that this review of 3D methods and applications will contain some useful nuggets for other practitioners in cultural heritage and encourage further development, research and maker start-ups in this exciting field.

Acknowledgements

Thanks are due to the following individuals and organisation who have supported ThinkSee3D and contributed directly or indirectly to this work: Dr Rachel Wood and Dr Kate Kelley, University of Oxford; Daniel Pett, previously British Museum and now at the Fitzwilliam Museum; Elizabeth Galvin, previously British Museum and now at the V&A; Dr Jennifer Wexler, British Museum; Dr Paola di Giuseppantonio di Franco at the University of Essex; Prof. Andrew Bevan, UCL Archaeology; Nigel Tallis, formerly at the British Museum; Dr David Shlugman, formerly Cranfield University; Nigel Larkin, Natural-history conservation; Nick Holmans at ThinkSee3D Ltd; Dr Adi Keinan-Schoonbaert and Emma Goodlife, The British Library; Prof. Nicky Milner, University of York; Claire Sawdon at the Malton Museum and many of the curators and educators at the Ashmolean Museum, Oxford and the British Museum, London. I would also like to thank those involved with the MicroPasts project and Thomas Flynn from Sketchfab.com. I am particularly grateful to Prof. Stewart Thompson at Oxford Brookes University and Prof. Alex Rogers of the University of Oxford for their comments on earlier drafts of this article.

---

[2] Clammer 2016.

References

Abel, R. L., S. Parfitt, N. Ashton, S. G. Lewis, B. Scott, and C. Stringer 2010. Digital preservation and dissemination of ancient lithic technology with modern micro-CT. *Computers and Graphics* 35/4: 878–84.

Clammer, P. 2016. Erasing ISIS. How 3D technology now lets us copy and rebuild entire cities', *The Guardian*, 27 May 2016.

Di Giuseppantonio Di Franco, P., C. Camporesi, F. Galeazzi, and M. Kallmann 2015. 3D printing and immersive visualization for improved perception of ancient artefacts. *Presence: Teleoperators and Virtual Environments* 24/3: 243–64.

Fletcher, A., J. Pearson, T. Molleson, R. Abel, J. Ambers, and C. C. Wiles 2014. Beneath the surface: Imaging techniques and the Jericho Skull, in A. Fletcher et al. (eds) *Regarding the Dead: Human Remains in the British Museum*: 91–102. London: British Museum Press.

Galeazzi, F., P. Di Giuseppantonio Di Franco, and J. L. Matthews 2015. Comparing 2D pictures with 3D replicas for the digital preservation and analysis of tangible heritage. *Museum Management and Curatorship* 30/5: 462–83.

Guennebaud, G. and M. Gross 2007. Algebraic point set surfaces. *ACM Transactions on Graphics* 26/3: no. 23.

Kazhden, M. and H. Hoppe 2013. Screened poisson surface reconstruction. *ACM Transactions on Graphics* 32/3: no. 29.

Larkin, N. R. and S. Dey 2017a. Recording the uncollectable with low cost low tech: successful photogrammetry in the field using a mobile phone to create digital 3D models. Poster presented at The 65th Symposium of Vertebrate Palaeontology and Comparative Anatomy, Birmingham University. http://www.natural-history-conservation.com/PhotogrammetryPoster.pdf

Larkin, N.R. and S. Dey 2017b. One way to 'collect' a massive specimen—simple photogrammetry in the field using a mobile phone. *Deposits Magazine* 52: 15–18.

Pavlidis, G., A. Koutsoudis, F. Arnaoutoglou, V. Tsioukas, and C. Chamzas 2007. Methods for 3D digitization of Cultural Heritage. *Journal of Cultural Heritage* 8: 93–8.

Remondino, F. 2011. Heritage recording and 3D modelling with photogrammetry and 3D. *Journal of Remote Sensing* 2011/3: 2072–4292.

Remondino, F., S. Del Pizzo, P. T. Kersten, and S. Troisi 2012. Low-cost and open-source solutions for automated image orientation—a critical overview, in M. Ioannides et al. (eds) *Progress in Cultural Heritage Preservation. EuroMed 2012. Lecture Notes in Computer Science* (Vol. 7616). Heidelberg: Springer.

Uueni, A. and H. Hiiop 2017. The Combination of 3D and Multispectral Imaging for Scientific Visualization – Tool for Conservation and Heritage Specialists, in S. Abrams et al. (eds) *Archiving 2017 Final Program and Proceedings*: 133-7.

Young, G. C., S. Dey, A. D. Rogers, and D. Exton 2017. Cost and time-effective method for multi-scale measures of rugosity, fractal dimension, and vector dispersion from coral reef 3D models. *PLoS ONE* 12/4: e0175341.

The potential of hyperspectral imaging for researching colour on artefacts

David Howell

Abstract

A rapidly developing technique that offers even greater advantages than infrared, visible, or UV imaging is full spectrum imaging, also variously described as multispectral imaging or hyperspectral imaging. Instead of trying to create an accurate representation or surrogate of an object, the imaging reveals information unavailable by simple inspection alone. The purposes of hyperspectral imaging can vary from simple enhancement for increased clarity of image or text, revealing hidden or obscured text or images, accurate colour measurement for a condition report, and chemical characterisation for a variety of reasons including material identification, change of state of condition, and condition at a chemical level.

Introduction

Multispectral and hyperspectral imaging are in increasing usage in the field of art conservation, art history, and archaeology, as is indicated by the number of recent journal publications on the subject.[1] Whereas normal or standard studio imaging often undertaken to digitise collections aims to recreate images as close to the original object as seen by the human eye, spectral imaging aims to record both visible and invisible features. The majority of this work has been in art galleries and libraries to reveal hidden texts and under-drawings.[2]

Multispectral images are usually created by using a high resolution digital camera. There are two common ways for producing spectral bands. One can illuminate the object with white light and then place narrow bandwidth coloured filters in front of the lens, taking an image through each lens in turn. Commonly 5–7 filters are used. Alternatively, the object can be illuminated by different coloured lights and the images taken under each colour (see Hameeuw, this volume). Coloured light can be produced by Light Emitting Diodes (LEDs) or by putting coloured filters in front of a white light source. LED systems commonly have up to around 20 bands whereas filter systems in one case has 70.[3] Whatever system is used, the result is a number of digital images taken in different spectral regions, typically with a spectral resolution of 100 nanometres (nm), of the visible spectrum, with sometimes further images taken in the infra-red (IR) and ultraviolet (UV) regions. Even with quite few bands, a great deal of information can be revealed by combining, subtracting, and other manipulation of the images. The use of statistical methods such as Principal Component Analysis (PCA) can be used to speed up the analysis. Because the images are taken at different times, possible movement and the slight difference in focussing of some lenses at different wavelengths can cause problems in aligning the images, so-called 'registration'. This can be quite complex and time consuming.

---

[1] Aalderink et al. 2010; Fischer and Kakoulli 2006; Grahn and Geladi 2007; Liang 2012, 309.

[2] See, for example, work on the Archimedes Codex: Netz et al. 2011.

[3] Aalderink et al. 2010.

These techniques are very effective for looking at relatively flat coloured objects where the whole object is seen from one direction. More spectral information can be found by using hyperspectral imaging where the number can be close to 1000 very narrow bands. A particular hyperspectral imaging system may be of most application to cylindrical seals will be described in the next section.

Hyperspectral imaging

Hyperspectral sensors, also known as imaging spectrometers, collect spectral information across a continuous spectrum at many narrow wavebands. Typical hyperspectral systems have several hundred wavebands with a spectral resolution of 10 nm or less. This is usually achieved by the use of a diffraction grating which, rather like a prism, separates the different wavelengths of white light. There are several suppliers of hyperspectral imaging systems and they can be either individually tailored for specific applications, off-the-shelf and ready to go systems, or self-made research systems for development.

The hyperspectral imaging system housed in the Bodleian Weston Library was purchased with a grant from the University of Oxford Fell Fund. It is part of an internal collaboration between the Humanities Division and individual academic colleagues from within its faculties and the Bodleian Libraries.

It is a bespoke 'push broom' system: a line scanner where the object moves past the scanning head in a similar way to a photocopier scanning a page. The 'starter set' comes with a motorized horizontal stage on which flat objects can be placed and then driven past the scanner. The Headwall system has 1600 spatial bands (pixels) and 973 spectral bands from 380 to 1000 nm. This region of the spectrum is Visible and Near Infrared (VNIR) and this spectral resolution is, at the time of writing, the highest available. At the highest resolution, with the scanner as close to the object as possible while still maintaining focus, the length of the strip scanned is 90 mm. This means that each pixel is 0.056 mm of the object, a resolution of 56 micrometres, adequate for most purposes. At this resolution, many library objects require more than one pass, but usually this high spatial resolution is not useful or required and so the scanner is moved further away from the object. For example a full stop in a printed newspaper is around 300 micrometres. Registration of the images is generally not such problem as with multispectral imaging described above since all wavelengths are measured at the same time, meaning no possibility of movement. The use of an achromatic lens means that all wavelengths are generally in focus at the same time. This is not always 100% accurate due to slight deficiencies in achromatic lenses, but the shift in pixels is at the maximum only two or three pixels at the edges of the image, which rarely causes problems in analysis.

Depth of field of focus in all imaging systems including hyperspectral is important when dealing with three dimensional object. It is important that those areas of the object further away from the lens are as 'in focus' as areas closer to the lens. This is obviously less important to flat objects where all areas of the object are the same distance from the lens. This means that for a flat object the lens can have a very open aperture to let in as much light as possible which in turn means that less light is needed to illuminate the object. This is extremely important for organic-based objects and light sensitive pigments and dyes which may fade or change colour very quickly at high light levels. Organic materials may also be damaged by temperature increases induced by high light levels. More robust objects, however, such as inorganics can withstand higher light levels and the aperture can be shut down if necessary to give a greater depth of field for more three-dimensional objects.

Many hundreds of pages from the Bodleian Library's vast collections have been scanned and analysed. The image capture is very easy and quick to set up and the scan time is usually from a few minutes for a small object up to an hour for a large object needing maximum accuracy. The scanning is carried out with bespoke software, HYPERSPEC III, written specifically for operating the equipment and is both simple and intuitive. An important aspect of any imaging system is calibration. This is to ensure that spectral information being measured is consistent and that measurements taken now can be compared with further measurements in the future. It also ensures that the spectra from different objects or parts of objects are all standardised to enable comparison and similarities and differences accurately recorded. Calibration for the Headwall system is carried out automatically by using Spectralon®, a 100 % reflective target across all wavelengths from 380 to 1000 nm, and by covering the lens for dark calibration. The speed of the stage has to be set according to the distance of the scanner to the object. This is also calculated automatically by scanning a scale with lines 10mm apart and the software setting the appropriate speed to achieve square pixels rather than elongated or squashed pixels. The technique has become more routine than project-based.

Most often a series of 'results' are given to the researcher who posed the academic question. These are usually in the form of a number of false colour images produced by ENVI® software, a high cost but extremely useful advanced hyperspectral image analysis software package written specifically for looking at multispectral and hyperspectral files. The development of ENVI® began in 1977 at the University of Colorado with a team of scientists from the Mariner Mars 7 and 9 space probes. Over subsequent decades the software has been developed for other applications, including military and environmental with the first version of ENVI® being released in 1991.

Because ENVI® is written for a wide range of users there are several hundreds of automated algorithms, most of which are not useful for the study of library materials. But the use of software is the only way that the vast amount of data can be interrogated. The mathematics are simple. Say a scan is taken of a square object. The Headwall scanner is 1600 pixels across so the total number of pixels in a square will be 2,560,000 pixels. Then each pixel is represented by 972 pieces of spectral data giving a data set of 2,488,320,000 components. And this is a square scan; the scanner can be left to scan a much longer strip giving even more data.

One of the most commonly used statistical methods for extracting information from hyperspectral data is Principal Component Analysis (PCA). In this the software tries to group spectra that have similarities across the whole spectrum. The software can do this automatically but there are several parameters that can be altered by the operator. When looking for hidden texts and other obscured items the results from PCA can be obvious; text becomes visible when looking at the different images produced by the PCA. To discover more complex and 'difficult' information a considerable number of other algorithms are available which can be set up to run automatically using the nicely named 'Automated Spectral Hourglass Wizard'. These include the vector dependent Spectral Angle Mapping (SAM) and Minimum Noise Fraction transform (MNF).

To some extent it is not really necessary to 'know what happens under the bonnet', that is, exactly how the software analyses the data. The purpose of using high-end software like ENVI® is exactly to avoid reinventing already existing and very good analytical tools. Obviously with experience the efficiency of the analysis can be improved incrementally. The first stage is to test and select the best routines to use for your particular applications. Secondly many of the routines allow parameters to be set, such as the number of Principal Components or the number of iterations of a particular process required. These two stages are mainly carried out by trial and error and experience. Finally there is the option to write your own routines using IDL®, the ENVI® programming language to automate and create your own tools. The data can also be pre-processed using other software such as MatLab.

Some uses of hyperspectral imaging

Routine scans as described above are usually turned around quite quickly by running the Wizard, quickly looking through various outputs, and sending the ones most likely to be useful to the client. An example of these 'quick wins' are some incunabula, books printed before 1501, which have been covered and bound with manuscript material. As soon as printing became possible, manuscript material became passé, but because parchment was expensive it was reused to bind the flashy new printed books. To make the books look uniform, the reused parchment was often coloured by painting over the original text and illumination, something we would baulk at now and consider vandalism. Because the original text, music notation, or illumination is now covered up scholars are now keen to recover the original designs. This was an extremely common practice. In the Bodleian, we have over 20 such items and they are being scanned to reveal the nature of the recycled manuscripts. Each volume was coloured blue and, although it is apparent that there is text and sometimes musical notation under the surface, the original decoration is not legible. Since these covers are flat, each item can be scanned in just a few minutes. Then the files can be analysed using automated image processing and results produced extremely quickly and with minimal human intervention. The only human intervention is to recognise outputs that contain readable information and to check with the 'client' that enough information has in fact been revealed (Figure 1).

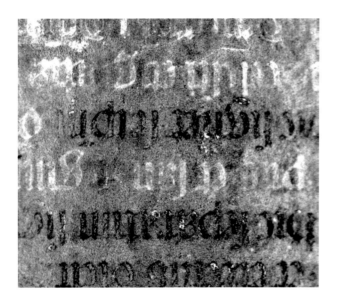 

Figure 1. Hyperspectral imaging on manuscript material from blue-painted incunabula in the Bodleian Library reveals left: text in two different colours; right: musical notation. Images © the author.

Another example of a 'quick win' was the set of results obtained from scanning the front cover of the manuscript of John Aubrey's *Brief Lives* (1680–81) in the Bodleian Library, MS Aubrey. The cover is of poor quality and shows no visible sign of a title (Figure 2). Aubrey expert Dr Kate Bennett (Magdalen College, Oxford) was keen to confirm that the title was there; she had in the past tried Infrared photography to this effect, but in vain. A quick scan and analysis revealed a very clear 'LIVES' and a perhaps more subjective 'Brief' (Figure 3).

Figure 2. Cover of *Brief Lives* manuscript, Bodleian Library. Image © the author.

Figure 3. The word LIVES revealed by hyperspectral imaging. Image © the author.

Not all objects are so accommodating at revealing their information. Perhaps the longest hyperspectral imaging project at the Bodleian's Weston Library was the work on a pre-Colombian Mexican codex, The *Codex Selden*, also known as *Codex Añute* (Bodleian MS. Arch. Selden. A.2). Studies in the 1950s had shown that parts of the codex formed a palimpsest, a re-use of an earlier document.

This is hugely significant for a number of reasons. Pre-Colombian Mexican codices are incredibly rare, with only 19 known to be extant. Also, Codex Selden, although of pre-Colombian style, is in fact slightly later, being said to date from shortly after 1556. What is below the surface, however, is most likely genuinely pre-Colombian. Despite using quite aggressive techniques in the 1950s, such as abrasion and soaking in solvents, it was not possible to identify any details of the original decoration due to the organic nature of the paints, and so further investigations were abandoned because it was felt that no more information would ever be revealed. In 2015, hyperspectral imaging was applied to selected pages of the Codex. The resulting scans were analysed over a year by Dr Ludo Snidjers of the University of Leiden, revealing unique genealogic information that will contribute to the historical and archaeological study of southern Mexico.[4]

Another use for hyperspectral imaging is the mapping and identification of pigments. The reflectance spectra of coloured materials tend to be quite broad and featureless, in the region of 400 to 1000 nm, making absolute identification of pigments problematic. However, recent experiments with Armenian manuscripts have shown that the technique is extremely efficient at mapping pigments as well as identification when used in conjunction with other techniques.[5] In these cases, the techniques used were Raman spectroscopy, which gives very diagnostic peaks for many inorganic pigments, and X-ray fluorescence spectroscopy, which gives information about the atomic composition, for instance the element mercury in Cinnabar (HgS).

Hyperspectral imaging of artefacts

Sometime the divide between manuscript and artefact can be quite obscure. An Indian birch-bark fragment, for instance, part of the 10th–12th-century Bakhshali manuscript (MS. Sansk. d. 14) in the Bodleian's collection, is materially no different to other wooden objects but by using hyperspectral imaging this mathematical text can more easily be read (Figure 4).

---

[4] Snijders et al. 2016.

[5] Maybury et al. 2018.

Figure 4. Fragment of the Bakhshali manuscript (MS Sansk. D. 14), 10th-12th century, Bodleian Library. Above: as visible to the eye. Below: the results of hyperspectral imaging. Images © the author.

Recently, there has been more interest in the applicability of hyperspectral imaging to more three-dimensional objects. One example of such work in progress is the hyperspectral imaging of the shrine of the ancient Egyptian King Taharqa in the Ashmolean Museum, which is the only pharaonic building in Britain (Figure 5). The shrine was dismantled shortly after its excavation and brought back to Oxford in 1936 in hundreds of wooden crates.

Figure 5. Shrine of Taharqa from Kawa, Sudan. c.680 BC. AN1936.661. Ashmolean Museum. Image © the author.

In its original state, the carved sandstone reliefs would have been painted in bright colours, now eroded over time. Soon after the arrival of the shrine in Oxford, the fragile painted surface was consolidated with cellulose nitrate and the shrine was rebuilt in its current location. The consolidant was not stable, however, and was beginning to flake off removing some of the surface of the stone with it, and so it was decided to remove the consolidant in 1989. Despite the lack of visible colour, the question of what the pigments would have been remained of great academic interest and, in 1990, microscopy was carried out on samples taken from the shrine prior to the removal of the consolidant. In 2015, photo-induced-luminescence study was carried out to ascertain the location of Egyptian blue. These investigations provided enough evidence for remaining pigmentation for further explorations to be carried out, starting in late 2017.

So far, exploratory photogrammetry, X-ray fluorescence, Raman spectroscopy, and, perhaps most importantly, hyperspectral imaging have been used in a new attempt to detect and characterise any remaining pigment traces. The hyperspectral apparatus had to be altered to carry out the scanning since the shrine is an immovable built structure weighing many tons, requiring the sensor to move past the object rather than the object moving under the sensor as per normal operation (Figure 6). Additionally, since the surface of the shrine is vertical, the hyperspectral sensor had to be rotated through 90 degrees. These adaptations were easily achieved, highlighting the versatility of the Headwall setup. As long as there is relative movement between the object and the sensor it does not matter how this is arranged, as long as the distance between the two does not vary too much and adversely affect focussing. While the shrine is overtly three-dimensional, however, the surfaces are relatively two-dimensional.

Figure 6. Hyperspectral imaging of the Shrine of Taharqa in progress. Image © the author.

Figure 7. Part of the Shrine of Taharqa as RGB image derived from hyperspectral data. Image © the author.

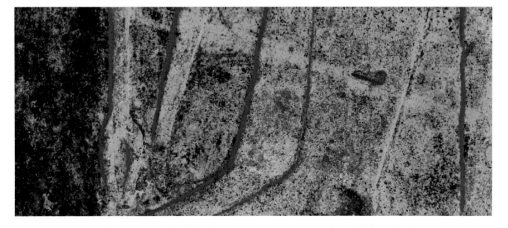

Figure 8. False colour image of the same area of the Shrine of Taharqa as Figure 7, mapping principal components. Image © the author.

Future potential for hyperspectral imaging of artefacts

The hyperspectral imaging system in the Weston Library has been in high demand for carrying out standard scanning on flat objects. But, as soon as time permits, experiments will be carried out on using the scanner on a rotating object. The similarities of the 3D scanning and push-broom hyperspectral imaging indicate that this could be an excellent method for recording colour information on cylinder seals. As stated above, all that is required is relative movement between sensor and object. It does not matter whether that movement is linear or rotational as long as the single line being scanned remains approximately at the same distance. All that is required is a turntable on which the object can safely be placed and a means for controlling the speed of rotation. This apparatus already exists and is being used by the project *Seals and Their Impressions in the Ancient Near East* to produce a flat image where the whole surface of a cylindrical seal can be seen at once rather than having to look at one side at a time (Dahl et al., this volume).

A further exciting outcome is the possibility to use the scanning of rotating artefacts on other three-dimensional objects such as some ceramics scanned for English Heritage, including a wine amphora (Figure 9). The distinctly curved surfaces of this object did present problems of depth of field, but since the ceramic is an inert inorganic object it was possible to have high light levels and a small lens aperture to overcome this (Figure 10). In these investigations, the aim was to reveal text on a curved surface, but using the same methodology as used for flat surfaces.

While the Mesopotamian cylinder seals studied by *SIANE* have a straight vertical profile, however, ceramic vessels tend to vary in profile, such as the concave neck of the amphora in Figure 10-11. This difficulty should be possible to overcome by angling the sensor to be orthogonal to whichever plane is being scanned. This would be a unique application of hyperspectral imaging and only possible with the push-broom imaging system of the type situated in the Bodleian Libraries. Using camera-based multispectral systems, the technique would not work without requiring a huge number of images from a multitude of angles, followed by a great deal of post-scan image analysis. With the scanner, however, the results will be in the same format as scans from a flat object and the analysis and processing will be the same.

Figure 9. RGB image of an amphora taken with a standard digital camera. Image © Historic England.

Figure 10. Text revealed by hyperspectral imaging but limited by low depth of field. Images © the author.

Conclusion

Hyperspectral imaging is a relatively new technique now being applied to Heritage Science; it is therefore being developed as it is being used. Like all new technologies, there are no manuals on how to get the best out of the apparatus and it is up to practitioners to experiment, develop, and disseminate results, such as at the workshop upon which this volume is based that gave an opportunity to share and publicise the capabilities of hyperspectral imaging to a diverse but specialist audience. An unexpected consequence, however, was that the sharing ideas at the workshop has resulted in a potential new methodology to be explored at the Bodleian.

References

Aalderink, B. J., M. E. Klein, R. Padoan, G. de Bruin, and T. A. G. Steemers 2010. Quantitative hyperspectral imaging technique for condition assessment and monitoring of historical documents. *The Book and Paper Group Annual* 29: 121–26.

Fischer, C. and I. Kakoulli 2006. Multispectral and hyperspectral imaging technologies in conservation: current research and potential applications. *Studies in Conservation* 51 (Supp.1): 3–16.

Grahn, H. and P. Geladi (eds) 2007. *Techniques and Applications of Hyperspectral Image Analysis*. New York: Wiley.

Liang, H. 2012. Advances in multispectral and hyperspectral imaging for archaeology and art conservation. *Applied physics: A: Materials science and processing* 106/2: 309–23.

Maybury, I. J., D. Howell, M. Terras, H. Viles 2018. Comparing the effectiveness of hyperspectral imaging and Raman spectroscopy: a case study on Armenian. *Heritage Science* 6/42.

Netz, R., W. Noel, N. Tchernetska, and N. Wilson (eds) 2011. *The Archimedes Palimpsest. Vol. 1: Catalogue and Commentary / Vol. 2: Images and Transcriptions*. Cambridge: Cambridge University Press.

Snijders, L., T. Zaman and D. Howell 2016. Using hyperspectral imaging to reveal a hidden precolonial Mesoamerican codex. *Journal of Archaeological Science: Reports* 9: 143–9.

A structured light approach to imaging ancient Near Eastern cylinder seals: how efficient 3D imaging may facilitate corpus-wide research

Jacob L. Dahl, Jonathon S. Hare, Kate Kelley, Kirk Martinez, and David Young

Abstract

This chapter presents the work of the 12-month project *Seals and Their Impressions in the Ancient Near East* (SIANE), a collaborative effort of the University of Southampton, Oxford University and the University of Paris (Nanterre). Recognising the need for improved visual documentation of ancient Near Eastern cylinder seals and the potential presented by new technologies, there have been several approaches to 3D-imaging cylinder seals in recent years (e.g. Pitzalis et al. 2008; Reh et al. 2016; Wagensonner *forthcoming*). SIANE focused on the development of equipment and workflow that can quickly capture the maximum amount of meaningful data from a seal, including 3D data from structured light and an automated production of 'digital unwrappings'. The project addressed some issues regarding the physical mounting of seals and developed a method of efficient data-capture that allows the imaging of large numbers of cylinder seals for research and presentation purposes. A particular research benefit from 3D image capture of entire seal collections is the potential for exploring computer-aided image recognition, which could contribute to comparative glyptic studies as well as helping to address the question of whether any original seals can be linked to known ancient impressions on tablets or sealings possibly separated across modern collections.

Introduction: ancient Near Eastern cylinder seals

Cylinder seals were used widely across the ancient Near East for three millennia, and tens of thousands are now held in modern collections (Wagensonner 2018), deriving from excavations and the antiquities trade. Invented in the late fourth millennium BC, as a part of a bureaucratic tool kit including clay sealings, bullae, and tablets, cylinder seals are simultaneously works of art, administrative tools, and sometimes also text objects, and are of significant import to understanding ancient near eastern societies. These objects are one of the most frequently surviving mediums for figurative art across many periods of Mesopotamian history. Like ceramics, seal styles can be important for archaeological periodization and for the study of regional identities and cultural contacts.

However, seals are also objects that often have especially complicated histories: they were used to make other archaeological objects (impressions on tablets and other clay objects) to which they are notoriously difficult to link in modern collections; they could become heirloom objects passed on for centuries; and could be re-carved for different purpose, as evidenced by remaining traces of former designs and inscriptions. Seals are known on a diverse variety of stones, presenting different reflectance properties (Hameeuw, this volume) and visual textures. The imagery on a seal is carved around the cylinder so that the whole scene is only observable upon rolling out onto clay or a similar material (producing a mirror-image of the actual carving) or by rotating the seal in hand. And seals are studied by specialists in different fields with different questions—these specialists are often art historians, but also Assyriologists and other epigraphists, and archaeologists interested in questions of technology and sealing practice. Because of the various functional and physical features of seals, imaging, cataloguing, and presenting them has proved a challenge but also an area with potentially high rewards including increased research possibilities.

SIANE's research

Corpus-wide research

The aim of the twelve-month project *Seals and Their Impressions in the Ancient Near East* (SIANE) was to develop equipment and explore methodologies for capturing and presenting cylinder seal collections on a larger scale in order to facilitate corpus-wide research. Over the course of the project, SIANE developed and tested imaging methods, collecting 3D data and other images for the entire collection of the Bibliothèque nationale de France (c. 850 seals) and the Museum of Archaeology and Anthropology, Cambridge (c. 150 seals), as well as the majority of the collection of the Ashmolean Museum, Oxford (c. 940 seals) and the 8 seals held in Charterhouse (Surrey, UK). It is hoped that this data, hosted online by the Cuneiform Digital Library Initiative (CDLI), represents the beginning of a much larger collection of seal records within the CDLI's open-access digital database.

The globally dispersed collections of ancient cylinder seals, if subject to consistent and comparable documenting, are suitable for corpus-based research from many different angles: studies of ancient trade in precious materials, of personal and bureaucratic networks, and of the spread of artistic expression and technological practice. A digital dataset would open up possibilities for art historical, archaeological, and textual studies that wish to exploit the corpus on the broader scale—yet the challenge is how to capture the most complete amount of information possible on the materiality of the seals and also how to present this data in a format that is most useful to researchers and collections managers.

Seals as material culture

Cataloguing practices contribute to the shape of research, and traditional print catalogues of seals can limit researchers in a number of ways. Seals are often presented in publication with photographs of modern rollouts, sometimes alongside a single shot of the seal in greyscale although increasingly in colour. SIANE recognises that while this type of presentation may encourage art historical study of the seal design since the rollouts can be useful for observing the carved scene, it discourages studies that approach seals from a material culture perspective. For example, the lack of colour images of the entire seal surface obscure the ways that the seal carver may have incorporated stone colour and texture into the design (Figure 2–3), or how the patterning of the stone sometimes obscures the carved image until it is rolled out (Figure 3); this aspect is better captured in the SIANE images of seals, presented in a form we call a fat-cross which consists of images of the side, top, and bottom of a seal along with a digital unwrapping, as shown in figure 1. The fat-cross format and the digital unwrapping that it includes are discussed further below.

A few other physical aspects of the cylinder seal are also conspicuously missing from traditional catalogues. Photographs of the short ends of seals are not usually included even though they may add useful information on the drill hole size and shape, stone composition, and occasionally carved decoration. In addition, the weight of cylinder seals is almost never recorded, but this basic information could be useful in a number of ways (Dahl and Kelley 2018). SIANE aimed to develop and test a system to capture 3D information on cylinder seals and at the same time address some of the current gaps in visual and other documentation of seals. We developed a workflow that included collection of the following data:

- Traditional catalogue information including dimensions, acquisition, and material information from collection records and print catalogues

- Weight of cylinder seals to 0.01 gram (see Dahl and Kelley 2018)

- Photographs, and ideally Reflectance Transformation Imaging, of existing modern rollouts

- At least ten microscopic images taken with a Dinolite digital microscope (Figure 1)[1]

- A structured light scan of the seal in the imaging equipment (first turntable rotation)

- A general set of photos of the seal in the imaging equipment (second turntable rotation)

- Photographs of the top and bottom and one side of the seal in the imaging equipment

While, ideally, researchers could work directly with objects to supplement the information available in catalogues, access to collections is not always possible or is limited for a variety of reasons, including staff availability and costs to researchers for travel to collections across the globe. The fullest possible capture for each seal was therefore a priority in designing SIANE's imaging equipment and data capture process.

---

[1] The Dinolite (see Morero et al. this volume) is a hand-held light microscope that can be powered through a USB connection to a laptop. SIANE used an AM 7115MZT model which has a magnification of x 10 to x 220. The Dinolite's portability and relative affordability have made it especially useful in recent years in fieldwork and museum contexts, and it offers more power than conventional low-powered microscopy as used in the past for general assessments of seal-carving techniques (e.g. Sax, Meeks, and Collon 2000). The Dinolite cannot compete in terms of resolution with scanning electron microscopy (SEM) equipment (for examples of SEM on cylinder seals, Gorelick and Gwinnet [1978, 1979], Sax and Meeks [1995] and Sax, Meeks and Collon [2000]), which can offer far greater resolution. However, depending on the particular SEM, this sometimes involves making silicon impressions of the seals that are then imaged (Sax, Meeks, and Collon: 2000) or coating the seal in conductive materials. This technique is therefore limited by effort, cost, and equipment availability, since not all seals collections can be brought to an SEM. By contrast, Dinolite captures are simple and quick, requiring no preparation of the seal, and can therefore be used to record entire collections. Unlike SEM, they also record the colour of stone.

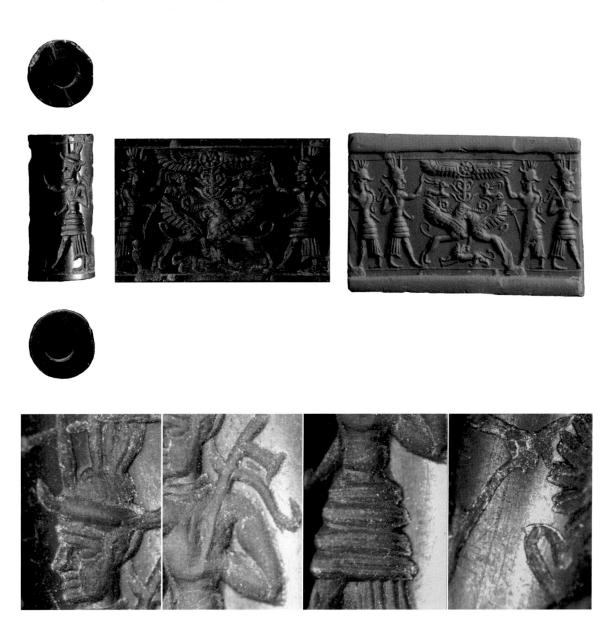

Figure 1. SIANE visual data-capture includes general images of the seals with their side, top, and bottom arranged in fat-cross format with a digital unwrapping (top left); images of modern rollout (top right) or virtual rollout; and microscopic images (below). Seal: Seyrig no. 25. © BnF Paris & AssyrOnline Project, LabEx Les passés dans le Présent, Université Paris-Nanterre, ANR-11-LABX-0026-01. Images by N. Ouraghi & K. Kelley.

Digital cataloguing of SIANE data

As with other archaeological datasets from the ancient Near East, both publication practices and modern collection histories impact upon research. Some collections are less accessible to researchers than others and the particular acquisition histories of the largest, most well-studied collections may influence our understanding of the broader history of seals and sealings. A unified, electronically searchable database would allow for testing hypotheses about widespread developments in seal carving and sealing practice that have traditionally been based upon studies of single collections.

One result of SIANE has been the addition of seal catalogue entries with visual data to the pages of the *Cuneiform Digital Library Initiative*. As a long-standing project, the CDLI is well-suited to host seals entries, but, most crucially, inclusion of seals on the CDLI reunites this dataset with those of seal impressions on tablets and bullae. For example, the seal of Aya-Kala, ruler of the southern Babylonian city of Umma in the Ur III period (c. 2100-2000 BC), has been assigned the unique seal number S000033 on the CDLI database, and 1056 clay tablets—all from the site of Umma—have been tagged as bearing an impression from this seal.[2] These objects are now held at dozens of different museums across the globe and have been published in different print publications (see https://cdli.ucla.edu/S000033). On the CDLI, the un-recovered, and possibly destroyed or re-carved, original seal object has been included as a catalogue entry and given the unique ID P430134 (see <https://cdli.ucla.edu/P430134>). In the CDLI database, P-numbers are reserved for physical objects, whether surviving or not, and S-numbers are used for the iconography of a seal. An S-number can therefore be associated with many P-numbers—tablets and sealings where it was rolled in antiquity—but a P-number is associated only with one physical object. In theory, however, in the case of re-carved seals where each re-carving represents one original object, more than one P-number can be associated with an object as it exists today. Seals are displayed on the CDLI in an approximation of the 'fat-cross' format used for clay tablets (Figures 1–3), where a side image of the seal is framed by images of the top and bottom, and accompanied by a 'digital unwrapping', a form of image presentation described in the following section.

Digital unwrapping: imaging, presenting, creating

One of the most immediately useful results of the SIANE data-collection method is the automated production of digital unwrappings—a virtual presentation of the seal as if a thin layer from the cylindrical surface had been stripped off and laid flat, retaining all its colour, surface details, and texture.[3] Digital unwrapping counteracts several of the problems with traditional documentation methods mentioned above: traditional photography fails to capture the carving in its entirety, while conventional drawings and photographs of modern roll-outs can show the design remarkably well but do not retain information on the colour and texture of the stone and how these may interplay with the incised designs. The digital unwrapping of seals is therefore useful for revealing the choices made by the artist with respect to seal design and stone texture. In cases where the stone texture renders the carving difficult to view, different light angles can be generated for viewing either aspect of the seal (Figure 8).

Yet, it should be noted that digitally unwrapping the seal presents modern audiences with an imaginary object, one that never existed, and this raises important questions about digital imaging and the display of images. Traditional modern rollouts of ancient seals, created in plaster, polymer clay, or plasticine, result in an impression of the object in mirror image to that carved on the seal. While these rollouts are also artificial, modern objects, they are more closely related to *potential* ancient objects—ancient impressions on clay. Unfortunately, ancient impressions of seals are rarely visible in full on uninterrupted or uninscribed surfaces, a fact that may have contributed to our inability of finding more than a handful of potential matches between recovered ancient seals and

---

[2] See Firth 2014 for discussion of the process of adding seal impression data to the CDLI.

[3] The practice of digitally unwrapping a cylinder seal was first trialled by the West Semitic Research Project. See for example, WSRP collaborative work at the Spurlock Museum of World Cultures (Illinois): http://www.spurlock.illinois.edu/collections/notable-collections/profiles/cylinder-seals.html

impressions on ancient artefacts (see Hallo 1973 and most recently Radner 2012). Sometimes we can show a difference between the types of seals in our collections and the extant ancient impressions: several hundred seals in the so-called 'schematic' style (see Asher-Greve 1985; Pittman and Potts 2009), dating to the Late Uruk and Jemdet Nasr periods (c. 3500–2900 BC), exist, yet no ancient impressions of this type of seal are known.

Viewing the carving as a whole via the digital unwrapping, however, creates an experience of the object that in some ways may be equally or more authentic to the experience of seeing an actual seal than viewing a modern impression. When holding and manipulating a seal as the ancient carver or owner could, the scene can in fact usually be comprehended in full. This experience of the object could be recreated by an animated 3D model of the seal (see below), but such models are not necessary for most research purposes and remain difficult to handle in an integrated online research environment. The 'unwrapped' image is therefore a tool of convenience for art historians and material culture specialists interested in efficiently understanding the motifs, but it is also more than that. It preserves far more information than modern rollouts on the materiality of the object and enables innovative searching and indexing of the visual textures (Cimpoi, Maji, Vedaldi 2015) as well as computational alignment of visual texture and engraved design.

Figure 2. Digital unwrappings offer information on the stone patterning and carving in a 2D publication format, sometimes revealing how the carvers used features of the stone as part of their composition. From top to bottom and left to right: Delaporte nos. 135, 398, 367, 170, 196, and 349 © BnF Paris & AssyrOnline Project, LabEx Les passés dans le Présent, Université Paris-Nanterre, ANR-11-LABX-0026-01. Images by N. Ouraghi & K. Kelley.

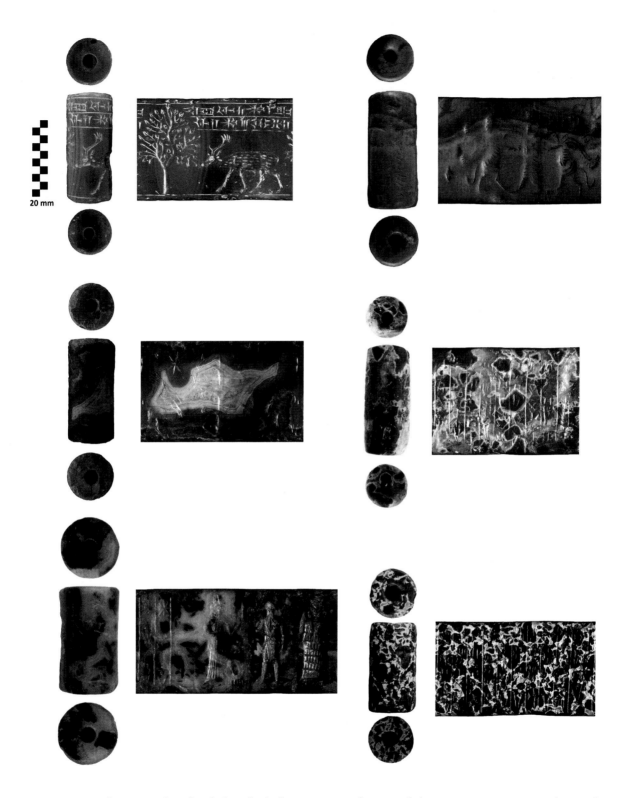

Figure 3. Further examples of seals for which the carver may have used the stone patterning to enhance the dynamism of the scene. The stones of some seals render the carving—perhaps intentionally?—very difficult to see on the seal itself, such as on two Kassite seals with cuneiform inscriptions (no.'s 295 and 302). From top to bottom/ left to right: Delaporte no.'s 307, 385, 191, 394, 295, and 302 © BnF Paris & AssyrOnline Project, LabEx Les passés dans le Présent, Université Paris-Nanterre, ANR-11-LABX-0026-01. Images by N. Ouraghi & K. Kelley.

The potential of 3D data

The most time and resource intensive of the types of data collected for SIANE (both in terms of capture and processing) is the 3D data, for which the acquisition process is described below. We suggest this data may also be among the most useful for innovative new studies of cylinder seal motifs and carving through the use of computer-aided image recognition.

Despite the many advances in imaging technologies and their increasingly common and diverse uses, the most frequent applications of 3D technology for artefacts (rather than archaeological landscapes) remain for research around a museum's most exceptional objects, as specific research questions or conservation needs arise. Few projects have proposed the use of 3D imaging for documentation and study of entire corpora or collections, although some projects have explored the potential of computer-aided matching of 3D data for larger datasets from a given site or context—for example, Koller (2008) applied several computer algorithms to help in the process of reconstructing fragments of a Roman marble map that had proven a time-consuming and difficult puzzle by conventional methods. Similarly, 3D data on the shape of pottery sherds is being exploited for projects interested in digital vessel reconstruction (Karasik and Smilanski: 2008).

Cylinder seals, however, are an excellent candidate for an even larger-scale 3D imaging project encompassing all known objects of this type in modern collections (estimated at c. 50,000 specimens worldwide, Wagensonner 2018). This is due to the convenience for imaging offered by their consistent cylindrical shape and general robustness. In addition, a consistent corpus-wide data-set would be particularly beneficial, since the research questions asked about seals are often dependent upon comparison with seals in other collections although seals are widely dispersed across collections and are in general poorly documented in print publications.

Developments in computer vision and machine learning can be exploited to find statistical patterns in large datasets (Bishop 2006; Prince 2012). In the case of cylinder seals, such patterns may offer evidence relating to their production, use, and development through time. As an initial example, relatively straightforward processing can elucidate the structure of the incised patterns. Standard operations such as thresholding, filtering, shape smoothing and region finding can be applied to a depth map of the surface to give a simplified map of the carving (Gonzalez and Woods 2006). This opens up the possibility of shape matching to identify similar motifs on other seals, and to systematically analyse the spatial arrangements of motifs on individual seals. Beyond this, machine learning can detect patterns and trends in data by finding and exploiting features that have not been specified *a priori* (e.g. Krizhevsky, Sutskever, and Hinton 2012). This may lead to the discovery of new groupings within the corpora of seals, with the potential to offer insights into cultural developments of their source regions. While art historical projects on seal iconography may continue to focus on corpus-wide descriptive terminology (e.g. http://www.diganes.gwi.uni-muenchen.de), computer vision can offer an alternative (and ideally, complementary) method to researching iconography across this large dataset.

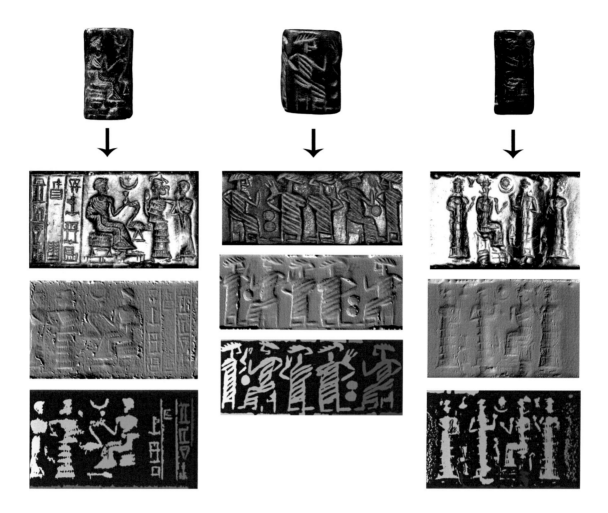

Figure 4. Different representations of cylinder seals. Each column is a seal from the collection at Charterhouse school (left to right: 2017.8, 2017.11 and 2017.12). The top row shows a normal side view of each seal. The second row is the digital unwrapping, showing the whole surface of the seal as if it could be peeled off and flattened. The lighting of these images can be controlled and altered during the creation of the unwrapping by selecting sections from the from the 120 images of each seal; here the light is chosen so that highlights on the stone make the incised pattern stand out. The third row shows 'virtual rollouts'. Generated from a 3D model of the seal, these give a rendered view of what a sealing from the seal would look like; again, the lighting is controllable. The bottom row shows the result of a simple image processing operation on the virtual rollouts: more advanced versions of such operations offer the possibility of automatic analysis and matching.

3D data may also help to address a problem in the study of seals and seal impressions: why have so few matches been identified between original seals and ancient impressions? Because of the size of the dataset, the large variety of scenes carved—sometimes with only minor variation in content from other seals—and the interruption of seal iconography on many impressed objects, computer vision may prove useful in identifying matches between objects impressed with the same seal, or, indeed, in matching seals to objects on which they have been impressed. Computational image analysis has the ability to remove the uncertainties of human choice in comparing images. In recent years, the idea of decomposing image content into 'visual words' (starting with the work of Sivic & Zisserman 2003, see also Bergel et al. 2013: 6), which are prototypical patterns learned across an image corpus, has had much success in image analysis research. These 'visual word' patterns are fuzzy in nature and incorporate the notion that a particular pattern will have some variation across images of different objects. By applying these techniques to images of seals, it will be possible to automatically index patterns within the images. Coupling these indexed features with supervised and unsupervised machine-learning techniques will allow scholars to identify and explore potential clusters of seals that reuse specific iconography.

During our pilot project we have tested open source online software developed by the University of Oxford Seebibyte project to match impressions of the same cylinder seal by searching for segments of one impression in defined corpora (using well-preserved impressions with known matches, see figure 5). These first results show that the basic algorithms are applicable for ancient Near Eastern seal impressions.[4] Further granulation of the code and improvement in image capture and image processing will improve the capabilities of the program. In a further step towards such research, SIANE staff imaged a seal held in the collection of Charterhouse in Surrey, UK, one of the few potential matches between an ancient seal and ancient impressions: see Dahl (forthcoming) for an assessment of the match.

---

[4] For a smaller but similar use in humanities see Bergel et al. 2013.

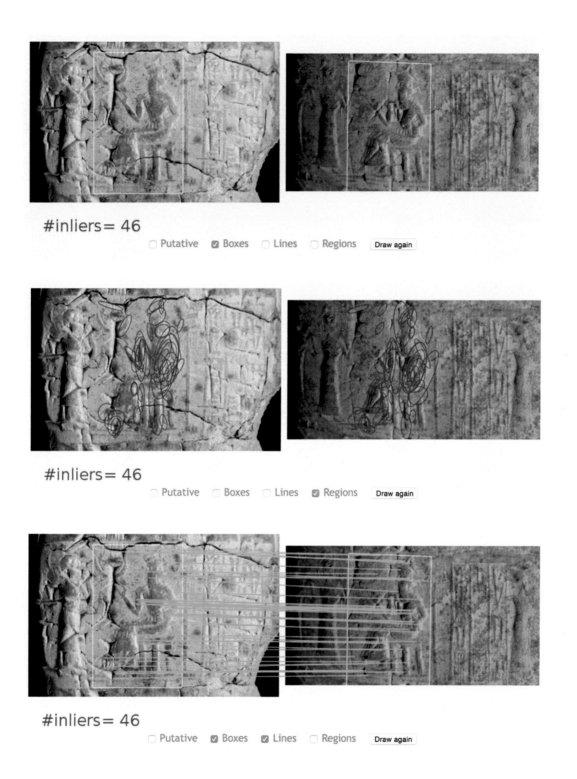

Figure 5. Upper row: two matching seal impressions computationally identified from a group of six. Middle row: regions or 'visual words' indexed by program. Lower row: matching of identical regions (Bergel et al. 2013). For an image of the tablet on the left, a tablet in Turin, Italy, see https://cdli.ucla.edu/P100257; for the right, a tablet in Los Angeles, California, see https://cdli.ucla.edu/P235442.

Practical considerations for digitally recording seal collections

In this section we set out the underlying considerations that guided the design of the system for creating the digital images described above: the data goals, spatial resolution, depth accuracy scanning time, consistency, and portability. The following two sections describe the general approach we chose and the prototype we built. We then discuss the post-processing of the data conducted to yield useful and easily shareable results, before looking briefly at how the system should be developed in the future and what advanced data processing may offer when applied to the large body of seal data.

Data goals

Given the broader research goals described above, the central objective of the scanning process is to capture as much information as possible about the physical object within a reasonable space of time, subject to the overriding requirement not to risk damage to the seal. To a large extent, the more time that is available to scan a seal, the greater the variety and quality of the information that we can obtain; for example, slower scans provide finer-grained surface detail. However, this basic trade-off spawns a variety of other issues, involving cost, portability, and data volume.

We aim to capture as complete a physical description of the seal as possible, comprising of two main components. The first is an accurate representation of the shape of the seal, including the details of carving and any other surface irregularities. This geometric information allows reconstruction of the seal as a digital object that can be manipulated and viewed from different positions, as well as generating a virtual roll-out—that is, a digital image representation of what an impression of the seal would look like. In principle, such information would also allow us to produce a precise physical replica using a fine-grained 3D printer. The second component is a record of the reflectance spectrum across the seal's surface. This describes how the brightness and colour of light changes as it is reflected from each point on the surface. This information allows us to render our digital 3D model of the seal so that it has the appearance of the original. It is also the information required to colour the surface of a physical replica to make it look like the original object.

The overall aim is to capture both of these kinds of information as fully as possible, recognising that it is impossible to do so perfectly. Our priority is the 3D model, as this captures the most information about the carving and is thus most likely to reveal meaningful patterns of design across collections of seals.

Spatial resolution and depth accuracy

The most significant parameter in the design is the spatial resolution of the measurements—the scale of the finest detail that is recorded. In a digital photograph, the resolution is related to the size of the patch of surface that corresponds to a single pixel in the image. The idea is essentially the same in 3D scanning, except that the information recorded for each cell in the mesh specifies 3D coordinates of the surface. It is clear that the resolution of our system needs to be sufficient to capture the finest details of the carving such as tool marks.

The choice of resolution has a strong impact on the design of the scanner. Whatever technology is adopted, increasing the resolution tends to increase both the cost and the amount of time needed to scan a seal as well as the volume of data collected. Although it would be possible to have a variable resolution so that, for example, smaller seals would be imaged with finer detail, this would add complexity and would mean that the results for different seals would not be directly comparable. We therefore chose to use a fixed basic resolution in terms of samples per millimetre.

We adopted a design goal of 0.02 mm resolution (meaning that a corrugated surface with 25 ridges per millimetre would be represented accurately). A sample of seals from the Ashmolean Museum, photographed at high resolution, indicated that this resolution captured the details of the carving, and indeed it would be surprising if the carvers were able to inscribe detail at finer scales. Sax and Meeks (1995) used a low-powered binocular microscope at magnification levels between x10 to x25 (0.01 mm to 0.004 mm) to make the majority of their assessments of seal-carving techniques in the British Museum collection of seals. As discussed below, significantly higher resolutions than 0.02 mm are difficult to achieve with digital imaging technologies, and we feel that this resolution allows a practical system to be built without compromising performance. Current archival standards for imaging tablets, adopted by the CDLI (see http://cdli.ox.ac.uk/wiki/submission_guidelines), specify a scan resolution of 600 pixels per inch, or 0.042 mm spacing. Our target resolution is better than 1200 pixels per inch.

While the resolution specifies the density of measurements across the surface of the seal, the depth precision specifies how well we can measure the depth of the surface relative to a perfect cylinder at each of these points (that is, it represents the height of the smallest ridges that could be detected). It is difficult to determine a target figure for this parameter in advance, but clearly the depth precision should be no greater than the resolution and possibly needs to be smaller in order to capture light and shallow engraving. As an interim aim, we expect to measure depth to better than 0.01 mm and to investigate this requirement further using the working system.

Scanning time

In order to deal with large collections in a reasonable time, the scan time for an individual seal needs to be as low as possible, particularly as access to collections is constrained by the availability of study rooms and staff. We proposed a target of 5 minutes per seal (from removal from its storage container to replacement). In practice, to scan over 800 seals at the Bibliothèque nationale de France in a campaign of six weeks, we worked at an average rate of 10 minutes per seal, allowing about 34 seals to be scanned in a typical working day. To achieve this with our current equipment, we needed to reduce the resolution of the 3D data, while retaining full resolution for the reflectance data. Reducing the time to 5 minutes would clearly reduce costs and increase the chances of successful large-scale data collection, and we are looking at how we might improve both the scanning speed and the setup time to reach this goal without compromising resolution.

Consistency

The data acquisition process needs to be as consistent and as standardised as possible to enable comparisons of seals from different collections using different capture equipment. We therefore needed to avoid sources of variability such as illumination, sensor changes, and movements of handheld equipment. In theory, a 3D model with a documented level of accuracy is device independent. The colour images could also be calibrated to sRGB for consistency.

Portability

It is important to have equipment that can easily be moved between collections and which can be set up quickly. Ideally, the system should pack into a single container that could be transported by one person using trains and aircraft. Our present system just meets this goal, but would benefit from being further reduced in weight and volume.

SIANE scanning equipment design

Approach to 3D imaging

The choice of method for obtaining 3D data is the central element of the design. We considered a number of technologies:

Laser scanning

In this approach, multiple laser beams are directed onto the object and 3D positions are inferred by measuring the time taken to reflect off the surface or by triangulation (Payne 2013). Until recently, systems of this type were either non-portable or did not achieve sufficient resolution. For example, the Konica Minolta Vivid 910[5] claims only to reach about one tenth of our target resolution. The technology is developing rapidly, but systems that might meet our resolution and portability requirements remain very expensive (in the tens of thousands of pounds) and testing would be needed to see whether these devices could meet our timing and consistency requirements. Due to these considerations, we did not pursue this strategy.

Photogrammetry

Images from multiple cameras with different viewpoints are compared in this high-precision version of stereopsis (Linder 2009). Although photogrammetric systems and software are readily available, most offer resolution much worse than our target. In addition, these methods depend on matching surface markings between the different images, and therefore perform badly on smooth uniform surfaces. Although cylinder seals have carvings and other texture, there are typically also significant smooth regions, and it is unlikely that a photogrammetric system would be sufficiently consistent and reliable.

Structured light

These methods project a pattern of light onto the surface. Viewed from one side, the projected pattern is distorted by the shape of the surface, and, by capturing this distortion using an offset camera, the 3D shape of the surface can be reconstructed (Zanuttigh et al. 2016). Structured light combines the robustness of laser scanning with the lower expense of photogrammetry. The main drawback for some applications is that it requires ambient light to be reduced so that the pattern is clear, but for small objects like seals this can be done using a box to enclose the apparatus. An advantage of this method is that images under general illumination accurately registered with the 3D data can easily be obtained using the same equipment. Reh et al. (2016) also adopted structured light for their system. Driven by 3D-printing demands, many commercial systems have emerged for small

---

[5] https://www.konicaminolta.com/instruments/download/instruction_manual/3d/pdf/vivid-910_vi-910_instruction_eng.pdf (4 June 2018).

objects, but these systems are currently of insufficient resolution for our research purposes (e.g. https://matterandform.net/scanner).

We opted for a structured light approach, as offering the best point on the trade-off between performance and cost. We then developed equipment specifically tailored to imaging cylinder seals.

Scanning geometry

The simplest form of structured light is a straight shadow edge. Alternatives include a variety of stripe patterns, including laser-generated interference fringes, random patterns, and coded patterns (Webster et al. 2016; Van der Jeught & Dirckx 2016). These have some theoretical advantages, but the simplicity of the shadow edge makes processing more straightforward and contributes to obtaining robust results at high resolution since there is little ambiguity in the shadow position. In addition, a sufficiently sharp edge supports very precise depth estimation, is easy to produce, and involves no additional parameters to adjust. We chose this pattern for the prototype for these reasons.

The shadow edge must be scanned across the whole surface of the object. Systems for scanning small objects generally use a turntable and a fixed light source to achieve this and, in the case of the seals, the cylindrical symmetry makes this arrangement particularly appropriate with the shadow edge oriented parallel to the axis of the cylinder. The contour formed by the shadow edge on the surface of the seal is normally recorded using one or more digital cameras offset from the light source. Commercial systems (e.g. https://www.scaninabox.com/) often use two cameras mounted on opposite sides of the light source, but this increases the size, the cost, and the data volume, so we chose a single-camera system. The angle between the camera and the projector, subtended at the axis of the seal, is an important parameter. Larger angles increase the depth precision but also increase the possibility of occlusion of the shadow edge by the sides of sharp and deep indentations. We addressed this by making the angle adjustable in the prototype system.

Images for appearance

The 3D measurements need to be complemented by images of the seal under general illumination rather than structured light. These give ordinary views of the seal as a solid object at many different angles of rotation—typically, this generated around 120 general images. These are used to produce the digital unwrapping discussed above. Each of these ordinary views offers an approximation to reflectance measurements, which combined with the 3D information allow a fully-rendered 3D digital reconstruction to be made. Our design therefore has provision for additional light sources to be mounted that allow these 'images for appearance' to be acquired while the seal is mounted in the apparatus, immediately following the collection of data based on structured light.

Seal mount

Mounting the seal on a horizontal turntable with its axis vertical is intrinsically safer than the mounting adopted by Reh et al. (2016). However, many seals have damaged or irregular end surfaces and many have a small radius compared with their length. These all require support at their upper end; however, this must not obstruct the camera's view at any stage of a 360° rotation, so the support cannot be mounted on the turntable.

Our solution is to mount the upper support on a bearing above the seal, allowing free rotation but no sideways movement. The bearing is mounted on a steel or aluminium rod sliding vertically, whose weight alone presses the support pad onto the seal. This means that the contact force on the seal is controlled and limited; a mechanism involving screws or springs would not offer this degree of safety. Slightly yielding high-friction material for the upper and lower pads holds the seal securely. This was effective even for most seals with broken ends or unusual features (Figure 6, bottom). For images of the edges of seals, the objects could simply be turned on their sides.

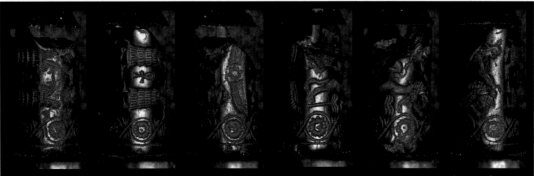

Figure 6. Above: The seal-mounting system used by SIANE with Chandon de Briailles 1 (Bibliothèque nationale de France) and the live view on the screen behind. Below: Seal Chandon de Briailles 106 shown at different stages of rotation on the turntable. The 3D-printed cap keeps the seal centred during rotation and functions well with even largely broken seal edges. © BnF Paris & AssyrOnline Project, LabEx Les passés dans le Présent, Université Paris-Nanterre, ANR-11-LABX-0026-01. Images by N. Ouraghi & K. Kelley.

A prototype scanner

Hardware

The prototype scanner implements the ideas above. We use an industrial computer vision camera from FLIR (the Grasshopper GS3-U3-91S6C-C), which has a 9 Mpixel sensor of 3.69 μm sensor size operating at 9 frames/second. This type of camera can capture frames much faster than normal digital cameras and connects to the computer via USB3. We fitted a 50 mm fixed-focus f/4 lens that gives us a resolution of 0.0156 mm, slightly better than our target, at a working distance of about 0.2 m. The distance between the camera and the seal ultimately determines the overall size of the equipment, and this is small enough to allow it to be portable.

The arrangement gives a field of view about 53 mm high, which places a limit on the length of a seal that can be scanned in a single operation. Although higher resolution cameras are available, they offer poorer performance in terms of noise, sensitivity, and, critically, lower data transfer rates. At present, this compromise between resolution, field of view, and cost appears to be the correct one.

The projector is based on an LED-based unit from Advanced Illumination fitted with an identical lens to the camera. The camera and the projector are mounted on manually operated linear translation stages for microscopy to allow fine control of focus by changing the distance to the seal. This also avoids changing the focal length of the camera, as happens with conventional lens focusing, which simplifies calibration of the scale of the images.

The turntable is a microscope rotation stage driven by a DC servomotor from Thorlabs. It provides positioning accuracy and repeatability to better than the equivalent of an image pixel at the surface of the seal. The upper seal support uses a 16 mm diameter rod, mounted in a plain linear bearing, with a small rotary bearing attached to its end. The seal sits between two 3D-printed soft plastic pads, the lower one a flat mat covering the turntable, the upper one a cone mounted in the upper bearing. The upper pad can easily be changed between different sizes to match the seal size.

Each seal needs to be positioned with its axis of symmetry aligned closely with the axis of rotation. We use a calibration object to line up the camera on the rotation axis at the start of a session and use the camera view to centre each seal manually. The seal is re-centred after a 90° rotation of the turntable to complete alignment.

The camera, projector, turntable, and seal support are mounted on an aluminium baseboard that provides alternative mounting positions for the projector and for general illumination. The camera and turntable are controlled by a purpose-built PC and the system can be disassembled and transported in a single case.

Figure 7. The current scanning equipment. The seal mount is at bottom left, the structured light projector at top right, and the camera at bottom right, with a mount for an ordinary LED between them. In operation, a light-excluding cover is placed over the whole apparatus.

Software and data

Data acquisition software was developed in MATLAB™. The software provides a live, magnified view of the seal for alignment and focusing of the camera and projector, controls the turntable, and handles image acquisition and data transfer to disk.

A 3D scan of a seal requires multiple images to be taken during a full rotation. Ideally, the seal surface would move 0.02 mm (the target resolution) between frames, but this would require too much scanning time. We increased the inter-frame rotation for all but the smallest seals, giving surface movement of 0.04 mm and 1700 images per seal, on average. The number of images was automatically adjusted for seal diameter. Each image was cropped in the camera to select a region of interest surrounding the shadow line, giving an average resolution of 1900×600 pixels. With lossless compression, the resulting data occupies about 4 GB per seal.

The raw data are stored for later processing on a large hard disk drive in a folder hierarchy that is organised by institution, seal acquisition number, scan type, and scan date/time. The timestamp allows repeat scans to be performed without losing data or changing the identifier. The institution name is based on the URL of the institution's main web site using the principles set out in the MuseumID proposal (http://museumid.net).

Limitations

There are a number of limitations to this prototype system, which will form the basis for future development:

- Long seals, over about 50 mm, have to be scanned twice, once each way up, and the results digitally spliced. These seals are relatively rare, but it would be preferable to scan them in a single pass.

- To keep the exposure time small and avoid motion blur, the lens apertures have to be fully open at f/4. The theoretical depth of field is thus only about 1 mm for full resolution; in practice, the image remains usably sharp for 2-3 mm on either side of the focus point. The depth of field limits the accuracy of the 3D reconstruction for very irregular seals and also reduces the quality of any general views of the seals 'in the round' taken with the camera.

- Manual focusing of the camera and projector using a magnified live view takes time and is sometimes difficult to do consistently.

- On average, the rotation time for 3D data is about 3 minutes and for appearance is about 1 minute. (The time of 10 minutes per seal given above includes the time taken to place the seal, focus the equipment, and other overheads.) These times are essentially determined by the frame rate of the camera and could be improved.

- Alignment of the seal axis with the axis of rotation of the turntable and illumination switching are currently manual operations that could be streamlined.

- The equipment can be moved by one person but is heavy and cumbersome to manage on public transport. Weight savings would be helpful.

- Scanning the seals at the Bibliothèque nationale de France generated over 4 TB of raw data. This is a substantial amount to transfer and archive, and it would be useful to reduce it by better compression and a tighter region of interest. However, modern hard drives (up to 10 TB at the time of writing) mean it is quite simple to store rather than risking data loss.

Processing for digital unwrappings

Digital unwrappings show what the seal would look like if a thin layer of the surface could be peeled away and flattened out while retaining the shape of the carving and the surface markings.

This is relatively straightforward to achieve. Strips of images taken during a full rotation under general illumination are spliced together, taking care to allow for the foreshortening of the surface if the strip is not directly facing the camera. Different strips can be chosen to generate images under different apparent lighting conditions. These images and the 3D model are complementary: the digital unwrappings record the appearance, including the colour and surface markings, but do not explicitly represent the surface shape, while the 3D model represents only the shape. A future extension would be to add a colour texture map using the image data.

Figure 8. Digital unwrappings of seal Chandon de Briailles 8 from the Bibliothèque nationale de France under different virtual light sources. © BnF Paris & AssyrOnline Project, LabEx Les passés dans le Présent, Université Paris-Nanterre, ANR-11-LABX-0026-01. Images by N. Ouraghi & K. Kelley.

Processing for 3D models

The central operation in creating 3D models is finding the exact position of the curved shadow boundary in each of the raw images. It is then straightforward geometry to convert this into a position in 3D and hence to get a detailed 3D digital model of the seal. The contour-finding stage involves several challenges:

- The position needs to be measured to sub-pixel accuracy to achieve the depth resolution we want.

- Variations in the colour and brightness of the seal surface can cause spurious edges to appear in the illuminated region.

- Highly reflective patches in the seal material can disrupt the contour.

- Translucent and transparent seal materials make the contour indistinct.

For these reasons, ordinary thresholding and edge detection (Szeliski 2011) in individual images are not adequate. Rather than treating the images independently, we stack them to form a 3-dimensional volume containing a surface representing the evolution of the shadow contour. This allows us to exploit the constraint that the seal surface is continuous in space. We currently use two main approaches: a modified Canny surface detector (Canny 1986) with sub-pixel output and orientation-specific sensitivity; and an adaptive surface (Blake & Isard 1998) fitted iteratively using Newton's method. The second of these is the more general approach and allows general properties of the seal to be incorporated into the algorithm.

Some results are shown in Figure 4. The 3D model has been used in each case to generate a synthetic image of a digital roll-out, and a simple segmentation algorithm has been used to pick out the incised regions.

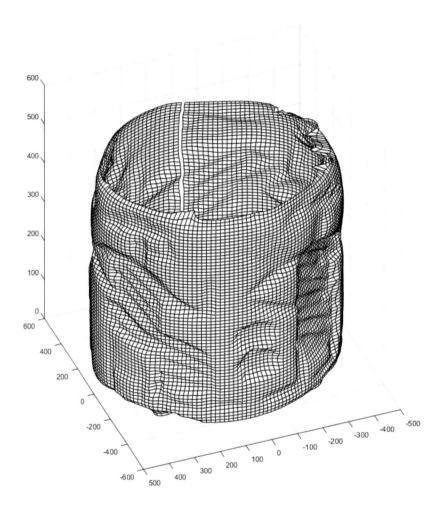

Figure 9. A 3D model of seal Charterhouse 2017.11 shown as a mesh drawn on its surface. The detail of the underlying model is far greater than this mesh can show.

Learning from the prototype

Our experience of the prototype hardware suggests three core areas of development for future systems:

- Lighting. Higher intensity lighting will allow shorter exposure times, and hence faster seal rotation and smaller apertures, giving greater depth of field. Different patterns of structured light may allow more robust and accurate shape determination. Light sources with controllable spectral content may allow more accurate analysis of the surface reflectivity, and more careful positioning of general light sources will give better surface appearance images.

- Weight and size. Lighter and more compact components will allow easier deployment.

- Software. A graphical user interface for the operator will improve the efficiency and reliability of data acquisition. The processing for 3D model extraction may also be further developed to be more robust and precise.

Overall, our experience with the prototype has allowed us to better understand and manage the design trade-offs identified above so that future systems can be more closely matched to the requirements for imaging large numbers of cylinder seals for research purposes.

Project results and conclusions

The approach to digital capture of data on cylinder seals adopted by SIANE required an initially large investment of resources; however, SIANE equipment is now theoretically capable of efficiently capturing virtually all known cylinder seals in modern collections within a timespan of around five years were it given the full-time effort of a handful of employees. The data required to produce 3D models like that in figure 9, as well as coloured 3D models, is now available for over 1,600 cylinder seals imaged by SIANE during its pilot project. While developments in imaging methods will continually improve the manner in which objects are imaged, presented, and understood (see Hameeuw, this volume), the sets of data collected through SIANE's capture methods are sufficient to begin supporting research on cylinder seals from a multitude of perspectives previously untenable due to the state of print catalogues.

References

Asher-Greve, J. M. 1985. *Frauen in altsumerischer Zeit.* Malibu: Bibliotheca Mesopotamica 18.

Bergel, G., A. Franklin, M. Heaney, R. Arandjelovic, A. Zisserman and D. Funke 2013. Content-based image recognition on printed broadside ballads: The Bodleian Libraries' ImageMatch Tool, *Proceedings of the IFLA World Library and Information Congress.*

Bishop, C. M. 2006. *Pattern Recognition and Machine Learning (Information Science and Statistics).* Berlin: Springer-Verlag.

Blake, A. and M. Isard 1998. *Active Contours.* London: Springer-Verlag.

Boon, P., and M. De Vries-Melein 2012. A new look at cylinder seals – digitization of 5 seals from the De Liagre Böhl collection, Leiden, The Netherlands, in R. Matthews and J. Curtis (eds) *Proceedings of the 7th International Congress on the Archaeology of the Ancient Near East 12 April – 16 April 2010, the British Museum and UCL, London*, Volume 3 (Fieldwork and Recent Research): 357–71. Wiesbaden: Harrasowitz.

Canny, J. 1986. A computational approach to edge detection. *IEEE Transactions on Pattern Analysis and Machine Intelligence,* PAMI-8/6: 679–98.

Cimpoi, M., Maji, , S. and A. Vedaldi. 2015. Deep filter banks for texture recognition and segmentation. *IEEE Conference on Computer Vision and Pattern Recognition.*

Dahl, J. L. and K. Kelley. A note on cataloguing ancient cylinder seals: including weight. *Cuneiform Digital Library Notes* 2018/2.

Delaporte, L. 1910. *Catalog of Oriental Cylinders and Assyro-Babylonian Seals, Persian and Syro-Cappadocian of the National Library.* Paris: Ernest Leroux.

Digard, F. 1975. *Répertoire Analytique des Cylindres Orientaux.* Paris : Editions du Centre national de la recherche scientifique.

Gonzalez, R. C. and R. E. Woods. 2006. *Digital Image Processing (3rd Edition).* Upper Saddle River, NJ: Prentice-Hall.

Gorelick, L., and A. J. Gwinnett 1978. Ancient seals and modern science: Using the scanning electron microscope as an aid in the study of ancient seals. *Expedition* 20/2: 38–47.

Gorelick, L. and A. J. Gwinnet 1979. Ancient lapidary, a study using scanning electron microscopy and functional analysis. *Expedition* 22: 17–32.

Firth, R. Notes on composite seals in CDLI. *Cuneiform Digital Library Notes* 2014/26

Hallo, W. W. 1973. The Seals of Aššur-remanni, in M. A. Beek, A. A. Kampman, C. Nijland and J. Ryckmans (eds) *Symbolae Biblicae et Mesopotamicae. Francisco Mario Theodoro De Liagre Böhl Dedicatae*: 180–84. Leiden: Brill.

Karasik, A. and U. Smilansky 2008. 3D scanning technology as a standard archaeological tool for pottery analysis: practice and theory. *Journal of Archaeological Science* 35:1148–68.

Koller, D. R. 2008. Virtual archaeology and computer-aided reconstruction of the Severan Marble Plan, in B. Frischer and A. Dakouri-Hild (eds), *Beyond Illustration: 2d and 3d Digital Technologies as Tools for Discovery in Archaeology.* BAR International Series 1805. Archaeopress: Oxford.

Lippert, M. 2016. 3D model of Cylinder Seal VA 00619, Vorderasiatisches Museum Berlin – Staatliche Museen zu Berlin, Cylinder Seals, Edition Topoi, DOI: 10.17171/1-5-1582-1 Accessed June 27 2018.

Maaten, L. van der, P. Boon, G. Lange, H. Paijmans and E. Postma 2007. Computer vision and machine learning for archaeology, in J. T. Clark and E. M. Hagemeister (eds) *Digital Discovery. Exploring New Frontiers in Human Heritage. CAA 2006. Computer Applications and Quantitative Methods in Archaeology. Proceedings of the 34th Conference, Fargo, United States, April 2006*: 476–82. Budapest: Archaeolingua.

Payne, E. M. 2013. Imaging Techniques in Conservation. *Journal of Conservation and Museum Studies* 10/2: 17–29. DOI: http://doi.org/10.5334 Accessed June 27 2018.

Olson, B. R., R. A. Placchetti, J. Quartermaine, and A. E. Killebrew 2013. The Tel Akko Total Archaeology Project (Akko, Israel): Assessing the suitability of multi scale 3D field recording in archaeology. *Journal of Field Archaeology* 38: 244–62.

Pitard, W. 2014. Circular signatures: Getting a better view of Mesopotamia's smallest art form. *Biblical Archaeology Review* 40/3: 55–9.

Prince, S. J. D. 2012. *Computer Vision: Models, Learning, and Inference.* Cambridge UK: Cambridge University Press.

Radner, K 2012. The Seal of Tašmetum-šarrat, Sennacherib's Queen, and its Impressions, in G. B. Lanfranchi et al (eds), *Leggo! Studies presented to Frederick Mario Fales,* Leipziger Altorientalische Studien 2, 687–98. Wiesbaden: Harrassowitz.

Reh, B. C. Seitz and S. Speck 2016. Seal rotation device – an automated system for documenting cylinder seals, paper delivered at the 40th ÖAGM & ARW Joint Workshop on Computer Vision and Robotics. Wels: FH Oberösterreich. DOI: 10.11588/heidok.00020769

Pittman, H. and D. T. Potts 2009. The earliest cylinder seal in the Arabian Peninsula. *Arabian Archaeology and Epigraphy* 20: 109–21.

Pitzalis, D., P. Cignoni, M. Menu, and G. Aitken 2008. 3D enhanced model from multiple data sources for the analysis of the cylinder seal of Ibni-Sharrum, in M. Ashley et al. (eds) *The 9th International Symposium on Virtual Reality, Archaeology and Intelligent Cultural Heritage (VAST).* The Eurographics Association.

Sax, M. and N. D. Meeks 1995. Methods of engraving Mesopotamian quartz cylinder seals. *Archaeometry* 37/1: 25–36.

Sax, M., N. D. Meeks, and D. Collon 2000. The early development of the lapidary engraving wheel in Mesopotamia. *Iraq* 62: 157–76.

Sivic, J. and A. Zisserman. 2003. Video Google: a text retrieval approach to object matching in videos, in *Proceedings of the Ninth IEEE International Conference on Computer Vision*: 1470–77. Los Alamitos, CA: IEEE Computer Society.

Stamatopoulos, M. L. and C-N. Anagnostopoulos 2016. 3D digital reassembling of archaeological ceramic pottery fragments based on their thickness profile. https://arxiv.org/pdf/1601.05824.pdf Accessed June 27 2018.

Szeliski, R. 2011. *Computer Vision: Algorithms and Applications.* London: Springer-Verlag.

Teissier, B. 1998. Sealing and seals: seal-impressions from the reign of Hammurabi on tablets from Sippar in the British Museum. *Iraq* 60: 109–86.

Wagensonner, K. 2014. Digitizing in the round. *Cuneiform Digital Library Notes* 2014/8.

—2018. Eine Welt in Miniatur. Ein Essay zu Aufnahme und Abbildung von Rollsiegeln, in G. J. Selz and K. Wagensonner (eds), *Orientalische Kunstgeschichte(n). Festschrift für Erika Bleibtreu*. Wien: LIT.

Van der Jeught, S. and J. Dirckx 2016. Real-time structured light profilometry: a review. *Optics and Lasers in Engineering* 87: 18–31.

Webster, J. G., T. Bell, B. Li, and S. Zhang 2016. Structured light techniques and applications, in J. G. Webster (ed) *Wiley Encyclopedia of Electrical and Electronics Engineering*. doi:10.1002/047134608X.W8298. Accessed June 27 2018.

Will, P. M. and K. S. Pennington 1972. Grid encoding. A novel technique for image processing. *Proceedings of the IEEE* 60/6: 669–80.

Krizhevsky, A., I. Sutskever, and G. E. Hinton 2012. ImageNet classification with deep convolutional neural networks, in F. Pereira, C. J. C. Burges, L. Bottou, and K. Q. Weinberger (eds) *Proceedings of the 25th International Conference on Neural Information Processing Systems - Volume 1* (NIPS'12), Volume 1: 1097–1105. USA: Curran Associates Inc.

Linder, W. 2009. Digital Photogrammetry: A Practical Course. 10.1007/978-3-540-92725-9.

Zanuttigh, P., Marin, G., Dal Mutto, C., Dominio, F., Minto, L., Cortelazzo, G. M. 2016. *Time-of-flight and structured light depth cameras: Technology and applications*. Switzerland: Springer International. DOI: 10.1007/978-3-319-30973-6.

The digital microscope and multi-scale observation in the study of lapidary manufacturing techniques: a methodological approach for the preliminary phase of analysis in situ

Elise Morero, Hara Procopiou, Jeremy Johns, Roberto Vargiolu, and Hassan Zahouani

Abstract

The study of ancient craftsmanship requires a solid knowledge of the technology employed in the workshops. Our first source of data for the reconstruction of these technologies is provided by analysis of tool traces recorded on artefacts' surfaces. Selection of appropriate techniques of observation and recording of the technical data, adapted to the morphology and size of the tool traces, is crucial. A large quantity of digital pictures and videos can be obtained directly in the field with ultraportable devices such as the digital microscope. However, although the digital microscope is perfectly appropriate to perform a first examination of the macro-traces at low magnification, more accurate methods of observation are also required. Complementary use of tribological analyses via interferometry enable us not only to obtain precise images and measurements of the macro-traces' topography and morphology, and also micro-traces that cannot be detected with the digital microscope.

Introduction

The study of ancient craftsmanship, such as stone vessels, glyptic, cameos, figurines, jewellery and ornaments carved in soft and hard stones, requires a detailed knowledge of techniques employed in the workshops.[1] The identification of manufacturing sequences, processes, and tools are essential elements allowing us to generate a series of wide-ranging hypotheses on different aspects of production, such as workshop organisation, type of apprenticeship, and degree of specialisation of the craftsmen. The study of ancient know-how also provides an invaluable source of data enabling us to apprehend other facets of ancient societies, such as their capacity to innovate or, on the contrary, to perpetuate ancient traditions. The progressive composition of a technical tradition, its evolution and transformations are deeply connected to the historical context that engendered them (Morero 2016: 218–33), indicating local innovations, potential transfers of technology from different centres of production, and also social and political consequences implied by the means of their diffusion, integration, or even rejection.

Reconstruction of ancient lapidary technology also requires a multidisciplinary approach involving the study of archaeological data and/or historical sources accompanied by the review of ethnographic accounts of traditional workshops, all supported by experimental replication of ancient processes and tools. Tool traces generated during the process of manufacture, still preserved on the artefact's

---

[1] The Mohs scale is employed to measure mineral hardness. The softest is talc (Mohs 1) and the hardest diamond (Mohs 10). Up to Mohs 5 indicates soft and medium-hard stones (soft limestone, marble, calcite, etc.). Above Mohs 6 indicates hard stones (nephrite jade, rock crystal, corundum, etc.).

surface, represent an important source of evidence as witness to the technology employed. Their analysis requires study at different and complementary scales of observation, the findings of which are to be set against a corpus of already identified traces of manufacture. The data for comparison is acquired through different systems of imaging that are adapted to each successive phase of examination and to the type of traces.

In this paper, we focus on the initial phase of observation of the material, generally executed in the museum or on the archaeological site. All documentation and images of the diverse tool traces are gathered during this crucial phase of work. In the course of our different research projects on lapidary productions of various periods and origins—for example, eastern Mediterranean Bronze Age stone vessel production, early Islamic medieval rock crystal vessels, and the Mughal (16th–18th centuries) hard stone industry—involving stone objects of various size, shape, fragility, and state of preservation, scattered through many museums and collections, we have had the opportunity to experiment with a number of specific devices, including the ultraportable USB digital microscope. Although this apparatus is the best option for initial observations and also for the creation of a comprehensive photo-documentation of the technical traces in fieldwork, it does have its limits linked to the nature of the stones and the degree of magnification applied. We shall see that other complementary systems of analysis and collecting images of tool marks—at a higher magnification and by applying parameters of use-wear characterisation developed by tribology—are thus essential to reconstruct ancient know-how.

The study of tool traces applied to the reconstruction of lapidary industries

Typology of traces on stone artefacts

The basic premise is that each operation in the chain of production (sawing, hammering, chiselling, drilling, successive abrasion processes, and final polishing etc.) leaves macro- (>1 mm) and micro-traces (<1/0.5 mm) on the surface of a given object (Figure 1), which are specific to the tool's shape and the material being worked, but also were affected by the way in which the worker handled and presented the tool to the stone (angle of attack, applied force etc.).

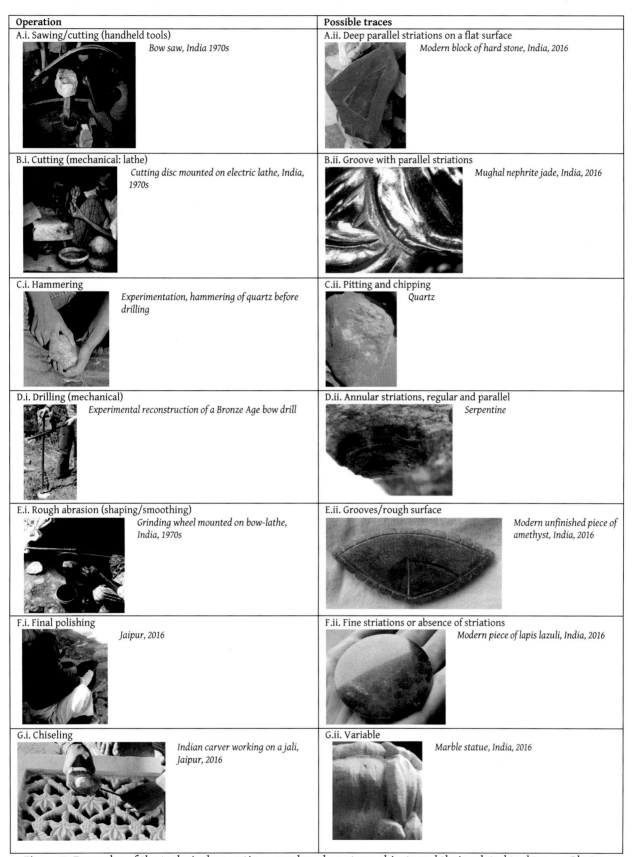

Figure 1. Examples of the technical operations employed on stone objects and their related tool traces. Photos: A.i, B.i, and E.i by R. Skelton; rest: Morero.

Traces generated during the manufacturing process are of a different range. Four main categories are generally observed on the surfaces of, for example, stone sculptures, figurines, or vessels: polishes, striations, pits, and small chips. Their size, shape, density on the object's surface, but also their organisation and interrelationships, are characteristic to specific technical actions such as cutting, abrasion, scraping, or hammering (Vargiolu 2008; Procopiou 2013; Morero 2016). For example, the processes of sawing, cutting, drilling, and smoothing or polishing the surfaces are a series of procedures that involve different calibres of abrasion. These procedures may include the addition of abrasive powders varying in coarseness and hardness, and a lubricant.[2] The movement of different elements in contact with each other (whether tool surface, abrasive particles, or the stone to be worked) generates the wear-process. If the abrasive particles are sufficiently resistant, their passage can cut or deform the surface of the stone object, causing the formation of striations (Georges 2000: 113–14). These striations take on a variable density, shape, and size according to the type of abrasive powder and lubricant employed. Their orientation and organisation are generated both by the use of a specific tool and by the manner in which the worker moves the abrasive particles against the surface. The nature of the tool's material (stone, metal, wood, leather, fabric etc.)–its hardness, flexibility, or roughness–is also an essential element in the formation of the traces, and can be identified through their morphology.

Multidisciplinary method of analysis

Analysis of traces was first exploited and developed for archaeological purposes by Sergei Semenov, the founder of use-wear analysis (Semenov 1964). This science is now largely employed in the study of prehistoric societies to identify the function or even the hafting system of metal and stone tools (Rots 2010). Micro-traces on the surfaces of artefacts are first observed and characterised using optical microscopes and then compared to a database of traces with known origin that were generated experimentally. This approach was later developed in association with other scientific methods, such as tribology (Anderson et al. 1996; Beyries et al. 1988; Procopiou 2013; Boleti 2017). More recently, the study of technical traces and tribological analyses has been employed and adapted to reconstruct manufacturing processes. The first applications, for the analysis of drilling techniques in Minoan stone vessel production, were initiated more than a decade ago (Morero et al. 2008; Vargiolu et al. 2007; Morero 2011, 2016, etc.), in collaboration with the researchers of the Laboratory of Tribology of the École Centrale de Lyon (Laboratoire de Tribologie et de Dynamique des Systèmes – LTDS).[3] Since then, it has been employed and developed for the reconstruction of the technology employed on a range of soft and hard stone products of the Bronze Age (Morero 2015; Morero and Prévalet 2015) and medieval period (Morero et al. 2013 and 2017).

---

[2] A large range of abrasive powders was employed in lapidary industries in different regions and periods. Processes such as rough shaping, smoothing of the surfaces, cutting, sawing or even drilling generally require hard abrasive powders, mostly made of natural sands or crushed stones such as garnet, corundum, emery, diamond, etc. Finer powders, made of metallic oxides (hematite, tin oxide, aluminium oxide, etc.) were also employed for operations such as polishing. The addition of a lubricant is usually required to allow a better distribution of the abrasive particles and improve the abrasion/cutting processes. According to the type of operation and stone to be worked, water or vegetable oils were employed.

[3] Project directed by Haris Procopiou and supported by the French National Agency of Research – ANR (2007–2009).

The interpretation of tool traces, as well as reconstruction of the organisation of workshops and production, involves analysis of other types of data. For pre- and proto- historical periods, archaeological evidence, particularly the excavations of workshops with their contents (tools, waste material, unfinished pieces etc.) are essential elements. However, such discoveries, clearly linkable to a given industry, are generally extremely rare, and may present problems of interpretation.[4] For historical periods—late antiquity, medieval, or modern—texts, including accounts by ancient travellers and scholars, constitute valuable sources of information for ancient processes and tools.[5] Since the 3rd millennium BC, numerous bas-reliefs, frescoes, and paintings depicting craftsmen at work also provide important data.[6] Although extremely valuable, this set of evidence is extremely variable in quantity and quality depending on the period and industry represented. Much information remains lost. Reconstructions of a past technology benefit also from other sources such as ethno-archaeological studies of traditional workshops. Research into pre-industrial systems of production is essential to reconstruct fundamental components, such as the manipulation of the different tools. For stone industries, workshops in India, Egypt, Iran, and China are particularly well studied and provide most of the documentation available to date.[7] All data collected from these assorted sources enable us to generate hypotheses about the ancient tools and processes employed, which need subsequently to be tested by experimental reconstruction. Through successive tests, a database of the known traces of different tools is created that can then be compared to the traces recorded on archaeological material. Any correlations that eventually emerge between the two sets may then enable us to identify the tools and techniques employed by the ancient craftsmen.

Multi-scale observation of the surfaces

Observation of surfaces at different scales is necessary for best study of various phenomena of wear.[8] The traces are of variable dimensions and thus demand to be studied by several systems of observation adapted to their morphology and size. The initial phase is macroscopic observation of the object's surface, which generally has to be carried out in museums or on archaeological sites. This

---

[4] Among the problems encountered is the disappearance of a large part of the tools. For instance, metal tools were often recycled, tools made of perishable material tend not to survive, and many tools were reused for other purposes.

[5] For stone industries, see, for example, ancient Greek sources (Halleux 2003), medieval and modern writings of al-Bīrūnī (1995), al-Tīfāshī (1998), Theophilus Presbyter (1961: 168–71), Natter (1754), Bernier (1916), de Thevenot (Sen 1949, Talboys Wheeler and Mac-Millan 1956), Fryer (1909), Bedini 1965, Koeppe and Giusti 2008.

[6] For example: bas-reliefs and frescoes from ancient Egyptian tombs depicting the process of drilling stone vessels, beads or even wooden furniture (Davies 1902: pl. XII; Davies 1943: pl. LII-LIV, etc.); Roman reliefs showing drilling tools and carving processes (for example: Boardman 2001: 380–81, Fig. 316); Starac 2007; Russell 2013: Fig. 7.20, 8.12); The Album of Jahāngir, with the painting of a *ḥakkāk* using a bow-lathe to polish or shape a gemstone (AH 1019/1610–11 AD) in the Náprstek Museum, Prague.

[7] See, for example, Indian sculpture and small objects in hard stone: Baden-Powell 1872: 192–4; Crosthwaite 1906, Chandra 1939, Murari et al. 1964, Dash 1981, Roux 2000, Procopiou et al. 2013; for Egyptian stone vessels: Hester and Heizer 1981; Iranian craftsmanship: Wulff 1950; Chinese jade industry: Hildburgh 1907, Hansford 1950.

[8] Beyries et al. 1988, Kimball et al. 1995, Zahouani 1995, Anderson et al. 1996, Beyries and Rots 2008, Dubreuil 2008, Skakum 2008.

preliminary phase, performed with the naked eye and under low magnification, has two main objectives. First, to identify the macro-traces and their interrelationship on the surface of the object. Analysis of their organisation, superimposition, and interrelationship is essential for establishing the sequence of operations carried out on the artefact, and thus in reconstructing the sequence of manufacture. The second objective is to create a good set of data – to isolate the relevant traces. Pictures of these traces must be able to establish and record their characteristics as well as their location on the surface of the object.

The characterisation (morphology and depth) of macro-traces requires more detailed observation under low magnification. Generally, apparatus such as an optical microscope (binocular, stereomicroscope, digital microscope, etc.) is employed. For this phase, we usually use a magnification ranging between x 30 to x 55. This phase allows us to observe smaller traces (<1/0.5 mm) that are usually linked to the macro-traces of polishing and cutting. It is usually during this stage that the image database of traces is composed. The macro- and micro-traces are classified and described. To a degree, at this point a hypothesis can be formulated regarding their place in the sequence of manufacture (distinguishing between traces belonging to the rough shaping, the hollowing-out sequences, the carving of the decoration, the smoothing or final polishing etc.).

To further characterise the traces of manufacture, the surface topography is then investigated through a different optical apparatus, with the aim of quantifying it according to the specific parameters developed by tribology.[9] Macro-traces of carving are measured from silicone replicas taken from the object's surfaces, using a confocal rugosimeter. The principle of this optical device is based on chromatic aberration, which focuses on different wavelengths of white light. The dimension of the surface measured for stone artefacts studied is generally 10 x 10 mm, with a resolution of 4 μm. This enables us to obtain three-dimensional images z (x,y) of the wear traces. The micro-traces (micro-polish and striations of <0.5 mm) that determine the specific abrasive powders and lubricants used, however, require other systems of analysis, such as the interferometer. Interferometry uses phase detection. Light reflected by the surface being analysed is compared to a standard. The resulting interference phenomenon is recorded with a digital camera, which produces a three dimensional map z (x,y) of the measured surface. The dimensions of the surface measured (x,y) are 122 x 92 μm. In this way, we can obtain three-dimensional views z (x,y) of polished surfaces (see below, p.89-90). Such valuable information on the morphology and topography of the tool traces cannot be obtained with optical and digital microscopes, not even through the scanning electron microscope (SEM), which is generally used for accurate observations on stone surfaces.[10]

Picture acquisition and the creation of a tool traces databases

Characterisation and interpretation of tool traces is a complex task requiring the existence of a good set of data, namely the compilation of a comprehensive photographic record of the traces at different degrees of magnification and angles of observation. This database has to be organised rigorously as it represents the only source of information through the long process of trace interpretation. The procedure is based mainly on the comparison of traces on archaeological objects with traces generated experimentally. All images have to be in an identical format and at an identical scale. Employment of the same optical devices seems thus to be the best option. For the general view, use of

---

[9] Especially the method of continuous wavelet transform (Zahouani 1995, 1997; Procopiou et al. 2013).

[10] See the studies of Twilley 1992; Sax et al. 2004, 2007, 2008; Gwinnett and Gorelick 1979, 1988.

a camera and raking light onto surfaces to create a contrast between traces and the surrounding areas is a relatively simple task. These macroscopic views of surfaces will be used to show the relationship of traces and their precise location on the object. Low magnification capture of tool traces, however, can be much harder to achieve. Although a camera connected to a simple microscope can be perfectly adapted to this phase of study, most of the objects to be studied are dispersed across museums and private collections. Some are fragile and so valuable that they cannot be taken out of their collection to be examined in the laboratory under constant conditions with the same apparatus.

The large size of some objects may also exclude the use of these systems of observation. Our various study campaigns, which included examination of Cycladic marble statues more than one metre high, as well as details of glyptics and gemstones measuring less than one centimetre across, have shown us that a portable digital microscope is the most suitable device for recording tool traces. This portable device has a wide range of applications across many fields.[11] For our work on the manufacturing techniques, we are using the Dinolite Premier digital microscope, which is equipped with white light (8 LED) and a polarized system (Figure 2).

Figure 2. Use of the digital microscope. Photo: Morero.

---

[11] Especially industrial (reparation and quality control for printing, textile, solar panel, automotives, etc.), health care (dermatology), forensic, etc. Handheld digital microscopes are generally employed in art restoration: the conservators also use them, for instance, to detect traces of pigments.

The digital microscope allows us to compile quickly pictures and video-coverage of up to five megapixels (2592 x 1944). As a USB device, it can be directly plugged into a laptop so that the relevance of the digital pictures, directly visible on the screen, can be quickly estimated and the morphological details of the traces enlarged and studied with precision. Although not especially powerful, it possesses the distinct advantage of being small, light, and thus easy to transport in the field and to move about over the surface of sizable objects. In this manner, good digital images of the traces and other characteristics are obtained that can be used as both working archives and illustrations in publications. However, the apparatus has its downside too, especially depending on the nature of the stone studied. Although the apparatus can magnify up to x 200, the images are not always very crisp and sufficiently precise.

Examples of application for the analysis of homogeneous stones

Early Islamic rock crystal vessels

Early Islamic rock crystal vessels are mainly small objects, usually miniature flasks, of varying qualities of execution. Alongside these rather simple pieces, rarer and more luxurious vessels attest to a higher degree of skill and a more elaborate technology. An especially famous group is made up of seven ewers, nicknamed the 'Magnificent Seven' (see Figure 6a, 7a, 9a).[12] All these pieces bear decoration carved in relief. Produced in the Islamic world between the 8th and 12th centuries AD, relief-carved rock crystal pieces are conventionally attributed to Fatimid Egypt (10th–11th centuries AD). Only two of the ewers bear an inscription indicating that they were produced for the court of the caliph. Other centres of production seem to have existed, especially in Iran, Iraq, Afghanistan, and Morocco. Workshops are also considered possible in Spain and in Sicily during the 12th century AD. Most, if not all, medieval Islamic rock crystal artefacts that have survived more or less intact seem to have been brought to Christian Europe during the 12th and 13th centuries and preserved in ecclesiastical treasuries where they were used as liturgical objects (Shalem 1998: 56–71, 177–226).

Our project was specifically aimed at reconstructing the technology employed for carving these rock crystal pieces with relief decoration.[13] The work also permitted us to test and refine our recording protocols. For the first phase of this research we focused on the group of the seven ewers. Our ultimate goal was, through the identification and comparison of the manufacturing techniques employed for each of them, to determine whether or not they were all produced in the same period and by the same tradition of production. The study corpus also comprised a group of twenty flasks and small objects considered as early Islamic. We compared data obtained from these objects with pieces manufactured at earlier periods—mainly early Byzantine (4th–5th century) and late Sasanian (6th–7th centuries) - and also with five artefacts produced much later (16th–17th and 19th centuries) in Europe.

In order to reconstruct the ancient techniques, we used the interdisciplinary approach described above. Archaeological, ethnographic, and historical sources provided us with an initial database of the

---

[12] For general bibliographical references on the early Islamic production and precise locations of the objects studies, see Morero et al. 2013 and 2017.

[13] Project realised with Jeremy Johns at the Khalili Research Centre for the Art and Material Culture of the Middle East (University of Oxford), funded by Ranros Universal.

tools and techniques that might have been used by ancient craftsmen.[14] Traces of manufacture still preserved on the rock crystal surfaces were examined and captured at different magnifications.

First phase of observation and imaging of the traces

Pure quartz crystals present a homogeneous and fine-grained structure almost ideal for observation of tool traces with the naked eye. Topographical differences on the surface appear clearly with the use of raking light. The natural transparency of the crystal is also an asset in the detection of tool traces. Indeed, viewed close up, the working marks show some opacity, compared to the transparent surrounding areas.[15] Examination of rock crystal also involves difficulties, however, especially for compiling macroscopic images. If the surface is very well polished, light reflection can be intense, creating glare that masks the decoration and tool traces. The database documenting the technical traces, therefore, was fundamentally based on images taken with the digital microscope at low magnification. The USB microscope, when applied directly to the surface of the object, confines the light source to the LED alone, partially mitigating the creation of an over intense and undesirable glare.

Analysis of the early Islamic rock crystal pieces raised other problems. First, the objects are preserved not only in many museums in Europe, USA, and Russia, but also in churches and private collections. The pieces are extremely valuable and often fragile, and so are virtually impossible to remove from their locations. But the main issue was certainly their size (H. 15.6–24 cm, D. ranging from 9.5–13.5 cm), and also the curved profile of the ewers, which meant that viewing their surfaces under fixed optical microscopes was not feasible. The handheld digital microscope was thus the only option to take the great number of pictures (50–100) required, including images of areas difficult to access, such as the interior of the ewers and small flasks, in order to examine the drilling and polishing traces (Figure 3a).

Following this procedure successfully and precisely captured the tool traces and generated a large image database. This in turn enabled us to select the most representative examples and take silicone impressions that were later analysed in the LTDS Laboratory.

Reconstruction of the manufacturing techniques

From analysis of these images, we were able to reconstruct the sequence of manufacture as follows. First, the craftsman employed saws with abrasive powders (corundum or emery) and water to rough out the exterior shape of the vessel (Figure 1.1). Contours were then shaped using a series of abrasive grinding wheels and tools powered by a horizontal bow-lathe (Figures 1.5 and 6b). Water was again used as a lubricant during the process. During the next phase, the worker proceeded to hollow out the interior of the vase, still using abrasive powders and water, initially with a tubular drill held vertically (Figure 3b). The cylindrical opening thus generated allowed the insertion of other drilling tools and

---

[14] The sparse references in medieval Arabic and Persian sources (al-Bīrūnī, al-Tīfāshī, Nāṣir-i Khusraw, etc.), and the accounts of early modern and modern European scholars and travellers in Asia (*cf. supra* n. 7) were valuable sources of data (Morero et al. 2013 and 2017).

[15] During the working processes, the rock crystal becomes locally opaque, but the natural transparency of the stone is restored at the end of the manufacturing sequence by polishing (Morero et al. 2017: 129).

gouges employed to enlarge the cavity and to create globular or piriform shapes. Finally, the relief decoration was carved and the surface polished.

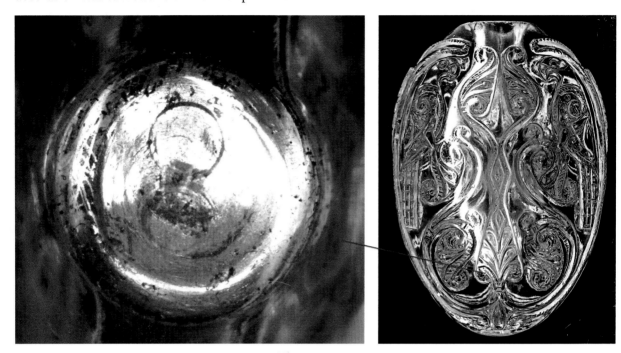

Figure 3a. Annular traces left in the bottom of the narrow cavity in an ovoidal flask (Keir Collection, R11, Dallas Museum), H. 10.3 cm, photographed with the digital microscope. Photo: Morero, Johns.

Figure 3b. Tubular drills employed for jade industry in India, 1970s. Photo: Skelton.

Traces of carving were documented the most thoroughly, allowing us to perform a more accurate analysis and reconstruct the different processes and tools employed. First, straight-sided raised islets of relief were cut using grinding tools (Figure 4) and cutting discs of different sizes. Then the worker carved the decoration into the islets using cutting discs to generate both straight and curved lines (Figure 5).

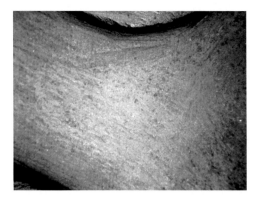 

Figure 4. (a) Traces generated during the preliminary phase of creation of the islets of relief observed on the fragment of unfinished dish (British Museum, 1959,0515.1), magnified x 50; (b) Grinding tool employed for identical purpose on rock crystal in lapidary workshops in Jaipur, 2016. Photos: Morero.

Figure 5. (a) Example of creation of a curved motif on the Mouflon Ewer (San Marco Treasury, Venice), magnified ~x50; (b) Small cutting disc employed in lapidary workshops in Jaipur, 2016. Photos: Morero.

Observation of tool traces at a low magnification was also sufficient to identify the use of a rounded drill bit to carve dot motifs. This was encountered only on the more luxurious pieces, such as the seven ewers (Figure 6a-b). Detailed images of drilling traces, especially the orientation and arrangement of striations (Figure 6b-c), were obtained with the digital microscope. From these, it was clear that a horizontal bow-lathe had been used to power the drill, rather than a vertical system such as was used for tubular drilling.

Figure 6a. Dot motifs of D. <1-1.5> mm on the Mills Ewer (Keir Collection, Dallas Museum of Art).

 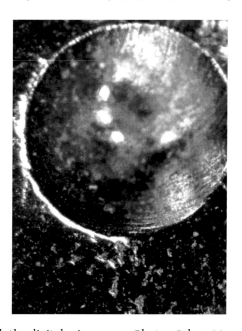

Figure 6b (left) view magnified ~x 50; (c, right) x 100 with the digital microscope. Photos: Johns, Morero.

However, accurate tribological analyses were still necessary to determine the shape and size of the cutting discs (Morero et al. 2013: 153–4 and 2017: 127). The detailed pictures of the micro-traces obtained with the confocal microscope both validated the observations made during the preliminary phase of observation and clarified further the wear mechanisms involved in the creation of the dot motifs. The method also provided us with views of the motif on the St Denis ewer (Figure 7) sufficiently accurate to reveal later modifications. The images obtained with the confocal microscope revealed the superposition of two types of traces and morphologies, realised successively on the St Denis Ewer, which were difficult to appreciate at lower magnification. A first series of dots were originally drilled using the rounded drill bit characteristic of the whole group of ewers (Figure 8a). But, after the St Denis ewer was originally produced, some of these same dots were re-carved using a very different tool (Figure 8b). The shape and organisation of the striations of this second group suggest the use of the grinding wheel (Morero et al. 2013: 132 and *forthcoming*).

Figure 7a. The St Denis Ewer (Louvre Museum). Photo: Johns.

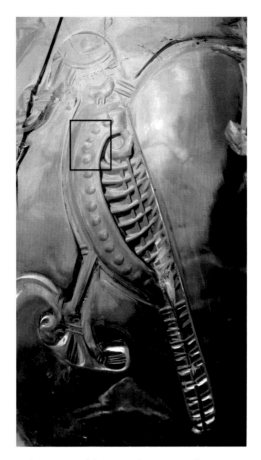

Figure 7b: Series of dot motifs re-carved using a grinding wheel of D. ~1.8 mm magnified x50 with the digital microscope. Photos: Johns, Morero.

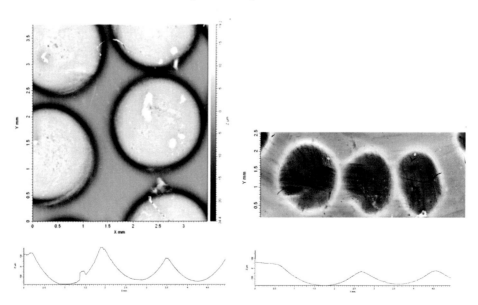

Figure 8. Views with the confocal microscope and profiles of the dots on (a, left) the Mills Ewer, made with the rounded drill bit, (b, right) on the St Denis Ewer, re-carved with the grinding wheel. Images: Vargiolu.

Finally, at the end of the process of manufacture, the pieces were polished using a series of abrasive powders of different hardness and coarseness. For the early Islamic pieces, this part of the manufacturing sequence could not be analysed with precision. The artefacts had been re-polished on several occasions over the years, erasing the traces of the original process. However, the analyses of a sample of polished surfaces examined through interferometry in the LTDS allowed us to observe that different polishing techniques were employed by the early Islamic worker and a 17th-century European counterpart (Figure 9a and c). The surfaces examined revealed dissimilar levels of roughness (Figure 9b and c), suggesting that distinctive polishing agents and processes were employed in the two workshops (Morero et al. 2013: 130–1). In the future, characterisation of these polished surfaces, using the method of continuous wavelength transform, could reveal the exact signature of the polishing processes.

Figure 9a. Two polished areas on the Fermo Ewer were measured by interferometry. Photo: Johns.

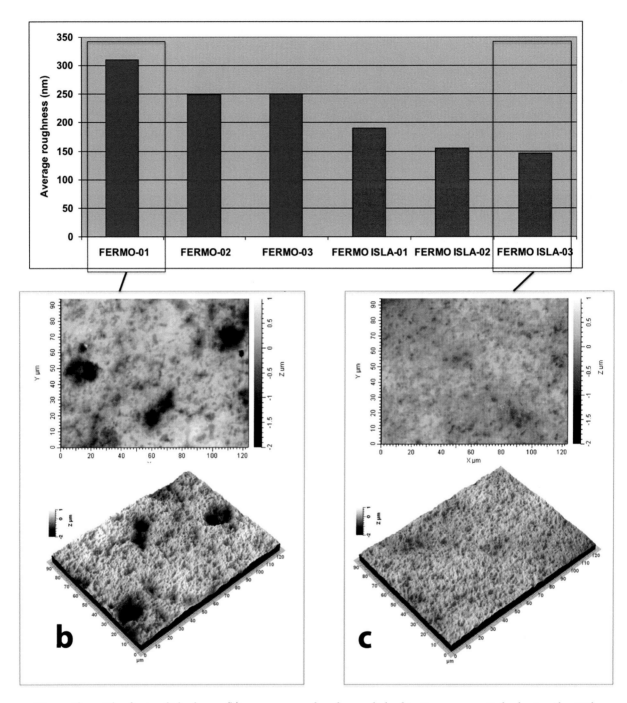

Figure 9b–c.. The first polished area (b) was re-carved and re-polished in Germany or Italy during the 17th century, and the second (c) is the original polished surface produced in the Islamic workshop. Images: Vargiolu.

In sum, using these complementary methods of observation, it was possible to demonstrate that all the ewers were made with the same tools and techniques. They were indeed produced in the same technical tradition. We observed later modifications carried out on some specimens. The St Denis Ewer is the only ewer to show later re-carving of the dot motifs, using the grinding wheel. Although the spherical drill bit seems to have been almost exclusively employed on luxury products, the grinding wheel was also very occasionally used at the final stage of the carving process to correct or deepen some of the dots on a few objects of the highest quality (Morero et al., forthcoming). This is maybe the case for the St Denis ewer. This operation could have been performed at the same time as the addition of a little palmette, at the point that would originally have been covered by the base of the handle, after the latter was broken. Analysis of the carving techniques employed indicates that the modifications were probably carried out before the ewer left the Islamic world (Morero et al., forthcoming). The St Denis ewer was maybe considered a second rate piece, damaged after manufacture, and then subsequently refurbished, possibly in order to be sold on the market, or presented to a recipient of less than the highest rank.

The grinding wheel, however, was more generally used to form the dots on rock crystal objects of lower quality and on early Islamic plain relief-carved glass. The technological links observed between these two productions suggest that they all grew out of the common technical tradition in which they were rooted (Morero et al., forthcoming).

Mughal hard stone production[16]

The study of hard stone carving technology employed in India between the 16th and 18th centuries essentially concerns vessels, dagger handles, boxes, mirror frames, jewellery, and other small objects produced in nephrite jade or rock crystal.[17] Workshops and/or craftsmen were operating in royal workshops for the court, and in the cities for a more 'open' market.[18] Mughal jade and rock crystal products demonstrate a variable degree of skill. The most luxurious products were decorated with carved relief and/or inlaid precious metals and gemstones (Bernier 1916: 422-3). It seems that the working of nephrite was introduced during the Mughal era (Chandra 1939: 80), especially during the reign of Emperor Akbar (AD 1556–1605). The production - on an extremely limited scale at this period - reached its full development in the first half of the 17th century during the reigns of his successors Jahāngir and, especially, Shāh Jahān (Markel 1992: 49–50). The first phase of our research, currently in progress, aims to reconstruct the techniques employed for jade and rock crystal carving. When combined with future analysis and comparison of technologies employed for the carving of these pieces, and also for the cutting of the inscriptions on a group of emeralds and spinels dedicated to the emperors (Figure 10), our studies will give us insight into the organisation of hard stone production in India.[19] This second phase, planned in 2018, will concentrate more specifically on the reconstruction and analysis of the development of the industry, and investigate potential transfers of technology between Iranian, Chinese, and European centres of jade production.[20]

---

[16] Project with Robert Skelton (former curator of the Victoria and Albert Museum, London).

[17] See for example in Markel 1992, Skelton 1995, Stronge 1982: Cat. 349–84.

[18] In 1666, Thevenot reported that lapidary craftsmen worked gems in the palace of Golconda (Sen 1949:138), for example.

[19] See, for example, Stronge 1982: cat. 349–56, 377, 380. Keene 2001, etc.

[20] On this problem of transfers of style and technology see for example: Skelton 1972 and 1995: 284, 291–5.

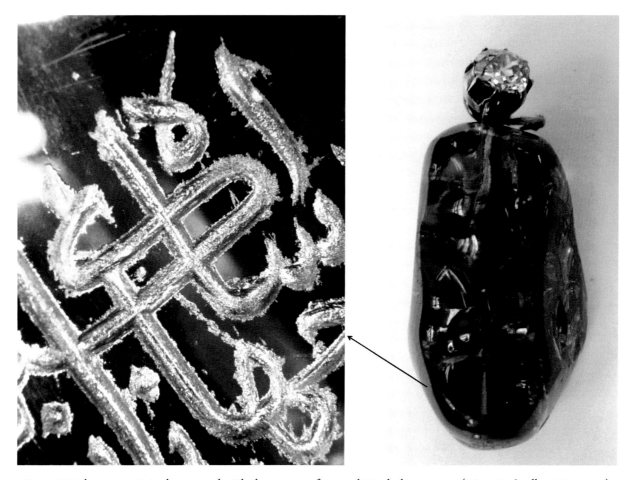

Figure 10. The Carew Spinel engraved with the names of several Mughal emperors (Victoria & Albert Museum), H. 4 cm, W. 2.3 cm. Left: detail of the name of Jahāngir, magnified ~x50, using the digital microscope. Photos: Morero.

To date, we have studied 20 jade and rock crystal pieces attributed with more or less certainty to the Mughal industry. We have again concentrated on the processes used to carve the relief ornament. For the reconstruction of the ancient processes, the different types of sources already mentioned for our previous research on early Islamic rock crystal were supplemented by an ethnographical study of the systems of production employed in a group of seven workshops in Jaipur.

First phase of observation and imaging of the traces

Study of Mughal jade artefacts presents the same practical constraints as that of early Islamic rock crystal. The corpus is largely distributed across museums and collections, and the pieces can be sizeable. Marks on the opaque and homogeneous surfaces of the pieces are easy to capture both with a camera using raking light and with the digital microscope in its polarized position. The same apparatus also permitted us to study other materials involved in Mughal production, such as gold inlay. Use of polarized light enabled detailed views of the scratching marks on the soft metal, which were almost invisible to the naked eye. Even though some contemporary workshops now use motorised devices, much of the process follows traditional techniques of carving jade, rock crystal, agate, and other hard stones. Their products consist of contemporary original creations and copies in the Mughal style. Beyond the study of systems of production themselves, this campaign was a rare occasion to study the traces and morphology left by modern tools. During this preliminary phase, use of the ultraportable digital microscope was perfectly suited to the circumstances, allowing us to obtain a valuable corpus of tool traces instantaneously.

Reconstruction of manufacturing techniques

The traces related to the decoration processes were analysed. The first observations, performed at low magnification, were then complemented by an accurate examination of a selection of tool traces in the LTDS, using the confocal microscope. A sequence of manufacture close to the one identified for early Islamic rock crystal production was recovered. Cutting discs and grinding wheels of different sizes and shapes were also employed, but Mughal craftsmen manipulated and applied these tools differently to the stone. Specific instruments such as diamond drill bits could also be observed in Mughal hard stone production (Figure 11).

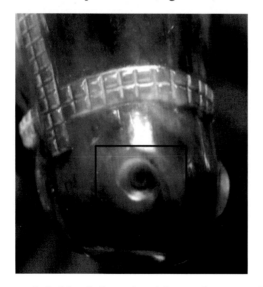 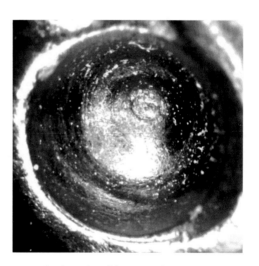

Figure 11. left: (a) Jade horse head dagger (private collection, London), right: (b) View of the horse's nostril (D. ~1.5/2 mm). Photos: Morero.

Motifs were carved in islets of low relief, using for the most part cutting discs with abrasive powders and a lubricant, and grinding wheels driven by a bow-lathe (Figure 12).

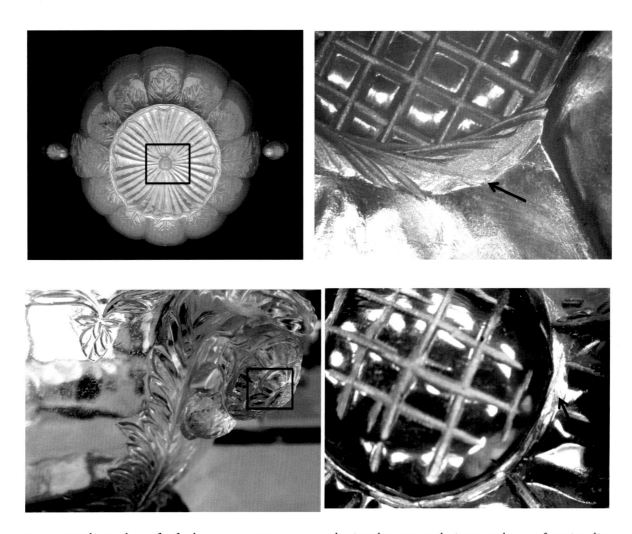

Figure 12. Identical motifs of a diameter <1-0.5> cm, carved using the same techniques and type of cutting disc (view ~50 x) on, above: (a) a jade cup (Victoria & Albert Museum, IS.25-1997) and, below: (b) a rock crystal cup (Ashmolean Museum, LI 2028). Photos: 5a, Victoria & Albert Museum; others Morero.

We also observed, and composed a database of, carving traces related to the engraving of dedicatory inscriptions to Mughal emperors on a sample of seven spinels, emeralds, and other hard stones. The traces are too small to be clearly observed with the naked eye. The tool marks observed with the digital microscope revealed both the use of the bow-lathe (Figure 10) and a handheld tool (Figure 13), certainly a stylus, to carve the inscription and decoration.

Figure 13. Cameo of Shah Jahān (Bibliothèque nationale de France), D. 6.7 cm: (a) areas magnified ~x 50; (b) View of the inscription magnified x 50 and x 100 (Photos: Morero).

Although the reconstruction of the Mughal industry is still work in progress, we have shown with certainty that both Mughal rock crystal and jade objects were made using exactly the same processes (Figure 12), probably in the same workshops. Finally, our work in modern Indian workshops allowed us to create a database of the tool traces on modern imitations of Mughal objects. These detailed pictures of the carving traces generated with motorised tools show a very different type of traces to the ones on original Mughal pieces. This database thus represents a valuable tool for the detection of modern forgeries.

Limits of the digital microscope

The digital microscope is an essential piece of equipment for the preliminary phase of observation and for composing a database of technical traces, all carried out in the field. The apparatus is perfectly adapted to homogeneous stones such as rock crystal and nephrite jade, but the study of the stones with a coarser surface structure can be more problematic.

We encountered such a difficulty during our research on eastern Mediterranean Bronze Age products. Among the coarser-grained stones, the examination of certain types of sandstone, granite, or marble can be difficult. For example, this is very much the case with large crystalline-structured marbles like those from the Cyclades. The Museum of Cycladic Art and the National Museum of Athens have recently developed a multidisciplinary project for the identification of manufacturing processes and painting of figurines and vessels made during the third millennium BC on the Cyclades.[21] Different types of marble are used in their production. On those with large crystals, shallow and/or fine tool-traces may be invisible. The information is lost among the natural irregularities and asperities of the stone, and remains undetectable at the low magnification of the digital microscope. Thus, most of the data comes from examination of larger traces observed with the naked eye. Although traditional microscopes (stereoscopic microscopes) give interesting results, the extent and edges of the traces become invisible when observed with the digital microscope in direct contact with the stone surface.

The examination of large traces of tools, such as those generated by the drilling techniques employed in the Bronze Age, presents the same difficulties. Striations that were formed during the operation are large, and their examination from a position too close to the surface can lead to the misinterpretation of patterns observed. It is thus preferable to study these macro-traces with the naked eye in order, for instance, to deduce whether the operation was performed by mechanical or handheld-tools (Figure 14). Subsequently, tribological analysis can reveal the mechanism of abrasion and potentially identify the type of abrasive powders and lubricants employed.

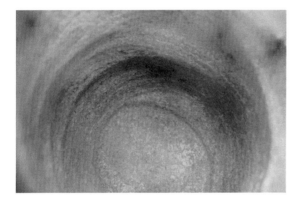 

Figure 14. left: (a) Annular striations of drilling in the cavity of a Cycladic *kandila* (National Archaeological Museum, Athens, 4791), right: (b) Striations are almost invisible with the digital microscope (Photos: Morero)

Other difficulties occur in the observation of the surface of any small item that presents a strongly curved shape, such as cylinder-seals, and cylindrical or round beads. Obtaining pictures of a precise area or motif on a surface showing significant variations of topography can be complicated: precise focus becomes difficult, and the surrounding areas in lower relief often become blurred, although mounting the device on a fixed stand can help keep the digital microscope steady during the observation. It is thus important to select and focus on the precise element about which information is desired.

---

[21] Coordinators of the project: Katia Manteli (Curator, National Archaeological Museum, Athens) and Nikolas Papadimitriou (Curator, Museum of Cycladic Art, Athens); other main participants: Kiki Birtacha (Akrotiri Excavations at Thera, Greece), Sophia Sotiropoulou (Ormylia Foundation Art Diagnosis Centre, Greece), Elise Morero (Oxford University), Athina Boleti (University of Paris 1, France), Francesco Paolo Romano (Consiglio Nazionale delle Ricerche, Italy), Andreas Karydas and Yiannis Bassiakos (National Centre for Scientific Research 'Demokritos', Athens, Greece). Project funded by the INSTAP Centre at Pachyammos on Crete.

Conclusion

In sum, it is essential to observe the surface of an object at different scales. It is critical to select the methods and imaging apparatus best adapted and appropriate to the type of tool traces extant, and to their dimensions, morphology, and topography. These are the necessary prerequisites to generate the most germane database of traces of manufacture, documenting the various features of the technical processes in order to reconstruct ancient know-how. The digital microscope is perfectly adapted to the initial phase of research and documentation *in situ,* but understanding the manufacturing process also requires accurate use-wear and tribological analyses, complemented by data derived from other sources, especially archaeological, textual, ethnographic, and experimental.

References

Anderson, P. C., L. Astruc, R. Sala, R. Vargiolu, and H. Zahouani 1996. Contribution of Quantitative Tribology Analysis to a Multi-Method Approach for Characterizing and Distinguishing Wear Traces on Flint Tools with 'Gloss', in S. Antonelli (ed.) *Colloquia of the XIIIth International Congress of Prehistoric and Protohistoric Science, 8-14 September 1996, Forli*: 157–8. Forli: Abaco Edizioni.

Baden-Powell, B. H. 1872. *Hand-Book of the Manufactures and Arts of the Punjab* (Vol. 1). Lahore: Punjab Printing Company.

Bedini, S. A. 1965. A Renaissance Lapidary Lathe. *Technology and Culture* 6: 407–15.

Bernier, F. 1916. *Travels in the Mogul Empire A.D. 1656-1668*, A. Constable (transl.). London: Oxford University Press.

Beyries, S., F. Delamare, and J. Quantin 1988. Tracéologie et rugosimétre tridimensionnel, in S. Beyries (ed.) *Industries lithiques. Tracéologie et technologie*: 115–32. Oxford: British Archaeological Reports.

Beyries, S. and V. Rots 2008. The Contribution of Ethnoarchaeological Macro- and Microscopic Wear Traces to the Understanding of Archaeological Hide-Working Processes, in L. Longo and N. Skakun (eds) *Prehistoric Technology, 40 Years Later: Functional Studies and the Russian Legacy, Proceedings of the International Congress Verona (Italy), 20-23 April 2005: 479-82.* Oxford: Archaeopress.

al-Bīrūnī. 1995. *Kitāb al-Jamāhir fī ma ʿrifat al-jawāhir*, Y. al-Hādī (ed.). Tehran.

Boardman, J. 2001. *Greek Gems and Finger Rings: Early Bronze Age to Late Classical.* London: Thames and Hudson.

Boleti, A. 2017. *L'émeri. Modalités d'exploitation dans le monde égéen protohistorique et antique.* Paris: Publications de la Sorbonne.

Chandra, M. 1939. The art of cutting hardstone ware in ancient and modern India. *Journal of the Gujarat Research Society* 1/4: 71–85.

Crosthwaite, H. S. 1906. *Monograph on Stone Carving in the United Provinces.* Allahabad: The Superintendent of Government Press, United Provinces.

Davies, N. G. 1909. *The Rock Tombs of Deir el Gebrâwi* (Vol. 1). London: Egypt Exploration Fund.

Davies, N. G. 1943. *The Tomb of Rekh-Mi-Rē at Thebes*. New York: Metropolitan Museum of Art.

Dubreuil, L. 2008. Mortar versus Grinding-Slabs Function in the Context of the Neolithization Process in the Near East, in L. Longo and N. Skakun (eds), *Prehistoric Technology, 40 Years Later: Functional Studies and the Russian Legacy, Proceedings of the International Congress (Verona, 20-23 April 2005)*: 169-177. Oxford: Archaeopress.

Fryer, J. 1909. *A New Account of East India and Persia: Being Nine Years' Travels, 1672-1681* (3 vols., 2nd series), W. Crooke (ed. and annot.), London: Hakluyt Society.

Georges, J. M. 2000. *Frottement, usure et lubrification. La tribologie ou science des surfaces*. Paris: CNRS Editions.

Gwinnett, A. J. and L. Gorelick 1979. Ancient Lapidary. A Study Using Scanning Electron Microscopy and Functional Analysis. *Expedition* 22/1: 17–32.

Gwinnett, A. J. and L. Gorelick 1988. Diamonds from India to Rome and beyond. *American Journal of Archaeology* 92/4: 547–52.

Halleux, R. 2003. *Les Lapidaires Grecs: Lapidaire Orphique, Kerygmes, Lapidaires D'Orphée, Socrate et Denys, Lapidaire Nautique Damigéron-Évax*. Paris: Belles Lettres.

Hansford, S. H. 1950. *Chinese Carved Jades*. London: Faber.

Hester, T. and R. Heizer 1981. *Making Stone Vases: Ethnoarchaeological Studies at an Alabaster Workshop in Upper Egypt*. Malibu: Undena Publications.

Hildburgh, W. L. 1907. Chinese Methods of Cutting Hard Stones. *The Journal of the Royal Anthropological Institute of Great Britain and Ireland* 37: 189–95.

Keene, M. 2001. *Treasury of the world: jewelled arts of India in the age of the Mughals*. London: Thames and Hudson in association with the al-Sabah Collection, Dar al-Athar al-Islamiyyah, Kuwait National Museum.

Kimball, L. K., J. F. Kimball, and P. E. Allen 1995. Microwear Polishes as Viewed Through the Atomic Force Microscope. *Lithic Technology* 20/1: 6–28.

Koeppe, W. and A. Giusti (eds) 2008. *Art of the Royal Court: Treasures in Pietre Dure from the Palaces of Europe* (Exhibition catalogue) New York: Metropolitan Museum of Art.

Markel, S. 1992. Inception and Maturation in Mughal Jades, in S. Markel (ed.) *The World of Jade*: 49–64. Bombay: Marg Publications.

Morero, E. 2011. Transferts techniques en Méditerranée orientale. L'exemple de la fabrication des vases de pierre à l'Age du Bronze. *Syria* 88: 207–24.

Morero, E. 2015. Mycenaean Lapidary Craftsmanship. The stone vases manufacturing process. *Annual of the British School at Athens* 110: 121–46.

Morero, E. 2016. *Méthodes d'analyse des techniques lapidaires. Les vases de pierre en Crète à l'âge du Bronze (IIIᵉ-IIᵉ millénaire av. J.-C.)*. Paris: Publications de la Sorbonne.

Morero, E., J. Johns, H. Procopiou, R. Vargiolu, H. Zahouani *forthcoming*, Relief-carving on medieval Islamic glass and rock crystal: A comparative approach to techniques of manufacture, in C. Hahn and

A. Shalem (eds) *Seeking Transparency: The Medieval Rock Crystal, proceedings of the international conference, Kunsthistorisches Institut in Florenz, Max-Planck-Institut, Florence, Italy, 19-20 May 2017.*

Morero, E. and R. Prévalet 2015. Technological transfers of luxury craftsmanship between Crete and the Orient during the Bronze Age, in J. Mynářová, P. Onderka and P. Pavúk (eds) *The Crossroads II, or there and back again, proceedings of the international conference, Charles University, Prague, 15-18 September 2014*: 59–83. Prague: Czech Institute of Egyptology, Faculty of Arts Charles University in Prague.

Morero, E., H. Procopiou, R. Vargiolu, and H. Zahouani 2008. Stone vase drilling in Bronze Age Crete, in L. Longo and N. Skakun (eds) *Prehistoric Technology, 40 Years Later: Functional Studies and The Russian Legacy, Proceedings of the International Congress held at Verona, 20-23 April 2005*: 479–82. Oxford: Archaeopress.

Morero, E., H. Procopiou, R. Vargiolu, J. Johns and H. Zahouani 2013. Carving and polishing techniques of Fatimid rock crystal ewers (10–12th cent. AD.). *Wear* 301: 150–56.

Morero, E., J. Johns, H. Procopiou, R. Vargiolu and H. Zahouani 2017. The manufacturing techniques of Fatimid rock crystal ewers (10–12th centuries AD), in A. Hilgner, S. Greiff and D. Quast (eds), *Gemstones in the first Millennium AD. Mines, Trade, Workshops and Symbolism, proceedings of the International Conference, Römisch-Germanisches Zentralmuseum, Mainz, 20-22 October* 2015: 119–35. Mainz: Verlag des Römisch-Germanischen Zentralmuseums.

Murari, P., R. Reeves, and P. K. Nambiar 1964-6. *Madras: handicrafts and artisans of Madras State* (Vol. 5: Icons in stone and metals), 9 vols. Delhi: Manager of Publications.

Natter, L. 1754. *Traité de la méthode antique de graver en Pierre fines comparée avec la méthode moderne.* London.

Procopiou, H. 2013. *Techniques, sens et émotions: Autour du polissage en Méditerranée orientale durant l'âge du Bronze.* Unpublished dissertation of habilitation à diriger des recherches, University of Paris 1 Panthéon – Sorbonne.

Procopiou, H., A. Boleti, R. Vargiolu, and H. Zahouani 2011. The role of tactile perception during stone-polishing in Aegean prehistory (5th–4th millennium). *Wear* 271: 2525–30.

Procopiou, H., E. Morero, R. Vargiolu, M. Suarez-Sanabria, and H. Zahouani 2013. Tactile and visual perception during polishing: an ethnoarchaeological study in India (Mahabalipuram Tamil Nadu). *Wear* 301: 144–9.

Rots, V. 2010. *Prehension and Hafting Traces on Flint Tools: A Methodology.* Leuven: Leuven University Press.

Roux, V. 2000. Cornaline de l'Inde, Des pratiques techniques de Cambay aux techno-systèmes de l'Indus. Paris: Éditions de la Maison des sciences de l'homme.

Russell, B. 2013. *The Economics of the Roman Stone Trade.* Oxford: Oxford University Press.

Sax, M., N. D. Meeks, C. Michaelson, and A. P. Middleton 2004. The identification of carving techniques on Chinese jade. *Journal of Archaeological Science* 31: 1413–28.

Sax, M., J. Ambers, N. Meeks, and S. Canby 2007. The emperor's terrapin. *The British Museum Technical Research Bulletin* 1: 35–41.

Sax, M., J. M. Walsh, I. C. Freestone, A. H. Rankin, and N. D. Meeks 2008. The origins of two purportedly pre-Columbian Mexican crystal skulls. *Journal of Archaeological Science* 53: 2751–60.

Semenov, S. A. 1964. *Prehistoric technology: an experimental study of the oldest tools and artefacts from traces of manufacture and wear*, M. W. Thompson (transl.). London: Cory, Adams and Mackay.

Sen, S. 1949. *Indian Travels of Thevenot and Careri*. New Delhi: National Archives of India.

Shalem, A. 1998. *Islam Christianized. Islamic Portable Objects in the Medieval Church Treasuries of the Latin West*. Frankfurt am Main: Peter Lang.

Skakun, N. 2008. Comprehensive analysis of the prehistoric tools and its relevance for paleo-economic reconstructions, in L. Longo and N. Skakun (eds) *Prehistoric Technology, 40 Years Later: Functional Studies and the Russian Legacy, Proceedings of the International Congress (Verona, 20-23 April 2005)*: 9–20. Oxford: Archaeopress.

Skelton, R. 1972. The relations between the Chinese and Indian jade carving traditions, in W. Watson (ed.) *The Westward Influence of the Chinese Arts from the 14th to the 18th Century*: 98–110. London: University of London, School of Oriental and African Studies, Percival David Foundation of Chinese Art.

Skelton, R. 1995. Islamic and Mughal Jades, in M. Kevern (ed.) *Jade*: 274–95. London: Lorenz Books.

Starac, A. 2007. A marble slab with relief of a stonemason. *Marmora* 3: 135–6.

Stronge, S. 1982. *The Indian Heritage. Court Life and Arts under Mughal Rule, Victoria and Albert Museum 21 April-22 August 1982*. London: Victoria and Albert Museum Publishing.

Talboys Wheeler, J. and M. MacMillan 1956. *European travellers in India* (India: past and present first series I). Calcutta: Susil Gupta.

Theophilus Presbyter 1961. *De Diversis Artibus: The Various Arts*, C.R. Dodwell (ed. and transl.). Oxford: Clarendon Press.

al-Tīfāshī. 1998. *Arab roots of gemology: Ahmad ibn Yusuf Al Tifaschi's Best Thoughts on the Best of Stones*, S.N. Abul Huda (transl. and annot.). Lanham, MD: Scarecrow Press.

Twilley, J. 1992. Scientific Description and Technical Analysis of Jades, in S. Markel (ed.) *The World of Jade*: 109–24. Bombay: Marg Publications.

Vargiolu, R. 2008. De la fabrication à l'utilisation d'objets archéologiques: apports de la tribologie. Unpublished PhD dissertation, École Centrale de Lyon.

Vargiolu, R., E. Morero, A. Boleti, H. Procopiou, C. Pailler-Mattei, and H. Zahouani 2007. Effects of abrasion during stone vase drilling in Bronze Age Crete. *Wear* 263: 48-56.

Wulff, H. E. 1966. *The Traditional Crafts of Persia*. Cambridge, MA: M.I.T. Press.

Zahouani, H. 1995. Filtrage tridimensionnel des surfaces rugueuses. *Bulletin de la Société des Sciences et des lettres de LODZ, Recherche sur les déformations* 20: 131–63.

Zahouani, H. 1997. Spectral and 3D motifs identification of anisotropic components: analysis and filtering of anisotropic patterns by morphological approach, in *Proceedings of the Seventh International Conference on Metrology and Properties of Engineering Surfaces*: 220–30. Götebo.

Imaging seals and coins with various light angles and spectra: consequences for understanding and representing colour and relief

Hendrik Hameeuw

Abstract

Stone seals are composed of translucent minerals that reveal complex reflectance and florescence effects when exposed to light from multiple angles or spectral bands. Similarly, the reflective responses of metal coins vary significantly depending on their alloy. There can be far-reaching consequences when these common ancient Near Eastern artefacts are recorded using imaging systems that produce representations based on principles of the reflective responses of the materials and/or photometric stereo. When multi-light imaging techniques are used to estimate reflectance characteristics and surface orientations of translucent or metal objects, the results can sometimes deviate from the appearance of the original. Applying multiple spectra on such surfaces provides insights, clues, and solutions to overcome these challenges.

Photometric stereo and normal maps

The presented study pertains to interactive imaging systems as applied to a selection of common Near Eastern artefacts. These systems are all derived from multi-light (directional) reflectance technologies (or MLR imaging), which are based on the principles of structure from shading. In short, the changing illumination and shading on a surface are used to understand the local surface orientations and, hence, the overall surface shape. This is possible because the apparent brightness of any particular point on a surface changes according to the angle between the local surface orientation and the incident illumination (the light that falls on a subject). In an ideal situation on a so-called Lambertian surface—a surface that appears the same from different viewing angles—three measurements on images illuminated under different conditions for each location suffice to determine the local surface property. These measurements are transformed and represented in a digital image by a pixel.

So, by observing a surface under different but well-defined illumination conditions, the components that contribute to the shading (i.e. surface orientation and albedo, the natural material colour) can be understood and used for an interactive virtual reconstruction of that surface. This technique is called photometric stereo (PS) and has been used for imaging heritage objects for several decades (Earl, Martinez, and Malzbender 2010; Einarsson, Hawkins, and Debevec 2004; Woodham 1980, 1989). The recovered parameters can also be used to simulate photo-realistic re-lightings of a surface. To achieve this, estimating correctly the albedo of each defined surface point (i.e. pixel) plays a key role. This albedo, or intrinsic colour of a surface, is a measure for reflectance (optical brightness). A photometric stereo algorithm scales the reflectance from zero (low albedo: all incident radiation is absorbed) to one (high albedo: all incident radiation is reflected). Based on these two estimations in a virtual rendering of the data, the imaged surface can interactively be inspected by visualizing that data in photorealistic and photo non-realistic manners.

101

For the results presented below, the Portable Light Dome (PLD) system of the KU Leuven was used for the acquisition, data processing and viewing. The acquisition domes count 260 (minidome) or 228 (microdome) LEDs installed on the inside of a black hemisphere. Two types of acquisition systems have been developed: domes equipped with white light LEDs (WL PLD, Willems et al. 2005) and domes equipped with multiple separate sets of LEDs with peak wavelength ranges (MS PLD, Van der Perre et al. 2016). The five selected peak spectra in the MS PLD (counting #228 LEDs) are in the infrared 850 nm (#43), red 623 nm (#48), green 523 nm (#48), blue 465 nm (#45) and ultraviolet 365 nm (#44). The applied macro lens is a CoastalOpt UV-VIS-IR 60 mm Apo, the light sensor an Allied Vision Prosilica GX 6600.

Reconstructing the colour and relief characteristics of stone seals and metal coins requires as accurate as possible an estimation of the surface orientations (i.e. relief); the PS algorithm stores these estimations in a 'normal map'. A 'normal' is the line or vector perpendicular to a given point on a surface. That estimation of a normal can be made for one point, but also for a whole range of points, defined by pixels, on one and the same surface. In this way, a normal is being defined for every pixel, and all these normals per pixel together are called a normal map. These pixel or raster images are similar to all digital photographs but, unlike photographs, the colour value attributed to these pixels does not represent those colours defined in standard RGB, sRGB eciRGB, CMYK, or LAB colour models. Colour models are related to the visual appearance of the represented surface. In normal maps, rather, each colour represents geometric information. Such raster images only represent normal vectors that point towards, or are visible by, a unique viewer; an approach that suits perfectly the setup of MLR imaging techniques. In the normal map images below (in each table and figure), an alternative RGB colour model has been used. The red channel is represented by the X axis (pointing the normals predominantly leftwards or rightwards), the green channel stores the Y axis (pointing the normals predominantly upwards or downwards), and the blue channel stores the Z axis (pointing the normals outwards, away from the surface). Thus, every shade of red, green, and blue represents a particular normal vector orientation. This approach permits storing very detailed geometric information in a fairly ergonomic way using a simple RGB raster image, drastically reducing the required storage volume. As the blue channel stores the normal vectors pointing outwards away from the main surface, in the direction of the camera, the overall look of these normal maps has a blue hue.

Malzbender, Gelb, and Wolters (2001) revealed the potential of MLR algorithms for the imaging and study of artefacts. When Hammer et al. (2002) demonstrated that PTM (Polynomial Texture Mapping) produced superior results compared to laser scanning of that time for low or subtle relief on particular surfaces, the method had sufficiently proven its value for high-end research on many types of artefacts. Since then, several distinct PS algorithms producing normal maps have improved further, some solutions for the field of heritage studies focussed on extracting robust visual properties others allow additional forms of visualization and analysis of the imaged surfaces as they mine more reflection components.[1] In the examples below, the same photometric stereo approach implemented by the PLD system has been used for all results. They demonstrate that the material or surface characteristics of the artefacts imaged with these methods influence the accuracy of the outcome, especially when focusing on the extracted 3D information. These inaccuracies can be minimal, and thus, during the workshop where this paper was presented, the question was raised:

---

[1] For the solution engineered in the PLD system see Willems et al. (2005: figure 6); for the enhanced MLR algorithm used in the contemporary RTI (Reflectance Transformation Imaging) methods, see Macdonald and Robson 2010.

why would we bother? It is my conviction that the technicalities of any high-end imaging technique should be thoroughly understood by all its users and observers, and, secondly, that not only the success stories should be communicated but also the failures, issues affiliated with a particular imaging method, and the acquisition strategies to overcome them. This is crucial if we want to trust the quality of the results and to assess their potential. In particular, imaging ancient Near Eastern artefacts with the highest standards is a task we must take very serious as recent, dramatic events have alerted us to: one day a satisfying yet inferior image can be produced, the next day the artefact may be destroyed.

Stone seals

All stone artefacts behave in a complex manner when the material interacts with incident light. Some of the light is directly reflected (a mirror or specular effect), while other light beams scatter when they penetrate the material, producing irregular diffuse reflections. A refraction effect is observed on translucent or transparent stones—the direction is changed when the incident light travels through the material, giving no reflection at all. On the other hand, part of the waves in a light beam will be absorbed by the material so, again, no reflection can be detected by the light sensor of a camera. In addition, almost all materials will use the absorbed light (energy) to emit light produced by its own molecules and atoms (i.e. fluorescence or luminescence), particularly when minerals are exposed to UV light. Thus, when the MLR technique is applied to stone seals, incident light coming from the pre-set directions is not reflected in a simple manner. In fact, some of the light registered by the light sensor mounted on top of a mini- or microdome will not originate from a reflection at all but instead from fluorescence or luminescence. These characteristics offer interesting challenges for the PS algorithms when applied to the imaging of these types of heritage objects.

Metal coins

Since its implementation in numismatics, MLR imaging methods have proved their value for conservation, curatorial, and research purposes (Gyselen and Mochri 2017; Hameeuw 2011; Mudge et al. 2005; Palma et al. 2013; Kotoula and Kyranoudi 2013). Studying and virtually reconstructing the surface morphology of coins, however, is impeded by their state of preservation and the degree of circulation wear. As a result, for many examples the relief is very shallow or almost gone, and often the metal has degraded dramatically. Additionally, the coins are made of various alloys and have undergone a wide range of physical conditions over the centuries. The physical and chemical condition of the surface will therefore interact with incident light in many different ways (Hameeuw 2017) and not all PS algorithms will have the same success rate in estimating correctly the albedo values and surface orientations.

Number of incident lights positions

As mentioned above, when dealing with a Lambertian surface, three images on which the incident light originates from another direction, are sufficient to estimate the normals for every recorded pixel. Unfortunately, the presence of shadows and specular reflections caused by the relief and the reflective responses of the materials demand an image-set to include a larger number of images. This means that light sources must be directed towards the surface from more positions. Although it is

103

possible to produce a normal map with so-called single-shot acquisitions (Chakrabarti and Sunkavalli 2016; Fyffe, Yu, and Debevec 2011), in practice, a sufficiently large number of images with different lighting conditions must be acquired for the recording of non-Lambertian surfaces such as those of most types of heritage artefacts. In applying MLR techniques, Earl, Martinez, and Malzbender (2010, 5–6) established that a dataset between 56 and 65 images can be taken as standard, although acknowledging—as per Hammer et al. (2002)—that an additional number of images with light positions will increase the quality of the normal map. They conclude that, when datasets of over 100 images are compared with a 65-light source dataset, the latter produces 'near equivalent results' and, similarly, the RTI branch of MLR techniques suggests an acquisition of 36 to 48 images.

To demonstrate the issue, Table 1 sets out two similar types of metal objects that behave in different manners. For each, datasets were acquired with a different number of light positions (24, 70, 131 or 260 respectively) and an indication of their even distribution on the inside of the PLD is given at the top of the table. For each recording, the PS normal map estimations of the algorithm used by the PLDviewer 5.0.04 (for WL) or 7.0.04 (for MS) are presented. The lead Sasanian coin (IR.3753-170, Gyselen and Mochri 2017) hardly shows true glossy behaviour. The random micro-scratches from circulation wear give the surface an ideal level of roughness, with virtually no glossy appearance, and the relief is very low; all closely resembling a Lambertian surface. As such, even with 24 light positions a nearly perfect estimation of the normals could be reached. The difference between the quality of the 24 light sources and 260 light sources normal map is negligible. Nevertheless, a slightly different conclusion must be drawn from recordings of an Iron Age silver plate bearing a standing figure in relief (O.3436a).[2] The main difference to the lead coin is that this metal plate has a glossy appearance. At first sight, the accuracy of the normal estimations seems similar throughout the four tests. Notice, however, that many normals in the field to the left and right of the figure's skirt have been estimated differently. When inspected more closely, many pixels have been attributed an inaccurate normal value in recordings with a limited number of light directions, as seen, for example, in the details of the figure's face. For this type of material and surface, the normal maps based on 131 and 260 light directions produced the more accurate results.

---

[2] To compare the WL PLD renderings with a professional exhibition catalogue photograph of this artefact, see Gubel and Overlaet 2007, 148.

Distribution of light sources

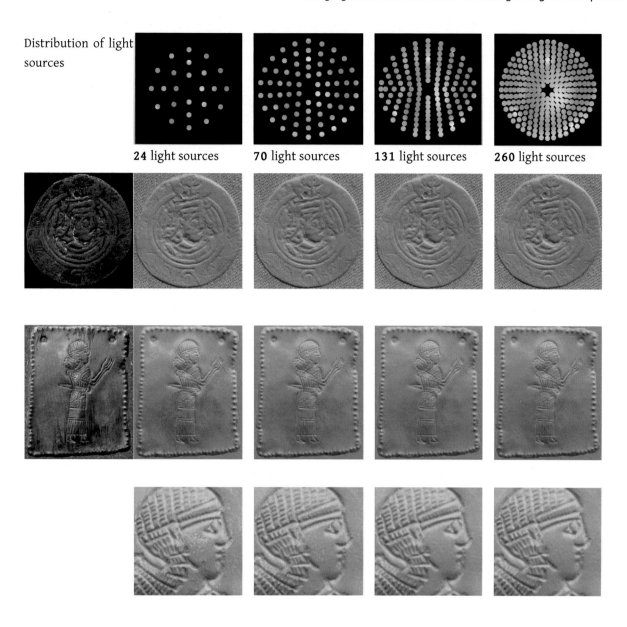

24 light sources   **70** light sources   **131** light sources   **260** light sources

Table 1. Compilation of colour visualization of two kinds of metal surfaces MLR imaged with four differently numbered sets of light sources. Above: Sasanian lead coin (© RMAH IR.3753-170 & KU Leuven); middle: Iranian Iron Age silver plate, detail below (© RMAH O.3436a & KU Leuven).

In conclusion, determining the ideal number of required images correlates to the degree in which the artefact behaves as a Lambertian surface; it depends on the characteristics of the artefact's material(s). The same observations can be made for surfaces with less shallow geometric features. A limited number of light directions is insufficient to allow enough emitters to irradiate features hidden deeper in the relief. The normals will not be estimated correctly for geometric surface elements inside relatively deep incised lines or depressions; the same is true for the estimation of the albedo. Therefore, the methods incorporated in MLR imaging techniques are designed to overcome these complicating effects; we therefore speak of robust photometric stereo. One of these strategies was demonstrated above: the more illumination directions introduced, the more it is possible to isolate a set of three pixels exhibiting purely Lambertian behaviour. In other words, the more complex a surface is, the greater the necessity for a sufficiently high number of light directions included in an image dataset. This will allow a correct estimation of both the normals and albedo's for every pixel included in the image. The drawbacks of capturing and using datasets with many incident directions of light, however, are the time needed for acquisition, processing times, and the required data storage.

Accuracy of the surface morphology

The electromagnetic spectrum can be subdivided by defining it by wavelengths. The longer these wavelengths, the more one shifts towards red and eventually near-infrared and infrared. When the wavelengths shorten, the colours blue, violet, and ultraviolet are reached. When PS and Multispectral Imaging (MSI) are combined, the phenomenon of wavelength-dependent reflectance plays a crucial role (Takatani et al. 2013). According to the Lambertian model, to obtain normals with the PS algorithm, the diffuse reflection is distributed uniformly in all directions. However, the actual directions of the outgoing light are determined by how the light is reflected and scattered within the material. Every kind of material will influence these reflections differently as they have other optical properties (see Bass 2009), and incident light is reflected wavelength-dependent. UV spectra (short waves) will almost never penetrate the surface, so they will therefore hardly be influenced by the internal materiality of the object. On the other hand, IR spectra (longer waves) do penetrate deeper into the surface's material, and the degree of penetration will even depend and differ with the incident direction. For most materials, longer waves will therefore reflect in a more complex manner, which impedes the ability of the PS algorithms to reconstruct surfaces accurately. Thus, when normals are estimated based on the PS principles with different multispectral bands, this phenomenon will produce different results (Kotoula 2015; Nam and Kim 2014). In this way, estimations of surface orientations of stone seals and metal coins are affected, and when the use of different spectral bands is applied wisely it can contribute to more accurate results.

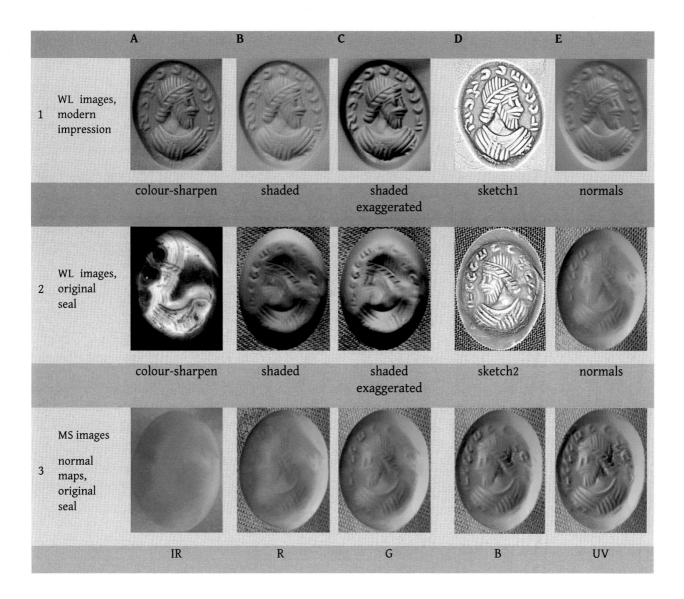

Table 2. Compilation of different visualizations of the surface of agate Sasanian seal IR.3584; based on 3 PLD recordings with white light (WL) and with multispectral imaging (MS) (© RMAH and KU Leuven)

It can sometimes be challenging to identify a stone seal's iconographic and epigraphic elements due to its material, colours, glossiness, translucency, or transparency. Table 2 presents images of a Sasanian stamp seal scanned with both the WL as well as with the MS PLD system.[3] The results offer interesting insights into the hazards involved in imaging this type of artefact. Specifically, the results demonstrate how the use of different light spectra strongly influences the ability to correctly reconstruct this type of material virtually. When MLR imaging techniques are applied to artefacts, there is a practical preference for the use of white light, i.e. a bundle or combination of wavelengths between 400 and 700 nm (the extended limits are 380 nm and 760 nm); or when flashlights are used, that includes even wavelengths into the near infrared. Table 2: 1E shows the normal map (with WL)

---

[3] For rows 2–3 the original seal was scanned, for row 1 the modern impression in clay. Columns A–E of rows 1–2 present a selection of visualisation filters made with PLDviewer 5.0.04 or 7.0.04 for the same recording; for row 3 the columns present only the results of the normal map visualisations, each time those based on the image-set made with five different spectral bands.

of a modern impression in clay, a material with a fair Lambertian behaviour. Using clay eliminates the problematic interaction of light with the stone minerals of the original seal and the resulting normal map offers a sound estimation of the surface orientations. For this example, this is our benchmark. Table 2: 2E shows the normal map, again with WL, of the original seal. In this case, the PS algorithm struggled visibly more with the interaction of the white light on this type of material and delivered a less accurate normal map.

The reason can be deduced from Table 2: Row 3. With the IR and Red datasets, the PS algorithm was incapable of reconstructing the surface orientation; it seems that the green, blue and UV respectively did gradually much better. This same phenomenon is fully demonstrated in Table 3. The IR (c) and red (d) waves have penetrated, interacted, and reflected in such a manner that the macro physical surface of this very translucent (a) red agate gem was not recognized by the algorithm at all. Notice that the surface profile line (black) of the selected section (yellow) is nearly flat. The calculations of the green (e), blue (f) and UV (g) waves estimated the surface orientations, pixel by pixel, with a much higher accuracy, because those waves penetrated the physical surface less deeply. They have therefore interacted and reflected more consistently according to the predetermined PS principles and parameters. This is what can be observed when MS is combined with MLR.

White light includes red waves as well, so the more complex and irregular reflective behaviour of these types of materials has influenced the overall ability of the PS algorithm to produce accurate normal estimations. Returning to the banded agate sealing surface of IR.3584, the WL normal map (Table 2: 2E) achieves the same level of accuracy as the result obtained with the MS dataset of green; the application of blue and UV can even visually be considered better. To conclude, WL MLR will produce good visual colour representations (albedo, Table 2: 2A) of glossy, translucent, and transparent stone artefacts, but for the reconstruction of their surface geometry it is recommended to exclude the longer wavelengths of the electromagnetic spectrum and to favour exclusive Blue or even UV spectral bands (Table 2: D and E or even more clear Table 3: e and g).[4]

---

[4] A number of commercial scanning systems already uses selected short wavelengths, for such a structured light scanner applied on cuneiform tablets see Graham et al. 2017, 288.

a1) Colour photograph

a2) Colour photograph with backlight

b) RGB false colour representation with underlying green normal map applied

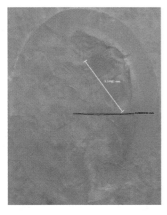

c) Normal map based on IR spectral band and profile of relief

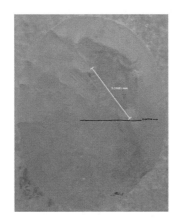

d) Normal map based on red spectral band and profile of relief

e) Normal map based on green spectral band and profile of relief

f) Normal map based on blue spectral band and profile of relief

g) Normal map based on UV spectral band and profile of relief

h) Normal map based on UV-fluorescent response in VIS and profile of relief

Table 3. Compilation of different visualizations of a red agate gem sealing surface of MB.Gl.30 (Baudot 1987–1988, 121) based on Nikon D800 photographs and MS PLD recordings (© KU Leuven).

UV-induced visible fluorescence imaging detects the white light emitted by materials when radiated with UV light (UV-A). This absorption, interaction, and transformation of UV energy into white light emission takes place at the outer limits of the surface. As Kotoula (2015) argued, the combination of MRL imaging and UV induced visible fluorescence—labelled by Kotoula as 'UVF RTI'—can contribute to the study of conservation materials and previous repairs on the surface of ceramics. Interestingly, normal maps based on the dataset of images with the reflected UV and fluorescent UV produce very similar high-quality results (compare Table 3: g and h).[5] Hence, highly accurate information is acquired by using UV light with any standard camera bearing a non-full spectrum light sensor. In addition, this also gives an insight into the influence of the fluorescence/luminescence effect when the photometric stereo algorithms are applied on image datasets.[6] Table 3: g presents the result when all the returned light energy (reflection and fluorescence) from the surface is detected and transformed into a normal map; whereas for the normal map in Table 3: h, only the fluorescence energy could be used. As stated above, the differences between these two are minimal but, when examined more closely, they are obviously not the same. In Figure 1, a pure reflectance and a fluorescence result are compared. On the left, only the UV reflection was registered; a LUV U II UVpass 360WB53 filter was mounted while the surface was irradiated by the MS PLD UV LEDs. On the right, only the fluorescence in the VIS was registered, by mounting a Schott BG38 bandpass filter, i.e. blocking the UV reflection and letting the fluorescing waves in the visual spectrum pass. Beside some minor variations in the local estimations of the normals, the most important difference is observed in the general understanding of the gem's shape. The curvature (see Figure 1, the profile lines in blue) diverges considerably: the height difference is almost double. Thus, even though the engravings in the stone surface are registered with an astonishing sense for detail, the overall geometry of the imaged surfaces is not estimated and understood consistently enough when the various combined MSI-MLR results are inspected. It raises the question: which of the blue, UV, or fluorescence results provides the most accurate curvature?[7]

---

[5] Table 3: h) consists an acquisition in which a Schott BG38 bandpass filter was mounted in front of the CoastalOpt UV-VIS-IR macro lens to register only the fluorescent emission triggered by the UV radiation of the MS PLD in the white light range of the spectrum. Table 3: g) gives the normal map based on the dataset for which the UV reflected light of the UV radiation was registered, but, as no filters were mounted, that included as well the light energy of the UV fluorescent emission in the white light range of the spectrum.

[6] Note that MLR techniques are based on the controlled irradiation of a surface and on measuring the reflection of that incident light by the surface; fluorescence is strictly spoken an entirely different phenomenon.

[7] For a recent study on how photometric stereo UV fluorescence can support heritage studies, see Salvant et al. 2017.

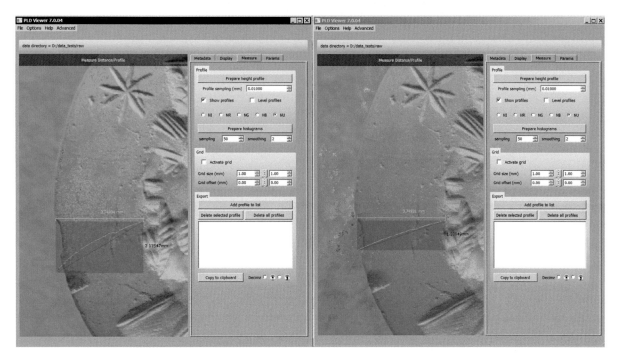

Figure 1: Detail of two recordings of MB.Gl.30 (© KU Leuven). Left: UV reflection of UV radiation. Right: White light emitting of the surface by UV radiation (fluorescence).

Something extra

The absolute advantage of the combined MSI-MLR imaging lies in the interactive approach of consulting the results in real-time, switching between the many renderings of the applied spectral bands. The discussion above determined that the Blue and UV datasets provide the best and most reliable reconstructions of the stone seal's relief, but other datasets may reveal additional information on the imaged artefacts as well. The highly polished surface of the gem is shown in Table 3: a; while the Table 3: b image with translucent light gives us hints on the interior conditions of the stone mineral. MSI-MLR imaging has detected some of these features, by means of the Red and Green spectral datasets. The normal maps in Table 3: b, d and e visualize (and makes measurable) several cracks inside the left part of the gem. This method can therefore be used to monitor the physical conditions of the materials on the surface and on the inside.

Porous, glossy, and varying materials

The MLR colour raster images presented here are photo-realistic, close to conventional digital photography. The PS algorithm has, however, excluded all potential specular highlights and consequently, these images do not show any of the glossy characteristics of the surface materials one would expect. They have an overall dim appearance, to which human perception is not accustomed for objects such as stone seals and metal coins. Another phenomenon the imaging of ancient artefacts with MLR techniques is faced with, is that spectra will interact differently on various materials and with the physical conditions of one particular material.

As seals and coins are often well-represented in collections, documentation strategies will seek to establish a fixed procedure of actions to image them. As demonstrated above for seals, the best fixed practice to settle on is not evident because of the challenges associated with the materiality and varying physical conditions of this type of object. A well-preserved coin has a smooth surface, reflecting light in a predictable manner for the robust PS algorithms, but the more this smoothness is affected by aging, the more porous the surface layer has become. As such, light will penetrate and interact with that layer and reflect light back in a much more unpredictable pattern. This makes it more challenging for the PS algorithms to estimate the correct colours and surface orientations per pixel. Under the same acquisition parameters (see Figure 2), the normal and albedo estimations for dark reflecting coins with deteriorated surfaces (left) will be much more problematic compared to well-preserved examples (right) that have a smooth, intact surface with a nearly Lambertian behaviour. Both in the albedo and normal maps in Figure 2, we observe that not all pixels have been defined correctly on the item on the left, whereas these inaccuracies do not occur on the coin on the right because it is easier to document with MLR techniques. Furthermore, the Æ alloy (left) appears darker because it absorbs most of the white light, and PS algorithms work with reflected light. The highly light-absorbing nature of this material also affects the ability of the method to estimate the reflectance values of each pixel as accurately as possible. Both effects explain the difference in quality between the MLR imaging of one coin compared to another, thus impeding the development of simplified acquisition strategies; an excellent setting for one coin, may lead to an unsatisfying result for another. Generally, good results can be obtained for each particular surface by adjusting settings during the acquisition process, such as exposure time, the number of light sources, or the alternations between spectral bands.

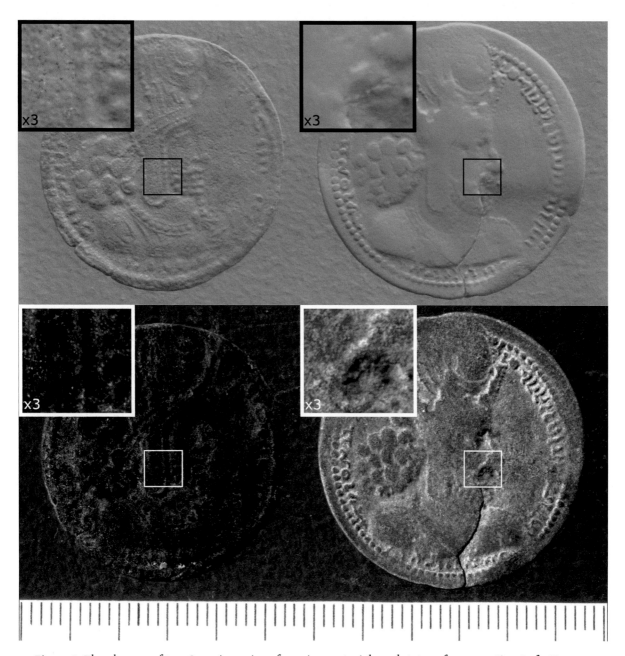

Figure 2. The obverse of two Sasanian coins of varying materials and states of preservation. Left: IR.3753-0185 (Gyselen and Mochri 2017), an Æ alloy; Right: IR.3753-0186 (Gyselen and Mochri 2017), a billon (potin) alloy (© RMAH and KU Leuven). Both coins have been imaged under the same lighting conditions by the WL PLD.

Finally, the manner in which even the smallest alterations in the physical composition of materials can influence the final results is be demonstrated with the recording of a banded stone agate stamp seal (Figure 3). These bands—on this seal, variations between white and red/brown/orange—are most probably a result of the conditions in which substances containing silica were deposited during their formation process, resulting in variations between chalcedony and crystalline quartz. Their compositions are dissimilar, hence they also reflect light differently. Geometrically, the sealing surface prepared by the seal cutter has produced a smooth, perfectly polished surface, in this case slightly concave. The transition from one band to another is seamless. MLR should allow the reconstruction of a perfect concave form with engravings. That is generally the case, but when examined more closely, this visualisation of the surface orientations also allows vaguely distinguishing the colour bands in the agate, as if these bands would have slight different surface orientation. All the datasets derived from the applied spectral bands with the MS PLD revealed this effect. Here, too, it proves to be particularly challenging to use light to reconstruct the macro-physical relief of multi-material surfaces that interact with light in a complex manner.

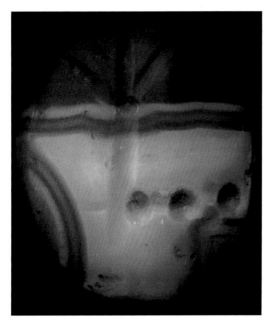 

Figure 3. Agate stamp seal (MB.Gl.23, Baudot 1987–1988, 120, © KU Leuven). Left: colour mode of sealing surface (MS PLD recording); Right: UV normal map of sealing surface (MS PLD recording).

Conclusions

These selected MLR recordings of the PLD system illustrate that, due to the behaviour of normal white light when applied to the reconstruction of the relief of stone seals and coins, the results are not necessarily fully satisfactory. Acquisition settings or strategies must be established for every sub-type, for every preservation condition, and for each object of mixed media. We must therefore conclude that imaging entire collections with a fixed pipeline of actions bounces against a number of limits that arise from the complex materiality and physicality of these types of artefacts and which are inherent to the operated imaging technique. The many (sub-)types of artefacts and definable surfaces require other settings and acquisition strategies to assure high-end results for all objects in entire corpuses. Some of the issues we are faced with when documenting large quantities of stone seals and metal coins with these imaging techniques remain to be addressed and discussed in depth; any solutions must be integrated in the further fine-tuning of the existing robust photometric stereo algorithms. Especially where MS MLR techniques are concerned, some effects are still insufficiently understood. That is certainly the case for the influence of the luminescence phenomenon on the PS method. The decision to image these types of objects with a combined MLR-MSI acquisition to obtain good texture maps and information on the surface orientations with one and the same acquisition effort has proven to deliver excellent results. In particular, the combination of the albedo maps provides photo-realistic images, whereas the separately rendered results of the spectral bands can highlight different features of the surface or even internal characteristics. The datasets obtained via an MLR-MSI imaging method can also be used to address new research questions. By understanding the reflectance responses of surfaces, the same interactive images can be used to identify materials.[8]

The cases presented above argue that the use of spectral bands with specific peak wavelengths is preferable if the focus lies on the accurate detection of the object's relief. Wavelengths below 500 nm, blue-indigo-violet-ultraviolet, are recommended. These observations are valid for multi-light reflectance imaging, but also apply to several other imaging technologies that use the reflective responses of light to estimate the surface orientations of artefacts.

Acknowledgements

I am most grateful to the editors for their enthusiasm and the invitation to share the results presented above. Special thanks go to Dr Bruno Overlaet (Curator Ancient Near East, Iran and Islam collections at the RMAH, Brussels) who granted access to the ANE seal and coin collections of his institution for this study; to Bruno Vandermeulen (KU Leuven, Digitalisation Lab) and Prof. Lieve Watteeuw (KU Leuven, Illuminare) for letting me experiment with some of the additional components of the PLD system; and to Prof. Marc Proesmans (KU Leuven, ESAT–PSI) for sharing his technical insights.

References

Baudot, M. P. 1987–1988. The Ancient Near Eastern Seals and Gems in the Biblical Museum at the Catholic University of Leuven. *Acta Archaeologica Lovaniensia* 26–27: 113–30.

Bass, M. (ed.) 2009. *Handbook of Optics (Volume IV): Optical properties of materials, nonlinear optics, quantum optics*. New York: McGraw Hill Professional.

Chakrabarti, A. and K. Sunkavalli 2016. Single-image RGB Photometric Stereo With Spatially-varying Albedo, in *Proceedings of the IEEE International Conference on 3D Vision (3DV), 2016*: 1–9.

Earl, G., K. Martinez and T. Malzbender 2010. Archaeological applications of polynomial texture mapping: analysis, conservation and representation. *Journal of Archaeological Science* 37: 2040–50.

Einarsson, P., T. Hawkins and P. Debevec 2004. Photometric Stereo for Archeological Inscriptions (Sketches 0338). *ACM SIGGRAPH '04*. Sketches: 81.

Fyffe G., X. Yu and P. Debevec 2011. Single-Shot Photometric Stereo by Spectral Multiplexing. in *Proceedings of Computer Communication and Processing, 2011*: 1–6.

---

[8] For an example with gold coins, see the results by Watteeuw et al. 2016.

Graham, C. A., K. G. Akoglu, A. W. Lassen, and S. Simon 2017. Epic dimensions: A comparative analysis of 3D acquisition methods. *The International Archives of Photogrammetry and Remote Sensing and Spatial Information Sciences* XLII-2/W5: 287–93.

Gubel E. and B. Overlaet (eds) 2007. *Van Gilgamesj tot Zenobia: Kunstschatten uit het Oude Nabije Oosten en Iran*. Brussels: Mercatorfonds and KMKG.

Gyselen, R. and M. I. Mochri 2017. Une collection de monnaies sassanides de billon, de cuivre et de plomb. R. Gyselen (ed.) Sasanian coins, Middle-Persian Etymology and the Tabarestan Archive (Res Orientales XXVI): 9–106. Bures-sur-Yvette: Groupe pour l'Étude de la Civilisation du Moyen-Orient.

Hameeuw, H. 2017. Appendix: The interactive 2D+ images of the Brussels Sasanian coins, R. Gyselen (ed.): *Sasanian coins, Middle-Persian Etymology and the Tabarestan Archive (Res Orientales XXVI): 102-6. Bures-sur-Yvette: Groupe pour l'Étude de la Civilisation du Moyen-Orient.*

Hameeuw, H. 2011. Digitalisering van het archeologisch roerend erfgoed met behulp van 2D+ en 3D technologieën - een casestudie met het archeologisch erfgoed uit Roeselare. *West-Vlaamse Archaeologica* 24: 60–68.

Hammer, Ø., S. Bengtson, T. Malzbender and D. Gelb 2002. Imaging fossils using reflectance transformation and interactive manipulation of virtual light sources. *Paleontologia Electronica* 5/4: 1–9.

Kotoula, E. 2015. Reflectance Transformation Imaging beyond the visible: Ultraviolet Reflected and Ultraviolet Induced Visible Fluorescence, in S. Campana, R. Scopigno, G. Carpentiero and M. Cirillo (eds) *Proceedings of the 43rd Annual Conference on Computer Applications and Quantitative Methods in Archaeology*: 909–19. Oxford: Archaeopress.

Kotoula, E. and M. Kyranoudi 2013. Study of ancient Greek and Roman coins using Reflectance Transformation Imaging. *E-conservation Journal* 25: 74–88.

Macdonald, L. and S. Robson 2010. Polynomial Texture Mapping and 3D representations. *International Archives of Photogrammetry, Remote Sensing and Spatial Information Sciences* XXXVIII (Part 5 Commission V Symposium, Newcastle upon Tyne, UK): 422–7.

Malzbender, T., D. Gelb and H. Wolters 2001. Polynomial Texture Maps, in L. Pocock (ed.) *SIGGRAPH '01: Proceedings of the 28th Annual Conference on Computer Graphics and Interactive Techniques*: 519–28. New York: Association for Computing Machinery.

Mudge, M., J.-P. Voutaz, C. Schroer and M. Lum 2005. Reflection Transformation Imaging and Virtual Representations of coins from the Hospice of the Grand St. Bernard, in M. Mudge, N. Ryan and R. Scopigno (eds) *The 6th International Symposium on Virtual Reality, Archaeology and Cultural Heritage (VAST 2005), Pisa*: 29–39. Eurographics Association.

Nam, G. and M. H. Kim. 2014. Multispectral Photometric Stereo for acquiring high-fidelity surface normals. *IEEE Computer Graphics and Applications* 34/6: 57–68.

Palma, G., E. Siotto, M. Proesmans, M. Baldassari, C. Baracchini, S. Batino and R. Scopigno 2013. Telling the Story of Ancient Coins by Means of Interactive RTI Images Visualization. in G. Earl, et al. (eds) *Archaeology in the Digital Era: Papers from the 40th Annual Conference of Computer Applications and Quantitative Methods in Archaeology (CAA), Southampton, 26-29 March 2012*: 177–85. Amsterdam: Amsterdam University Press.

Pevar, A., L. Verswyvel, S. Georgoulis, N. Cornelis, M. Proesmans, L. Van Gool 2015. Real-time Photometric Stereo, in D. Fritsch (ed.) *Proceedings of the 55th Photogrammetric Week pages*: 185–206. Belin and Offenbach: Wichmann/VDE.

Salvant, J., M. Walton, D. Kronkright, Ch.-K. Yeh, F. Li, O. Cossairt and A. K. Katsaggelos 2018. Photometric Stereo by UV-induced fluorescence to detect protrusions on Georgia O'Keeffe's paintings, in F. Casadio et al. (eds) *Metal Soaps in Art - Conservation and Research*: 1–25. Springer Nature.

Takatani, T., Y. Matsushita, S. Lin, Y. Mukaigawa, Y. Yagi 2013. Enhanced Photometric Stereo with Multispectral Images, in *Proceedings of the International Conference on Machine Vision Applications* 13: 343–6. Kyoto: MVA Organization.

Van der Perre, A., H. Hameeuw, V. Boschloos, L. Delvaux, M. Proesmans, B. Vandermeulen, L. Van Gool and L. Watteeuw 2016. Towards a combined use of IR, UV and 3D-Imaging for the study of small inscribed and illuminated artefacts, in P. M. Homem (ed.) *Lights On... Cultural Heritage and Museums!*: 163–92. Porto: FLUP.

Watteeuw, L., H. Hameeuw, B. Vandermeulen, A. Van der Perre, V. Boschloos, L. Delvaux, M. Van Bos, M. Proesmans and L. Van Gool 2016. Light, shadows and surface characteristics. The multispectral portable light dome. *Applied Physics* A 122/976: 1–7.

Willems, G., F. Verbiest, W. Moreau, H. Hameeuw, K. Van Lerberghe and L. Van Gool 2005. Easy and cost-effective cuneiform digitizing, in M. Mudge, N. Ryan and R. Scopigno (eds) *The 6th International Symposium on Virtual Reality, Archaeology and Cultural Heritage (VAST 2005), Pisa*: 73–80. Aire-la-Ville: Eurographics Association.

Woodham, R. J. 1980. Photometric method for determining surface orientation from multiple images. *Optical Engineerings* 19/1: 139–44.

Woodham, R. J. 1989: Photometric Method for determining surface orientation from multiple images. B. K. P. Horn and M. J. Brooks (eds) *Shape from Shading*: 513–31. Cambridge, MA: M.I.T. Press.

Prehistoric stone sculptures at the Gregorio Aguilar Barea Museum, Nicaragua: photogrammetry practices and Digital Immersive Virtual Environment applications for archaeology

Alexander Geurds, Juan Aguilar, and Fiona McKendrick

Abstract

During the summer of 2016, photogrammetric acquisition was completed on a corpus of more than fifty pre-Columbian stone sculptures idols on display at the Gregorio Aguilar Barea Archaeological Museum (MAGAB) in Juigalpa, Nicaragua in order to create digital three-dimensional copies. Using computer vision, the goal is to analyse and compare these monumental objects and come to new observations on indigenous clothing, body adornment, weaponry, and possible post-funerary customs, in combination with an increased understanding of sculpting technology. This particular practice of sculpting large stone human and animal-like figures represents a unique case in the pre-Hispanic Americas, in light of the presumed absence of institutional political hierarchy in this region and the high volume of sculpture production. The MAGAB houses the single largest collection representative of this tradition. However, hardly any data on the context of these igneous rock sculptures was available until recently. These lacunae provided impetus for some of the research questions of the Central Nicaragua Archaeological Project (PACEN), initiated in 2007 and directed by Dr. Alexander Geurds. This chapter reports on the particular methodological challenges of creating a photogrammetric record of large worked monoliths in a closely spaced exhibit setting, as part of the ongoing PACEN investigations in stone sculpture production and use. We also provide details of efforts to generate a digital museum reimagining of MAGAB, presenting the needed steps from data collection to data presentation, and argue for the potential of Virtual Reality for engaging with existing and new audiences worldwide. To build a digital rendering of the original stone sculpture collection to be enjoyed and fully explored online, all 3D models were imported into the freely available Unreal Engine 4 Editor, a computer game engine tool to design virtual walkable worlds and tell new stories. In keeping with Aguilar Barea's collaborative vision, this archaeological imaging research works together with the MAGAB for purposes of knowledge exchange and exhibit improvement: the digital possibility to be able to freely rearrange massive and anchored sculptures, and redesign the museum to improve object lighting and overall visibility enables new ways to disseminate this unique but rarely exposed collection and its particular history of collecting.

'When the idol was perfect, its mouth was open, into which the blowing of the wind made a mournful, whistling sound, exciting suspicions that it was the incarnation of one of those ancient 'demonios' of the Indians. The pious priests demolished it in consequence.'

—Ephraim Squier, 1852

Introduction

In this chapter, we discuss the use of digital photogrammetric recording of a corpus of more than fifty prehistoric stone sculptures on display at the Museo Arqueológico Gregorio Aguilar Barea (MAGAB) located in the city of Juigalpa, central Nicaragua (Figure 1), completed in the summer of 2016. Using computer vision, the goal set was to re-analyse and compare these monumental monoliths and come to new observations regarding prehistoric indigenous clothing, body adornment, weaponry, and possible post-funerary customs, in combination with an increased understanding of technologies involved in sculpting the objects. The large volume of sculptural production combined with the presumed absence of institutional political hierarchy in this Central American region make this particular practice of creating large stone human and animal-like figures an extraordinary case for the pre-Hispanic Americas. Alongside improving archaeological understanding, our digital archaeological project also aims to actively support and advance MAGAB's efforts in preserving their collection, as well as promoting local cultural heritage valorisation in Nicaragua—a country marked by economic challenges and cultural divisions as a result of a modern history defined by authoritarian regimes and civil war during the 20th century.

In this contribution, the particular methodological challenges of collecting data and creating a digital photogrammetric record of large worked monoliths in a closely spaced exhibit setting are outlined. We also provide insights into efforts to generate a digital sculpture museum reimagining MAGAB, and make a case for the potential of using Digital Immersive Virtual Environments (DIVE) for engaging with existing and new museum audiences worldwide. Finally, we also want to put forth ideas concerning how this digital museum project can benefit existing local and national heritage narratives. In doing so, this archaeological digital imaging research works with the MAGAB for purposes of knowledge exchange and exhibit improvement: the digital possibility to redesign the museum enables new ways to disseminate this unique but rarely exposed collection and its particular history of collection.

Before discussing digital photogrammetry in archaeology and highlighting DIVE's manifold possibilities for cultural heritage management and museology, we set out how the MAGAB is at the centre of our on-going research. The intrinsic motivation behind the digital stone sculpture collection project flows from how the project relates to this small family-run museum and its founder's vision of caring for the past.

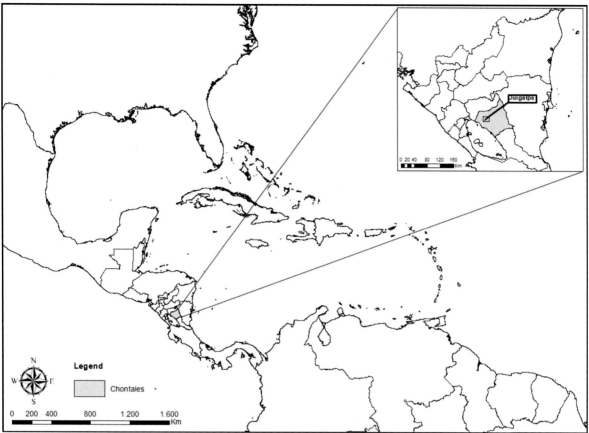

Figure 1. General map of Middle America, indicating Nicaragua, the Chontales region and its capital Juigalpa (map courtesy of Simone Casale).

The MAGAB and its prehistoric stone sculpture collection

The pedigree of the collection is centred around Gregorio 'Goyo' Aguilar Barea. Born in Juigalpa in 1933, Aguilar Barea became one of the protagonists of a remarkable push in promoting local heritage in the Nicaraguan province of Chontales from the 1950s onwards. He is considered the driving force behind the founding of multiple local public cultural institutions in Juigalpa including a zoo, an orchestra, a public library, numerous other cultural organisations, a local history circle or 'intellectual clan', and, most importantly perhaps, a museum devoted to local material culture, whether pre-Hispanic, colonial, or contemporary. He acquired objects for the museum collection from near and far. These donations include dozens of stone sculptures, some of which are several metres in height. Many were donated by ranchers who found them in their lands around Juigalpa. In this way, and through subsequent donations, Aguilar Barea amassed a significant collection of archaeological artefacts alongside the stone sculptures.

After more than a decade of planning and building, bringing together funds and building materials through a form of local crowdfunding *avant la lettre*, the museum opened its doors in January 1967, attracting national attention as well as the presence of several foreign archaeologists, an unprecedented feat at the time. The collection of sculptures was already sizeable and gradually expanded in the years thereafter. However, the majority of the stone sculptures were anchored in the ground in what was originally designed as an outdoor patio in front of the main museum building (Figure 2). The placement of the sculptures was largely in service of the building architecture with three rows of seven or eight sculptures parallel to either side of a stone-paved path leading from the street to the museum entrance, and six larger sculptures facing the street. The spatial result of this is a highly linear 'chessboard' setup (Figure 3), while overall impressive on the beholder, it makes individual appreciation of sculptures challenging.

Figure 2. Photograph showing initial outdoor patio layout. SItuation c. 1970 (photo: courtesy MAGAB).

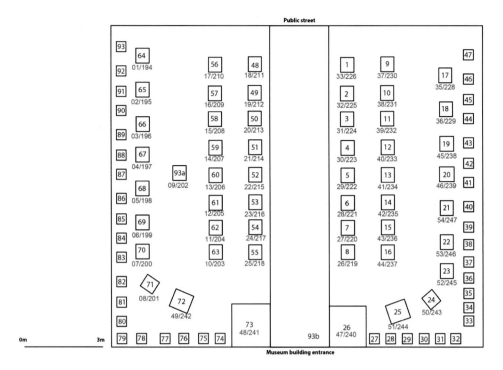

Figure 3. Schematic plan drawing of current patio space, indicating individual sculptures and reference numbers (drawing: Alexander Geurds).

Regrettably, Aguilar Barea prematurely died in a tragic car accident in 1970, abruptly leaving behind a local cultural legacy exceeding that of many national figures in Nicaraguan history. To this day, he remains an iconic figure revered in Juigalpa. The museum, posthumously named the *Museo Arqueológico Gregorio Aguilar Barea*, is visited by all primary and secondary schoolchildren of Juigalpa, visitors from outside of Chontales, as well as a steady trickle of national and international tourists. Since Aguilar Barea's death, the day-to-day management of the museum has been the almost uninterrupted responsibility of Gustavo Villanueva, one of his staunchest collaborators. Since the onset of the 21st century, Villanueva has gradually transferred this task to a legally recognised friends association. The vacuum left by Aguilar Barea's death led to a power struggle, with the museum becoming a bone of contention in the 1970s and multiple stakeholders bitterly arguing over ownership and authority of the collection, the museum building, and adjoining lots of land. For now, this conflict remains in want of a mutually agreeable solution, and the emotions and legal battles that have made up this conflict perhaps speak to the local importance of this museum and, central in this, its collection of stone sculptures.

Since its inception, the MAGAB has witnessed several modifications to the entrance space where the sculptures are placed. This has included filling up the grassy spaces in between sculptures, roofing the patio area (effectively making it an indoor space), and modifying the original iron fencing separating the patio from the public street (Figure 4). Whilst closing the space negates some threats posed to exposed sculptures, these adjustments have in turn also generated new issues to do with lighting, cement dust, and climate control. Overall, the condition of the stone sculpture collection is continually threatened, and although the museum staff are ambitious and caring, funding for improving the collection's preservation is limited - a stark contrast to the vision and initial community push demonstrated during its founding period.

Figure 4. The patio interior, c. 2010. Note the concrete foundations of sculptures and raised wall facing the public street (photo: Alexander Geurds).

Another issue affecting the stone sculpture, however, originates from the time before the building of the museum. In accordance with amateur collecting practices of the time when the sculptures were transported to Juigalpa by Aguilar Barea and his collaborators (Figure 5), little attention was awarded to physical and wider landscape contexts of these monoliths. In combination with a lack of subsequent archaeological research in the area, hardly any data on the context of these igneous rock sculptures was available until recently. These lacunae provided impetus for some of the research questions of the *Proyecto Arqueológico Centro de Nicaragua* (PACEN), initiated in 2007 by Alexander Geurds. In this sense, the digital imaging work presented here is part of a larger endeavour to investigate how the sculptures were created and preserved. We ask how raw materials were carved, including from where and how these materials were quarried, and the nature of the technologies involved in shaping them. The project also investigates the sculptures' monumental contextual settings: how do the surrounding anthropogenic mounds relate to the sculptures, and can the individuals depicted be linked to those settings?

Figure 5. Photograph showing Aguilar Barea (at centre, with cap) and a group of his young explorers with a sculpture found at the Copelito farmstead (photo: courtesy MAGAB).

The Chontales stone sculptures from an archaeological perspective

Ancient Nicaragua was a diverse cultural landscape. It was a key transition zone in Central America between the Mesoamerican and Isthmo-Colombian cultural areas (Baudez 1970; Drennan 1995; Healy 1980; Hoopes and Fonseca 2003; Lange 1992; Lange and Stone 1984; McCafferty and Steinbrenner 2005). Linguistically, it was a patchwork of speakers of many languages, pertaining to multiple language families (Constenla 1991; Lehmann 1920; Van Broekhoven 2002). When we speak of prehistoric Nicaraguan cultural identities, therefore, these are mostly known through references to ethnicities in 16th-century Spanish written accounts.[1]

In different regions of Nicaragua, stone sculptures were typically set in monumental environments defined by a planned arrangement of stone and earthen mounds serving a communal function. Such monumental sites emerged in several regions of Central America during the last millennium BC and lasted up to the period of the Spanish Conquest in the early 16th century. In the material world of prehistoric Central America monumental stone sculpture played a visible and connecting role in and between communities. In Nicaragua specifically, the use of monumental stone sculpture flourished perhaps from AD 600 up to the Spanish Conquest, but its development and link to monumental

---

[1] These identities remain complicated to attest archaeologically, as research in Pacific Nicaragua has repeatedly demonstrated (McCafferty and Dennett 2013; Steinbrenner 2010) through the study of 'foreign' pottery decorative motifs and more recently through analysis of pottery technology.

architecture is hardly known. We are unable to evaluate what role sculptures played in these complexes and it remains obscure how these monumental centres figured in regional settings.[2]

The regional investigative focus of PACEN is in the geographically diverse area of central Nicaragua, where the stone sculptures were procured, fashioned, and placed in communal ceremonial settings. Given the transitional geography in this region, it is thought that societies here were culturally related to both the Caribbean tropical forest lowlands towards the east, as well as the drier and volcanically active region around Lake Nicaragua and the Pacific coast to the west. Geographically, central Nicaragua is best described as a bridging zone between on the one hand the fertile soils and freshwater lakes of the Pacific coastal areas, while the other side is defined by the remnants of volcanic ridges separating central Nicaragua from the wide lowland expanses of the Caribbean to the east and northeast (Figure 6). Central Nicaragua itself is geomorphologically marked by Tertiary volcanic rock (Ehrenborg 1996) featuring abundant basalt and andesite outcrops used in the production of these sculptures.

Accordingly, the archaeological record shows significant differences to the Pacific in terms of settlement pattern across the landscape, domestic structures, as well as public architecture. Until recently, the prehistory of central Nicaragua lacked chronological precision and relied upon a rather crude categorisation by the Western explorers who travelled the region in the second half of the 19th century (e.g. Belt 1874; Boyle 1868; Pim and Seemann 1869; Squier 1852). Entire archaeological periods still remain undetected, including the initial peopling during Paleoindian times (2000–500 BC) as well as the transitional period at the onset of the Spanish colonization (c. 1522–1600 AD). For now, the earliest pottery types in central Nicaragua have been associated to materials from the second half of the last millennium BC and ranging up to the early part of the 16th century AD (Gorin 1989). What little we know of the prehistory of central Nicaragua points to hunter-gatherer and horticulturist societies gradually spreading across the geographically diverse landscape and subsequently developing monumental practices including earthworks and anthropomorphically-carved monoliths, as documented by the Spanish when they arrived in the region in the early 1520s. By then, the use of stone sculpture in combination with monumental public architecture was vibrant and probably widely dispersed across central Nicaragua and neighbouring regions. This we can conclude on the basis of the presence of stone sculpture preserved in museum collections throughout Nicaragua. This pervasive use demonstrates that these objects formed an integral part of the indigenous social world. Anthropomorphic sculpture occurred along the Pacific coast, on the interior lake islands, and in the tropical lowland Caribbean region (for an overview see Haberland 1973). This indicates that those who commissioned the sculptures not only used them to increase community coherence, but also to proverbially 'fix' particular regional memories and histories by means of the hardness of the sculptures' basalt.

---

[2] Some of these questions have led to pioneering work worldwide on the relationship between settlement context and stone sculpture in prehistoric Western Europe (Robb 2009), the Greek Neolithic (Nanoglou 2008), and parts of prehistoric Mexico and Costa Rica (e.g. Cyphers 1999; Holmberg 2005).

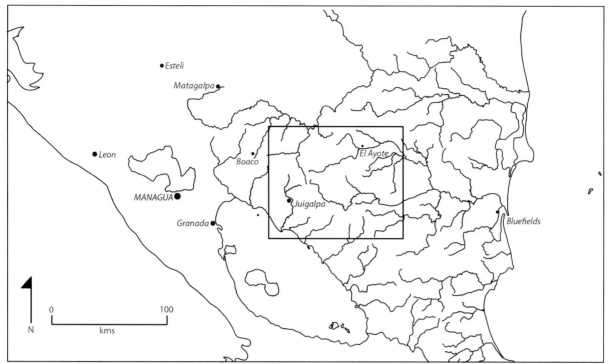

Figure 6. Map showing central Nicaragua depicted by the indicative rectangle. Note watershed division between Lake Cocibolca and the Caribbean Sea (map: Alexander Geurds).

Two principal focus areas are traditionally defined for Nicaragua: the Chontales region, and a second region in Pacific Nicaragua that includes the islands of Ometepe and Zapatera. Historically, the Zapatera island sculptures have received most attention, likely due to the proximity of the island to the Colonial period capital city of Granada. From the 19th century onwards, a mix of clergy, adventurers, and early scholars reported on, sketched, published, and removed many of these Zapatera sculptures. More recently, archaeology has taken a renewed interest in the island context of these sculptures.

Overall, the sculpting of large figures in bas relief on monoliths adheres to a wider shared preference for a style that can be characterized as ambiguous. Certainly present is an emphasis on the human body combined with renderings of animals and supernatural creatures, albeit in forms that are often hard to interpret. This combination of sculpting the human body in conjunction with the (super)natural world may index stages of transformation. The technology involved in quarrying the monoliths varies from heat-induced fracturing of individual polygonal columns from extrusive basalt outcrops to the extraction of entire monoliths from exposed sections of andesite. Some level of labour organisation is presumed in the extraction and transport due to the considerable mass of most monoliths, measuring up to five metres in height and weighing several tons each.

Despite their significance, the monumental stone sculptures have stood silent in much of the regional scholarly analysis, generally relegated to a separate treatment from a classificatory or iconographic perspective. Partly responsible for this was the scarcity of their systematic archaeological documentation (but see work by Navarro Genie 2005, 2007), a condition that has for example led to museum panels devoid of any specific contextual information for the sculptures on display. Within this limiting setting, stone sculptures in Nicaragua were used to construct public memories through the formation of local museum collections (Whisnant 1995). On the basis of these collections, existing studies on sculptures have focused on stylistic descriptions, emphasizing style coherence and outlining iconographic aspects such as clothing, weapons, and animals (Baudez 1970; Falk and Friberg 1999; Haberland 1973; Richardson 1940; Rigat 1992; Thieck 1971; Zelaya-Hidalgo et al. 1974).

In response to this scarcity of sculpture data, PACEN designed exploratory research to detect and record sculptures and fragments thereof in close context, leading the documentation of several dozen previously unknown sculptures (Geurds 2010; in press), to add to the existing body of knowledge on this sculptural tradition unique to the archaeological landscape of Nicaragua.

Scanning the museum's stone sculpture collection

Digital documentation of the known stone sculptures on site at the museum was, however, complicated by a number of challenges. As a method to generate digital 3D models by taking well-framed photographs from various angles, digital photogrammetry by definition heavily relies on the liberty to freely position the photo camera anywhere inside the given space. MAGAB's interior architecture, however, imposed several restrictions on photogrammetric data acquisition. On one hand, the mentioned 'chessboard' setup of the stone sculptures with very limited space in between, combined with the fact that all sculptures were anchored in the ground, called for new Structure from Motion (SfM) strategies. With little space to move the camera between the sculptures and without being able to move the sculptures or the museum wall, in order to capture the maximum extent of a sculpture's geometric structure, every possible camera angle had to be used to assure sufficient overlap during the posterior processing of the photogrammetric data (Figure 7). On average, 60 high resolution photographs including a scale bar were taken with a 21.1-megapixel Canon 5D Mark II on a Manfrotto tripod.

Figure 7. The photogrammetry work process, showing Juan Aguilar. Note the limited room for positioning (photo: Alexander Geurds).

Alongside the spatial factor, we also had to account for particular lighting conditions. The roofing of the patio had significantly reduced the amount of natural light inside the museum building. Consequently, a mobile lighting system was installed and all photographs had to be taken with long exposure times to compensate for the scarcity of available light as well as the almost closed camera lens iris required to guarantee full depth of field. A CamRanger remote control and image preview system in combination with an Apple iPad were used to remotely trigger the camera to avoid vibration and shaking during the long exposure times as well as to immediately check photograph quality on the larger computer tablet screen. Raising the ISO number to make images brighter and/or shorten exposure time would not have been favourable because so-called colour noise, a visual distortion, in the photographs would have diminished the overall quality. In general, the camera settings revolved around an aperture value of 22 (f/22), an ISO number of 200–400, and an exposure time around 1 second.

Despite these challenges imposed by the museum's interior architecture and the arrangement of the collection, all steps of the photogrammetric capturing process could be carried out by one person with the aforementioned adjustments in place. However, all data collection had to be completed in one month. Strict time management as well as occasional assistance from other PACEN members helped complete the photo scanning of 52 stone sculptures within the available four weeks. Especially with regards to the time-consuming repositioning of lights and camera for each photograph, the time saved by working in a team raised the quality of the 3D models since more time could be invested to meet the best possible photographic quality standards and thus later allow the production of high resolution textures without shadows or blurriness.

In an effort to reduce long computation times later, a telescopic background system was used to create a large white backdrop behind each sculpture (Figure 8). In doing so, a stone sculpture could be visually isolated from all neighbouring sculptures, which in turn made placing a digital mask on each photograph in Adobe Photoshop significantly easier (Figure 9). This way, the photogrammetry software would only concentrate on a particular stone sculpture and avoid unwanted rendering of other sculptures.

Figure 8. Use of telescopic background system (photo: Roosmarie Vasclamp).

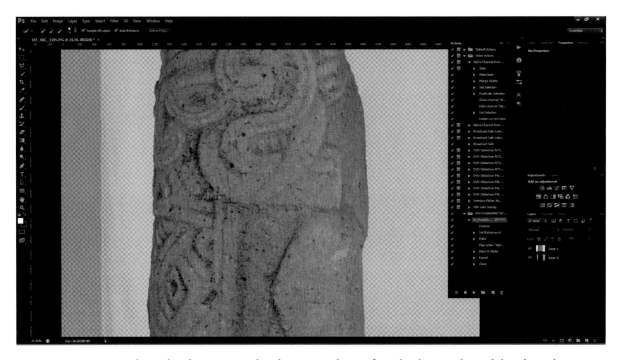

Figure 9. Screenshot taken by Juan Aguilar showing isolation from background in Adobe Photoshop.

As a precautionary measure, photogrammetric data of selected stone sculptures was sent via the remote desktop software Teamviewer from an iPad to a PC in Europe with larger computer resources. This step of performing a quick rendering of a complete model was necessary to detect errors in camera alignment or potential gaps in the geometric structure due to the possibility of insufficient overlap between photographs. After this error analysis, new photos could be taken on site in Juigalpa to fill the gaps (Figure 10).

Figure 10. Recording the sculptures from particularly cramped positions (photo: Alexander Geurds).

Towards the end of the four-week data collection phase in Nicaragua, the idea to rebuild the stone sculpture collection in digital space came forth out of on-site discussions. In Agisoft's digital photogrammetry software Photoscan Pro, all 52 digital 3D models were generated (Figure 11), producing around 34.84 million faces per sculpture and 1.812 billion faces for the entire collection.[3] The high number of faces is necessary to maximize the accuracy of the digital copy and to digitally preserve the details of the sculptures' carvings.

The most promising results were achieved by importing all 3D models into the freely available 3D post-processing software Meshlab. Its *radiance scaling shader* adds a high contrast filter to the 3D mesh, which makes even minute depressions on the geometric surfaces clearly visible (Figure 12). In combination with the high face number, and without the distraction of the current stone-coloured texture, all carvings on the sculptures became easily identifiable, which is of particular interest for iconographic analysis (Figure 13). The ability to reposition a virtual light and to capture and export snapshots taken from any angle provides iconographic analysis with the ability to produce high-resolution images for study and publication.

In the absence of physical weight and dimensions, and without the disadvantageous circumstance of museum artefacts being completely immobile, the stone sculptures in their digital form enable new kinds of scientific observations and measurements. Furthermore, the way to conduct these analyses changes by the simple fact that archaeologists do not need to be on site in the field. Pressure to complete archaeological documentation in a certain period of time is partially removed and digital photogrammetry presents itself as a complementary method to analyse artefacts remotely.

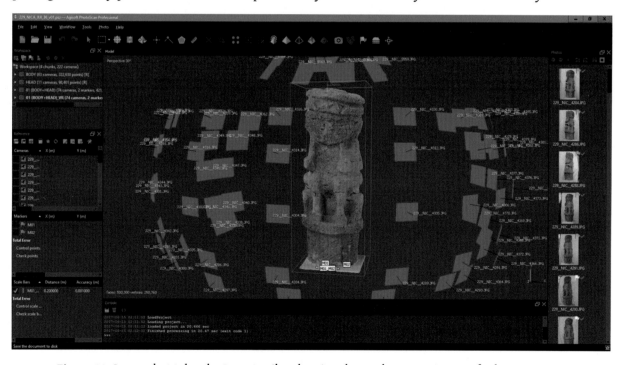

Figure 11. Screenshot taken by Juan Aguilar showing the work process in Agisoft Photoscan Pro.

---

[3] Another term for 'face' can be 'triangle' which is the smallest two-dimensional unit of any 3D mesh, consisting of at least three connected vertices.

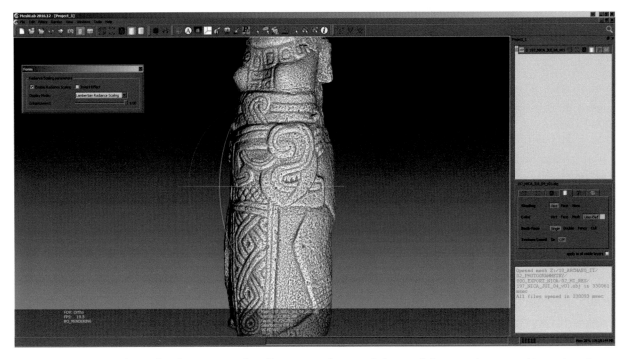

Figure 12. Screenshot taken by Juan Aguilar illustrating the possibilities of object radiance scaling using the Meshlab software package.

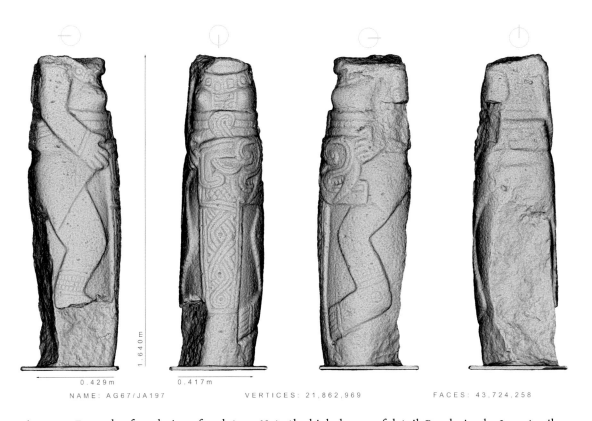

Figure 13. Example of rendering of sculpture. Note the high degree of detail. Rendering by Juan Aguilar.

Public engagement

These preliminary results seem primarily to benefit an academic audience, by providing resources for further research. However, since the first generation of a 3D model, the question arose if there was potential to do more with the data. Not only had PACEN the means to re-analyse the sculptures, but the detailed digital copies represented an opportunity to engage project members with questions of cultural heritage preservation and promotion. Should our role as archaeologists merely be limited to scientific analysis? Perhaps in using the sculptures to ask questions about prehistoric regional identity, we were at risk of neglecting their social context and meaning to current populations. The special case of Nicaragua's history and how heritage is seen and negotiated impelled the project to rethink both how results might be presented, and with which audiences in mind. Engaging public audiences with these materials is underpinned by an understanding of national as well as local recent history.

Since the middle of the 20th century, Nicaraguan history has been marked by political fragmentation and various forms of economic and cultural exploitation (cf. Babb 2001; Chavez 2015). As part of this traumatising process, multiple efforts of cultural negotiation and policy making have transformed historical awareness, and repeated efforts to redefine priorities and values in culture have thereby increased the potential to engage audiences with indigenous archaeological heritage (Whisnant 1995). These cultural policies build on the legacies of the colonial epoch and its relationship to the indigenous presence. The 16th century brought formal Spanish and informal British colonisation and the decimation of indigenous demographics. After independence in 1821, there followed a period of westernisation that reinforced colonial structures but were based on US cultural ideals, which culminated in the 20th-century cultural repression of the Somoza regime. After the Sandinist Revolution of 1979 and its ensuing Contra War, a period of destructive civil conflict took place that still resonates strongly in civic society. Each of these periods announced yet another programme of cultural reforms.

In such a national history, realisation of indigenous identity does not equate to national or regional identity. With important regional exceptions, most people do not self-identify as indigenous in Nicaragua. Similarly, people place intrinsic value on archaeological sites and have local knowledge of ruins in a practical sense: as a source of building materials, yet as something of a delicate nature that they would not want damaged or destroyed. As a result of this ambiguity and the twists and turns of Nicaraguan history, knowledge about prehistory is difficult to access, often not valorised, and considered alien to many.

This historical context, while destructive in many ways, makes Nicaragua a pressing case study for studying the role of indigenous archaeological heritage at both governmental and local levels. Throughout the many national programmes and policies, its prehistoric material culture continues to take up a central place. At the same time and paradoxically, local valorisation of precolonial heritage research remains poorly defined.

In focusing on public engagement in archaeology, we make reference to a growing body of work that is concerned with the role of the past in the present and which reports on archaeologists embracing collaborative approaches in their discipline (e.g. Richardson 2013; Skeates et al. 2012; and the journal *Public Archaeology*). Such initiatives focus on stakeholders who maintain ties with the archaeological heritage being studied. Examples of such collaborative work ranges from increasing research communication and involving stakeholders, to outright co-design of research projects. In designing this project, we ask how can such approaches take form in countries with a recent history of repression and internal armed conflict? Which methods might generate lasting impact on archaeological research in societal settings where national heritage priorities are repeatedly redefined? Lastly, we are also interested in examining whether digital imaging innovations in archaeological knowledge production can contribute to sustainable heritage valorisation in such culturally fragmented surroundings.

Digital Immersive Virtual Environments

One way to define a possibly successful strategy for public outreach is to look for ways to meet the public on platforms already used by general audiences. In recent years, we have seen digital immersive virtual environments technologies, or to put it in more general terms, technologies that reproduce 'a sense of 3D', gradually becoming part of daily life and increasingly familiar to wider audiences. It can be argued that the latest consumer product release to help usher in shared familiarity with DIVE and visual immersion is the computer game Pokémon Go. Released in 2016 on mobile devices, Pokémon Go aims to combine the physical world with 3D digital gaming content, thus creating a so-called augmented reality experience.

In contrast to 3D films, where the 3D experience is limited to constantly staring in the direction of a fixed rectangular screen, Pokémon Go and also Google's 2014 release entitled Cardboard, grant the spectator several kinds of freedom to change perspective at any time. Google Cardboard, for instance, allows a mobile device to constantly analyse a viewer's head rotation and tilt movements, which contributes to a fluent and physically correct viewing experience when watching 360-degree photos or videos. This sensory experience increases a person's level of 'presence', an accepted calibrating factor in the evaluation of digital virtual environments (Smolentzev et al. 2017).

In other words, photographs and videos no longer have to be defined by conventional 2D reproduction techniques and a person is free to experience more than just a rectangular-shaped part of reality. However, the point of view (POV) will always be defined by the position of the recording omnidirectional camera. This issue of bodily movement is addressed in augmented environments such as Pokémon Go, which uses a GPS signal and the mobile device's built-in camera to blend computer game elements with the image of real locations on the device's display. These examples show the increased potential for interaction between the physical and any given virtual environment. This is made possible by hardware and software tracking a viewer's movements and position, and using this data as a reference to correctly display digital content from a specific viewing angle.

Archaeological recording and use of digital 3D

For the past fifteen years or so, these developments in the entertainment industry have increasingly informed object-focused disciplines such as archaeology, art history, and museology on the integration of virtual reality. Since the advent of various 3D data recording techniques at the turn of the millennium, many archaeological sites, excavation trenches, architectural elements and structures, sculptures, and small finds around the world have been 3D-scanned either by using a laser scanner, structured light scanner, or digital camera, whether in the air, on the ground, or underwater (see discussion in Sapirstein and Murray 2017).

After the 3D recording stage is complete, the subsequent activities also need specification. The required methods and techniques to visualise, improve, or expand analysis and disseminate digital archaeological content are therefore also increasingly under consideration (Kersten and Lindstaedt 2012). In most cases, satisfactory solutions revolve around the two-dimensional representation of three-dimensional data on a computer screen, given the worldwide presence of flat displays and traditional one-dimensional viewing habits. This flattening of 3D data in combination with both a viewer and a (mostly immobile) visualisation system, however, dramatically reduces the possibility of gaining more information about a specific 3D-scanned archaeological object or context. With the sole option on the computer screen of rotating and/or zooming in on an object with a mouse to get 'a sense of 3D', the paradox of current digital 3D representation becomes obvious.

In our project in Nicaragua, we wanted to move beyond the discussed 2D representation of 3D and use or adapt the technology and concepts first widely distributed through Google Cardboard or augmented reality computer games like Pokémon Go.[4] Therefore, the creation of a fully walkable DIVE museum with the help of the freely available video game creation software Unreal Engine 4 Editor, by video game developer Epic Games, allowed new options for museum design, cultural heritage management and interaction between archaeology and the public in digital space to be explored (Remondino and Campana 2014). In this way, we propose that using a popular video game design software as a new medium constitutes a practical solution to present 3D archaeological data in more appealing and immersive ways than traditional audiovisual productions or printed articles.

Building a walkable MAGAB virtual museum

A virtual museum would be an opportunity to nullify some of the limitations imposed by the architecture of the current museum building. How the stone sculpture collection at the MAGAB is presented to the public is currently marked by two major problems: the narrow spaces between individual sculptures, and, depending on the time of the day and weather, the scarcity of light. In Unreal Editor, the rearranging and lighting of the massive anchored sculptures in a circular setup within a Guggenheim Museum-inspired setting was accomplished without much effort and in a timespan of hours (Figure 14).

---

[4] Some opinions would argue that there is a significant difference between 2.5D (three-quarter perspective) and true 3D like in computer games, yet the final representation happens on a stationary two-dimensional computer screen which eventually would also render true 3D as 2.5D.

Figure 14 . Screenshot taken by Juan Aguilar of a possible virtual museum, rendered in the Unreal Editor software package. The robot-like figure is not relevant, but a standard feature of Unreal Editor.

An initial compromise that had to be accepted was one of drastically reducing the number of faces for each sculpture model to avoid computer instabilities and allow better render results. As discussed above, a digital stone sculpture model counts a high face number which, in combination with the simultaneous rendering of other sculptures, is not suitable for any DIVE application because of the immense number of computations. Plans to show high-detailed 3D models had to be abandoned, and subsequently the high-resolution textures without shadows played a vital role in adding realism again to the virtual museum (Figure 15). In this regard, computer rendering capabilities define the complexity of the virtual museum.

Figure 15. Screenshot taken by Juan Aguilar showing a possibility for rendering a virtual museum, note increased spacing and alternative 'ceiling' illumination.

A second compromise was the decision to include 3D models with occasional gaps. As described above, some parts of a stone sculpture were difficult to reach and, as a consequence, were hard to photgraph, which resulted in insufficient photogrammetric material for digital reconstruction. These 3D models are incomplete and gaps can only be filled with the help of special algorithms in Meshlab, which can only estimate how the missing structure of the original might look.

Both compromises were needed in order to create a functioning and stable running DIVE experience. As a consequence, the DIVE comes with significant reductions concerning the overall 3D model quality and accuracy. However, the ability for archaeologists to create this DIVE themselves, using freely available software, helps avoid other possible forms of distortion. The rebirth of the stone sculptures as 3D models gives archaeologists the agency to communicate directly and immediately to wider audiences instead of indirectly and with limited decision-making in consultancy roles for film production companies or video game developers.[5] In these latter cases, producers request consultation from archaeologists, resulting in non-specialists deciding which content needs to be enriched with scientific facts and to what degree. In our case, we believe we do not have to lend the Juigalpa sculptures to third parties to see them come to life, for example, as part of the decoration in an entertaining audio-visual product. However, to bypass the unintentional restrictions imposed by the video game design tool Unreal Editor and avoid the situation that the stone sculptures can only be experienced as part of a video game, having a look at what the entertainment industry has produced since the release of Google Cardboard and Pokémon Go helps find solutions.

---

[5] The subfield of archaeogaming analyses the representation of archaeology in gaming, alongside attempting to conduct archaeological research of video games themselves. One of the initial aims was to analyse and question how archaeological data was portrayed in games (Reinhard 2017). Archaeogaming also takes part in debates on audiences of archaeological heritage (Mol et al. 2017).

An adequate solution to simultaneously combine head-tracking as well as the ability to freely move around in a DIVE through ambulation in the real world (in contrast to a so-called point and click solution) was offered through the Bridge headset, released in late 2016 by US-based technology company Occipital Inc. This head mount is similar to Google Cardboard, but with the significant difference that it is equipped with a laser scanning device, the Structure Sensor (Figure 16). In combination with a mobile device that serves to render and display any 3D content, the Bridge headset allows positional head-tracking and 3D image rendering to be calculated by the mobile device itself. As a consequence, Bridge is not connected by wires to any external rendering computer, which allows for greater autonomy than other positional tracking headset devices. With the possibility to define a viewer's position in physical space and the direction in which they are looking—or, put simply, change the POV at any time—the virtual experience or 'presence' in a DIVE is significantly increased.[6]

Figure 16. The Structure Sensor (photograph: Juan Aguilar).

As a consequence, the liberty to experience a DIVE museum without any physical restrictions not only makes the existing virtual MAGAB museum more real, but it also allows the rethinking and perhaps redefinition of the idea of a museum itself: With so much autonomy in virtual reality, the established idea of putting objects on display in one single place may no longer be the only option when stone sculptures are able to leave the museum building and virtually 'go back to' their place of origin.

Embedding a DIVE museum in the landscape of central Nicaragua

In applications of digital technology for public engagement purposes in archaeology, the goal of method advancement conferred by the new technology must be matched by the aims of improving access and designing outreach strategies. We believe that a series of tailored VR, AR and Mixed Reality experiences using the digital sculptures can enrich the abovementioned needed discussion on contextual information in archaeology as well as address the briefly discussed notion of 'presence'. Ultimately, our aim of outreach should benefit specific audiences of the museum, promote the iconic prehistoric monolithic sculptures, and give archaeological heritage in Nicaragua, including museum collection and sites, greater exposure to aid in their sustainable valorisation.

---

[6] 'Presence' in relation to 3D virtual environments can be defined as a human sensory reaction to immersion in such environments, leading to virtual objects being experienced as actual ones and having educational and enjoyment purposes (Lee 2004).

When the sculptures were reborn as 3D meshes and visuals, and were freed from the restraints of their museum environment, real or virtual, we decided to display the sculptures in a way that could go beyond the limitations of their current space and position them in an environment that in itself acts a teaching resource, implying or replicating the landscape and sense of space within which the megaliths originally stood (most sculptures used have approximate provenience data). Digital reconstructions allow for the return of sculptures to their original context as part of prehistoric indigenous communities, without fear for the preservation or conservation of the stone originals.

In relation to the potential of outreach to national and international tourism, a few days camping, visiting beaches, climbing a volcano, hiking, or following nature trails can be interspersed with the introduction of an AR experience. In destination tourism dynamics, there is a need for experiences that are natural, 'authentic', and remarkable. Such a demand for location-specific points of interest can motivate the designs of in situ digital reconstructions.

Virtually engaging audiences

We aim to expand the experiential possibilities of the sculpture in the MAGAB through the use of VR and AR, with a series of solutions tailored to the numbers, mobility, and technology of a spectrum of forms of alternative tourism, ranging from adventure and ecological tourism to leisure and educational tourism.

Backpacker tourism characteristically is characteristically travelling in small groups with an above-average preference for mobility and technology (access to mobile devices). In this case, a VR installation within the museum, composed of a headset and relay screen, could act as a primer for nature walking or hiking in the area. A VR experience that integrates the sculptures into a digital landscape would leave viewers excited to find these places and make those connections themselves through landscape exploration. This might further be achieved with an AR component triggered at the original location of one of the museum's sculptures, converting the contemporary natural surroundings into a VR enhanced archaeological landscape, a museum in and of itself.

Local visitors in smaller numbers would also benefit from the VR headset and relay screen installation within the museum. Their local knowledge and familiarity with the landscape might make AR 'place-finding' unnecessary, but since they bring particular knowledge and familiarity with archaeological sites in the vicinity, they are likely able to convert the landscape context of the objects into a mechanism to enrich their sense of place with the museum collection.[7] In this sense, the combination of VR experiences and the museum collection can also enrich the school curriculum with knowledge of Nicaraguan prehistory and its material culture, thus creating an outreach platform for community cohesion and preserving local identity.

In the case of more educationally-interested leisure tourism, larger groups are more likely and the number of persons would make it too time consuming for each person to take a turn with the VR headset. However, this could be remedied by investing in a number of Google Cardboard sets. With each person having access to their personal mobile device, and access to free wireless internet, the experience could be downloaded while perusing the museum.

---

[7] This sense of actively involving people's experiences can be applied to other parts of the MAGAB collections as well, such as the agricultural history of the region being connected with people's livelihoods.

Nicaraguans in diaspora (immigrant or migrant communities) are an audience that lacks the direct physical contact with the museum sculptures. For them, replicating size, physicality, and spatiality is central to an experience of the sculptures. Here we would suggest using a set of VR Google Cardboard glasses so each member of a large group is able to experience the VR walkthrough from anywhere in the world. There is also potential with VR to show the sculptures as they once stood in examples of likely original settings with a series of layered experiences that give audiences an immersive observation of what the indigenous cultural landscape may have looked like in pre-colonial times.

Finally, in a physical context, the photogrammetry data allows us to produce 3D prints of some of the sculptures so as to give a sense of the texture and weight of the objects that is missed in the purely visual VR and AR experiences. These experiences (both virtual and 3D printed) could serve, for example, in workshops centring on Nicaraguan culture past and present, with customs, performances, food, handicrafts as well as innovation and industry on display.

Conclusions

At some point in the mid-first millennium AD, indigenous communities in central Nicaragua began to quarry and carve monoliths and position them in the landscape at particular locations. These larger-than-life stones carved with anthropomorphic designs became the site of salient identity comparison, functioning as what we could call 'fixing agents'. Relatively minimalist in their carved expression, the sculptures added to everyday life in formal, essential terms. The sculptures were carved with a model in mind but maintaining a sufficient amount of fluidity in the iconography to allow for people to relate across a regional context.

A similar sense of relating to these sculptures is what we are proposing to here. Despite the extensive amount of time passed since their creation, these sculptures maintain the agency to tell stories, and impress and engage audiences. VR approaches offer multiple promising avenues to realize such engagement. In general, approaches to archaeological materials from the past, including archaeology and art history, are increasingly advancing in a process of digitisation. Especially with regards to recording, digital technologies are often deemed an almost non-negotiable signal of improvement. What we have tried to argue here is that the potential for increasing the quality and diversity of recorded artefact details is indeed substantial, but that basic procedures need to be in place to properly assess the feasibility and intensity of the work and its projected digital products. The illustrated case of the corpus of prehistoric stone sculpture in the Museo Arqueológico Gregorio Aguilar Barea has shown both the complexity in photogrammetry recording as well as the potential for mass diffusion through incorporation in virtual reality museum environments.

References

Babb, F. E. 2001. *After Revolution: Mapping Gender and Cultural Politics in Neoliberal Nicaragua.* Austin: University of Texas Press.

Baudez, C. 1970. *Central America.* New York: Barrie and Jenkins.

Belt, T. 1874. *The Naturalist in Nicaragua.* London: John Murray.

Boyle, F. 1868. *A Ride Across a Continent: A Personal narrative of wanderings through Nicaragua and Costa Rica.* London: Richard Bentley.

Chavez, D. 2015. *Nicaragua and the Politics of Utopia: Development and Culture in the Modern State.* Nashville: Vanderbilt University Press.

Constenla Umaña, A. 1991. *Las lenguas del área intermedia: Introducción a su estudio areal.* San José: Editorial de la Universidad de Costa Rica.

Cyphers, A. 1999. From stone to symbols: Olmec art in social context at San Lorenzo Tenochtitlán, in D. C. Grove and R. A. Joyce (eds) *Social Patterns in Pre-Classic Mesoamerica*: 155–81. Washington DC: Dumbarton Oaks Research Library and Collection.

Drennan, R. D. 1996. Betwixt and between in the Intermediate Area. *Journal of Archaeological Research* 4/2: 95–132.

Ehrenborg, J. 1996. A new stratigraphy for the Tertiary volcanic rocks of the Nicaraguan Highland. *Geological Society of America Bulletin* 108: 830–842.

Falk, P. and L. Friberg. 1999. *La estatuaria aborigen de Nicaragua.* Managua: Academia Nicaragüense de la Lengua.

Geurds, A. 2010. Monolitos misteriosos. *National Geographic en Español* 27/4: 12.

Geurds, A. In Press. *Monumental Stone Sculpture in Central Nicaragua*, in C. McEwan, B. Cockrell, and J. Hoopes (eds) *Toward and Archaeology of 'Greater' Central America.* Washington DC: Dumbarton Oaks Research Library and Collection.

Gorin, F. 1989. Archeologie de Chontales, Nicaragua. Unpublished PhD dissertation, Sorbonne University.

Haberland, W. 1973. Stone sculpture from southern Central America, in D. Easby (ed.) *The Iconography of Middle American sculpture*: 135–152. New York: Metropolitan Museum of Art.

Healy, P. 1980. *Archaeology of the Rivas Region, Nicaragua.* Waterloo: Wilfrid Laurier University Press.

Holmberg, K. 2005. The voices of stones: unthinkable materiality in the volcanic context of western Panama, in L. Meskell (ed.) *Archaeologies of Materiality*: 190–211. Oxford: Blackwell Publishing.

Hoopes, J. W. and O. Fonseca 2003. Goldwork and Chibchan identity: Endogenous change and diffuse unity in the Isthmo-Colombian area, in J. Quilter and J.W. Hoopes (eds) *Gold and Power in Ancient Costa Rica, Panama, and Colombia*: 49–89. Washington DC: Dumbarton Oaks Research Library and Collection.

Kersten, T. P. and M. Lindstaedt 2012. Image-based low-cost systems for automatic 3D recording and modelling of archaeological finds and objects, in M. Ioannides et al. (eds) *Progress in Cultural Heritage Preservation. Euromed 2012. Lecture Notes in Computer Science 7616.* Berlin: Springer.

Lambers, K., Eisenbeiss, H., Sauerbier, M., Kupferschmidt, D., Gaisecker, T., Sotoodeh, S., and T. Hanusch. 2007. Combining photogrammetry and laser scanning for the recording and modelling of the Late Intermediate Period site of Pinchango Alto, Palpa, Peru. *Journal of Archaeological Science* 34: 1702–12.

Lange, F. W. (ed.) 1992. *Wealth and Hierarchy in the Intermediate Area.* Washington DC: Dumbarton Oaks Research Library and Collection.

Lange, F.W. and D. Stone (eds) 1984. *The Archaeology of Lower Central America:* 165–94. Santa Fe: School of American Research Press.

Lange, F. W. and P. Sheets (eds) 1992. *The archaeology of Pacific Nicaragua.* Albuquerque: University of New Mexico.

Lee, K. M. 2004. Presence, explicated. *Communication Theory* 14/1: 27–50.

Lehmann, W. 1920. *Zentral-Amerika.* Berlin: Dietrich Reimer.

McCafferty, G. G., and C. L. Dennett 2013. Ethnogenesis and Hybridity in Proto-Historic Nicaragua. *Archaeological Review from Cambridge* 28: 191–212.

McCafferty, G. G., and L. L. Steinbrenner. 2005. Chronological implications for Greater Nicoya from the Santa Isabel Project, Nicaragua. *Ancient Mesoamerica* 16: 131–46.

Mol, A. A. A., C. E. Ariese-Vandemeulebroucke, K. H. J. Boom, and A. Politopoulos (eds) 2017. *The Interactive Past: Archaeology, Heritage, and Video Games.* Leiden: Sidestone Press.

Monaco, J. 2000. *How to Read a Film: The World of Movies, Medias, and Multimedia. Language, History, Theory* (3rd edn.). Oxford: Oxford University Press.

Nanoglou, S. 2008. Representation of humans and animals in Greece and the Balkans during the earlier Neolithic. *Cambridge Archaeological Journal* 18: 1–13.

Navarro Genie, R. 2005. Statuaire préhispanique de l'ile de Ometepe, in C. Giorgi (ed.) *De l'Altiplano mexicain à la Patagonie: Travaux et recherches à l'Université de Paris 1* (British Archaeological Reports, Paris Monographs in American Archaeology 16): 133–50. Oxford: Archaeopress.

Navarro Genie, R. 2007. La statuaire du versant Pacifique du Nicaragua et du Costa Rica et son contexte archéologique (500-1830 apr. J.-C.). Unpublished PhD dissertation, Sorbonne University.

Pim, B., and B. C. Seemann. 1869. *Dottings on the Roadside, in Panama, Nicaragua, and Mosquito.* London: Chapman and Hall.

Reinhard, A. 2017. *Archaeogaming: An Introduction to Archaeology in (and of) Video Games.* Oxford: Berghahn Book.

Remondino, F., and S. Campana (eds) 2014. *3D Recording and Modelling in Archaeology and Cultural Heritage: Theory and Best Practice* (British Archaeological Reports International Series 2598). Oxford: Archaeopress.

Richardson, F. 1940. Non-Maya monumental sculpture of Central America, in S. Lothrop and H. Shapiro (eds) *The Maya and Their Neighbors:* 395–416. New York: Appleton.

Richardson, L. 2013. A digital public archaeology? *Papers from the Institute of Archaeology* 23/1: Article 10.

Rigat, D. 1992. Préhistoire au Nicaragua: Région de Juigalpa, Département de Chontales. Unpublished PhD dissertation, Sorbonne University.

Robb, J. 2009. People of Stone: stelae, personhood, and society in prehistoric Europe. *Journal of Archaeological Method and Theory* 16/3: 162–83.

Sapirstein, P. and S. Murray. 2017. Establishing Best Practices for Photogrammetric Recording During Archaeological Fieldwork. *Journal of Field Archaeology* 42: 337–50.

Skeates, R., C. McDavid and J. Carman (eds) 2012. *The Oxford Handbook of Public Archaeology*. Oxford: University of Oxford Press.

Smolentsev, A., J. E. Cornick and J. Blascovich 2017. Using a preamble to increase presence in digital virtual environments. *Journal of Virtual Reality* 21:153–64.

Squier, E. G. 1852. *Nicaragua: Its people, Scenery, and Monuments and Proposed Interoceanic Canal.* New York: Appleton.

Steinbrenner, L. L. 2010. Potting Traditions and Cultural Continuity in Pacific Nicaragua, AD 800–1350. Unpublished PhD dissertation, University of Calgary.

Thieck, F. 1970. *Ídolos de Nicaragua: Álbum 1.* Managua: Universidad Nacional Autónoma de Nicaragua.

Van Broekhoven, L. N. K. 2002. *Conquistando lo invencible. Fuentes históricas sobre las culturas indígenas de la región Central de Nicaragua.* Leiden: CNWS Publications.

Whisnant, D. E. 1995. *Rascally Signs in Sacred Places: The Politics of Culture in Nicaragua.* Chapel Hill: University of North Carolina Press.

Zelaya-Hidalgo, G., K. Olsen-Bruhns, and J. Dotta 1974. *Monumental Art of Chontales.* San Francisco: Treganza Anthropology Museum.

A multispectral imaging and 3D modelling project on the Arundel Marbles

Alison Pollard

Abstract

The Arundel Collection of Greek, Roman, and Neoclassical sculpture and inscriptions in the Ashmolean Museum has recently undergone a resurgence in interest prompted by the 2013 redevelopment of the Randolph Sculpture Gallery. In this space, the marbles and their story are displayed, alongside new epigraphic and historical research undertaken as part of the Ashmolean Latin Inscriptions (ASHLi) project. In collaboration with the Web Science Institute at the University of Southampton, 3D Scanning Ireland, and Artas Media, the freestanding and relief sculpture from the Arundel Collection is undergoing investigation using new and exploratory technologies including multispectral imaging, 3D scanning, RTI, and photogrammetry. The results will be presented to the academic community and general public by means of an interactive, online resource through which visitors can learn about the creation and display of classical sculpture in ancient contexts alongside its more recent collection history, and individual objects will be used to highlight and discuss polychromy, ancient and modern restorations, the carving and recarving process, and the epigraphic habit.

A history of the Arundel Marbles

The Arundel Marbles, as the Greek, Roman, and Neoclassical sculptures and inscriptions of the private collection of Thomas Howard (1586–1646) are known, have been displayed in various locations around the University of Oxford and the Ashmolean Museum over the last 350 years. They arrived in Oxford as two separate gifts: the first in 1667, when the Greek and Latin inscriptions from the collection were bestowed by their then owner Henry Howard (1628–1684), later the 6th Duke of Norfolk, and the second in 1755, when Henrietta Louisa Fermor, the Countess of Pomfret (d. 1761), gave the Arundel sculpture in her possession to the university. Today, much of the freestanding and relief sculpture from the Arundel Collection can be seen in the Randolph Sculpture Gallery in the Ashmolean Museum (Figure 1) and many other objects and inscriptions are displayed in neighbouring galleries.

Figure 1. The Randolph Sculpture Gallery. © Ashmolean Museum, University of Oxford.

The collection itself was amassed by Thomas Howard, the 14th Earl of Arundel, in the early 1600s. Howard's own exploratory voyages to Italy and the work of his agents who scoured Greece, the Aegean, and western Turkey for antiquities culminated in the first significant English art collection, which was renowned by scholars and antiquaries throughout Europe for its diversity and its novelty since it marked the first time that such an assemblage had been brought together in England. Indeed, its arrival caused such excitement that after seeing the inscriptions newly-installed in the gardens of Arundel House on the Strand in London, the antiquarian Robert Cotton urged John Selden to work with him on deciphering them the very next day. Within a year, Selden's *Marmora Arundelliana* was published, transcribing 29 of the Greek and 10 of the Latin inscriptions.[1] Yet eyebrows may have been raised at the fragmentary state of some of the antiquities, since a contemporary remarked that the Reverend William Petty, the most successful of Arundel's agents, 'hath raked togither 200 peices, all broken, or few entyre'.[2]

Accordingly, as was the fashion of the time, marble sculptors were employed to restore and 'complete' the headless torsos and battered faces, leading to Roman togate statues elevated to the status of Cicero and Marius, and a dancing satyr promoted to Dionysus himself. Although written documentation pertaining to the original provenance and quantity of the sculpture from the collection is scarce, particularly in comparison with the paintings and drawings that were catalogued in 1655 as part of a family dispute over ownership, the various stages of restoration can be traced

---

[1] Johnson 1835,160–1.

[2] Letter from Thomas Roe to George Villiers, November 1626 (Roe 1740, 571).

through sketches and paintings made of the most celebrated statues. These include the commemorative portraits of the Earl and his wife, Alathea Howard (née Talbot), sitting among the most prized items from their collection in 1618 (Figures 2 and 3).[3]

Figure 2, left. Daniel Mytens, *Thomas Howard, 14ᵗʰ Earl of Arundel.* © National Portrait Gallery, London.

Figure 3, right. Daniel Mytens, *Alatheia Talbot, Countess of Arundel.* © National Portrait Gallery, London.

Near the end of Thomas Howard's life, civil war broke out and so, being a staunch royalist and prominent member of the Stuart court, he fled at first to the Low Countries and then to Padua, leaving Arundel House soon to be occupied by a Roundhead garrison, and the more saleable items within the property sold off to fund the army.[4] Although Howard stipulated in his will that the collection be kept intact after his death, which came only a couple of years later, still in exile in Padua, family disputes over the following years meant that eventually most of the sculpture was awarded to Thomas' grandson, Henry Howard. Clearly not as enamoured with the antiquities as his grandparents, Henry allowed the collection to fall into a state of disrepair and damage until, in 1667, he was persuaded by the diarist John Evelyn to give the remaining inscriptions (around half of what had originally been collected) to the University of Oxford.[5] Many of the ancient busts were bought by Lord Pembroke of

---

[3] The so-called Amersfoot Inventory. Hervey 1921, appendix v.

[4] A document drawn up by a certain B. Vermuyden, probably the regimental commander Bartholomew Vermuyden, lists the jewels and objects made of precious metals at Arundel House to be handed over to Parliament. Hervey 1921, 442.

[5] Evelyn writes in his diary on 19 September 1667: 'When I saw these precious monuments miserably neglected, and scattered up and down about the garden, and other parts of Arundel House, and how exceedingly the corrosive air of London impaired them, I procured [Henry Howard] to bestow them on the University of Oxford.' Bray 1901, 38.

Wilton House in 1678, and the more intact freestanding sculpture was sold for a relatively meagre £300 to Sir William Fermor in 1691, whose country pile in Northamptonshire was to be its home for the next 60 years.

It was here at Easton Neston that the infamous restorations by the sculptor Giovanni Battista Guelfi were carried out on a number of the statues, which were later so reviled that the classical archaeologist Adolf Michaelis felt compelled over a century later to write:

> The task could not easily have been entrusted to more unfortunate hands. Great as has been the blundering perpetrated in all quarters in the shape of so-called 'restorations', yet hardly ever have any antiques been so shamefully tampered with as in the tasteless additions made by this shallow botcher.[6]

In 1755, the Arundel and Pomfret marbles were given to the University of Oxford by Henrietta Louisa, the Countess of Pomfret and daughter-in-law of William Fermor, where they were received with great acclaim (including a dedicatory marble inscription, now displayed in the main Beaumont Street entrance to the Ashmolean Museum, and a laudatory poem for the countess).[7] They were initially housed in the Old Schools – later known as the Logic School but now the gift shop of the Bodleian Library – and were commemorated in 1763 by their first (and, to date, last) comprehensive catalogue, Richard Chandler's *Marmora Oxoniensia*.[8] In 1845, they were transferred to their current home on Beaumont Street, to be displayed in Charles Cockerell's new University Galleries, now the Ashmolean Museum.[9]

The pilot project

In 2013, with funding from the DCMS/Wolfson Museums and Galleries Improvement Fund, the Randolph Sculpture Gallery was renovated, with the original paint scheme from the 1840s restored and the original Portland stone floor refinished. After new research and a long period of planning and design, the sculpture was redisplayed with the aim of narrating and illustrating the story and history of the Arundel Collection from its ancient beginnings to its modern reception. To mark the reopening of the gallery, a study day was organised in collaboration with the University of Oxford's Classical Art Research Centre.[10] A common theme to emerge from the focus groups was the difficulty in assessing the restoration history of the sculpture, particularly that which had not been recorded in the (usually

---

[6] Michaelis 1882, 39. Further information about Guelfi and his restorations can be found in Giometti 1999.

[7] Vickers 2006, appendix, *On the Pomfret statues*.

[8] I am indebted to Julian Munby, Head of Buildings Archaeology at Oxford Archaeology, for clarifying information concerning the 'Old Schools' as depicted in William Westall's watercolour showing the Arundel Marbles on display in 1831.

[9] Adolf Michaelis' descriptive list of the Arundel Marbles in Oxford suggests that he was only able to study those on display in the University Galleries in the early 1880s, omitting several which must have been in storage at the time – most of it Neoclassical – including the two 'Roman generals' which were created by Egidio Morretti in the 1610s, and the bust portraits of Rupert of the Rhine and Henry VIII.

[10] Held at the Ashmolean Museum in May 2013. Lectures on the Arundel Collection were given by Susan Walker, Peter Stewart, and Alison Pollard and were followed by a workshop in which select pieces of sculpture were discussed by small groups, led by the speakers, R. R. R. Smith, Michael Vickers and Julia Lenaghan.

pictorial) documentation from the preceding centuries, alongside the relative neglect of many of the pieces in recent scholarship outside of the immediate museum context.[11]

The clear need to reinvigorate interest in the collection led to collaboration with the Web Science Institute at the University of Southampton in the development of a pilot project in which select pieces of sculpture would be analysed using non-invasive, new technologies and the results published for the general public and academic community. Funding was generously awarded by the Henry Moore Foundation and the Oxford University Museums Partnership Innovation Fund to investigate the sculpture using multispectral imaging, photogrammetry, 3D laser scanning, and RTI (reflectance transformation imaging), with a view to testing out the technologies in the investigation of traces of polychromy, ancient and modern restorations, and toolmarks on the marble, as well as the curious reports about a shipwreck in the Aegean in 1625. The results would be published in a free and interactive web resource accessed through the Ashmolean Museum website, and would not only explore the specific research questions but would bring the story of the Arundel Collection to a wider audience by creating a 'virtual research environment', thus allowing viewers to interact with virtual representations of the objects on display in the galleries and consider them in their ancient, Jacobean, and 21st century contexts.[12]

Four pieces of sculpture were selected for multispectral photography based on their potential to illustrate the different research areas: the so-called 'Oxford Bust', a composite made up of different pieces of sculpture, probably assembled in the 1600s (ANMichaelis.59); a colossal head of either Apollo or Dionysus, which was subject to extensive plaster restorations in the early 1900s (ANMichaelis.60); a Roman marble head considered to be a 'Kassel-type' portrait of the emperor Claudius, possibly reworked from an earlier head of Caligula (ANMichaelis.69); and a funerary monument from Rome dedicated to the Greek doctor Claudius Agathemerus and his wife Myrtale, which bears traces of polychromy and modern restorations (ANMichaelis.155).[13] These examples were also selected for 3D laser scanning and photogrammetry, alongside a colossal Roman statue of Athena Parthenos (ANMichaelis.19) and a marble restoration, probably from the early 1700s, in the form of a left hand and forearm once attached to the Athena statue, with an attachment on the wrist showing the positioning of an incorrectly restored shield (ANMichaelis.19b). RTI was carried out alongside the multispectral photography and was additionally undertaken on the Greek and Latin funerary inscriptions from the Arundel Collection which form part of a newly-reconstructed section of the 'Garden of Antiquities' in the Story of the Ashmolean Gallery.

Process of scanning and photography

The involved nature of the data capturing and object scanning meant that suitable days needed to be found when the museum was closed to the public and no events were scheduled to take place in the

---

[11] The key recent works on the sculpture are Vickers 2006 and Haynes 1975.

[12] Discussion in Beale and Earl 2010.

[13] Regarding ANMichaelis.56, the Ashmolean Museum's Annual Report of 1909 records: 'A few more restorations in plaster have been attempted. In particular, a colossal head of Apollo, of the Hellenistic age, which had been so badly restored in marble that it was kept in the basement, has been satisfactorily completed in plaster by Mr. Rost, and placed in the Randolph Gallery' (p.20). The earlier report of 1908 describes Mr Rost as a sculptor who was working alongside the museum's own W. H. Young in the restoration process (p.13). On AN Michaelis.69, see Vickers 2006, 80.

relevant galleries. Erato Kartaki from the University of Southampton carried out the photography for the multispectral analysis, the photogrammetry, and the RTI using a Nikon D700 camera with a series of visible light, ultraviolet and infrared filters (Figure 4). The 3D laser scanning was undertaken by Pat Tanner of 3D Scanning Ireland, who used a FARO Platinum Arm and Laser-line Probe to capture a three-dimensional point cloud with data points at a geometric accuracy of ± 0.07 mm (Figure 5). As the FARO Platinum Arm only records monochrome data, the models lack any surface colour detail since the capturing of colour would create unmanageable file sizes. Colour was therefore added in the processing stage using data from the photogrammetry. Simon Horton from FARO Technologies carried out further 3D scans using a FARO Focus X330 Laser Scanner (a terrestrial laser scanner with a radius range of 330 m, and accuracy of +/- 1 mm and capable of capturing up to 700 m points) and the FARO freestyle objects hand laser scanner (with a range of 300–1000 mm and an accuracy of 0.5 mm) (Figure 6).

Figure 4. Erato Kartaki carrying out multi-spectral photography on the Roman tombstone (ANMichaelis.155) © the author.

Figure 5. Pat Tanner uses the FARO platinum arm to capture a 3D laser scan of the Roman portrait head (ANMichaelis.69) © the author.

Figure 6. Simon Horton creates a 3D laser scan of the colossal Athena statue (ANMichaelis.19) with the FARO freestyle objects hand laser scanner attached to a pole © the author.

Since funding for the project was limited, it was not possible to move the heavier pieces of sculpture because of the costs of stone moving. This ultimately led to difficulties in achieving a true 360-degree laser scan of the larger objects and those displayed in niches and corners. Similar problems were encountered with the photogrammetry and it was impossible to capture the back of the head of the colossal Dionysus/Apollo, for example, since it is currently mounted on a Hellenistic marble altar and positioned in a confined corner of the gallery. Uneven display lighting was also problematic, causing shadowing that was replicated in the photogrammetry (visible in Figure 14, although correctible in the processing stages). Similarly, the pale green paint on the walls of the Randolph Sculpture Gallery initially caused colour distortion in the photography, and so a light reflector was held between the objects and the wall, and a large, portable, daylight lamp strategically positioned to correct the shadowing.

Results

Multispectral photography

The sculptures selected for multispectral analysis were photographed using ultraviolet, infrared, and visible light filters. The results showed that, overall, ultraviolet light was the most successful in allowing the processes of ancient and more recent carving and restoration to be discerned. UV photography revealed that the colossal head was more extensively restored than originally thought, and certainly to a greater degree than can be seen by the naked eye. Plaster was therefore used in the early 20th century to secure an earlier marble restoration that fills the right side of the face, recreating the apparently missing eyes, nose, lips, ears, and a large band around the neck (Figure 7).

Figure 7. From left to right, photographs of the colossal head (ANMichaelis.60) using visible light, ultraviolet and infrared filters © the author.

Interesting results were also achieved in the use of ultraviolet photography on the Roman portrait head which, unusually for the Arundel Collection, bears no signs of attempted modern restoration (Figure 8). Hans Goette includes the head in a list of portraits of the Roman emperor Claudius (AD 41–54) possibly recarved from earlier representations of his assassinated predecessor, Caligula (AD 37–41).[14] The Ashmolean head bears many features usually associated with recarving, including an overly thick neck, evidence of hair at the nape and the sideburns having been tidied up or shortened (portraits of Caligula traditionally having a longer hairstyle than those of Claudius), and retouching of the ears.[15] The ultraviolet light highlighted likely areas of recarving and exposed surfaces that may have been altered more recently than others. This is particularly visible in the hairline where the locks of the fringe appear to have been recut from an earlier formation and the characteristic crab-claw locks of Claudius' Kassel-type portrait sit 'above' the earlier fringe, best seen in the photogrammetry model of the head (Figure 9). Alterations also seem to have taken place around the eyes and the nasolabial folds in an attempt to age the portrait from a man in his twenties to one in his fifties, as again indicated by the colour variations in the ultraviolet photography.[16]

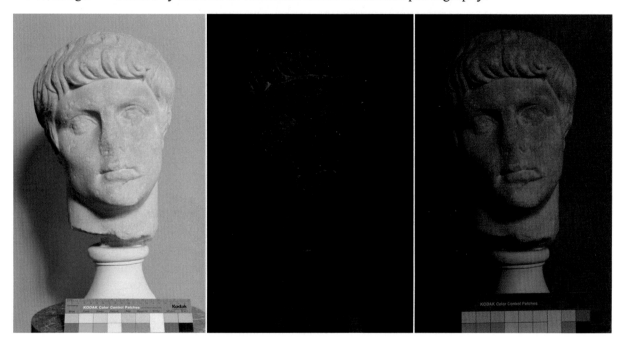

Figure 8. From left to right, photographs of the Roman portrait head (ANMichaelis.69) using visible light, ultraviolet, and infrared filters © the author.

---

[14] Goette 1986.

[15] Discussion and further examples of portrait re-carving in antiquity in Varner 2004.

[16] Kotoula 2015, 20. Further information on the application of ultraviolet imaging in archaeology in Verhoeven and Schmitt 2010.

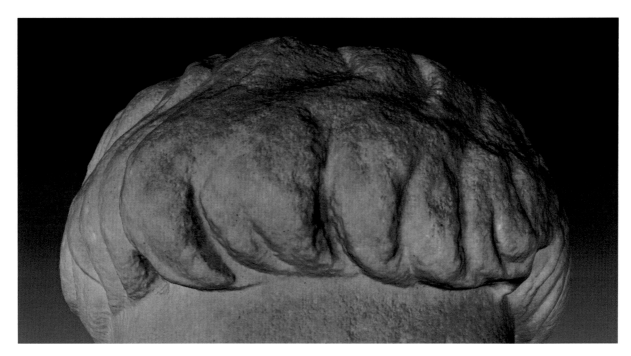

Figure 9. Detail from the photogrammetry model of the Roman portrait head (ANMichaelis.69) © the author.

Infrared photography was unable to reveal any features not already visible to the naked eye since its application is best suited to penetrating painted and encrusted layers, most of which were removed from the marble after years of weathering, restoration works, and cleaning in the early history of the collection. Traces of polychromy, in the form of reddish brown paint (possibly red ochre) visible on the funerary portrait of the doctor's wife Myrtale (ANMichaelis.55), particularly in her hair/wig and on her forehead where the paint has run in the intervening years, are not particularly discernible in the infrared photography (Figure 10). This is probably due to the composition of the ochre itself, since other pigments (Egyptian blue, for example) emit infrared radiation when excited with visible light, as recent analysis on the so-called 'Treu Head' in the British Museum has revealed.[17] Any further investigation into traces of ancient paint on the Arundel Marbles may therefore be better served by the use of ultraviolet- and visible-induced luminescence imaging (UIL and VIL) alongside Raman and Fourier transform infrared (FTIR) spectroscopy, which were together able to confirm the authenticity of the Treu Head and its polychromy. This may prove a particularly fruitful programme of research on the funerary monument in the Ashmolean which, based on the hairstyles of the deceased couple, probably dates to the first decade of the second century AD, thus within the same half century as Treu Head, and with the same city of Rome provenance. As questions have been informally raised pertaining to the authenticity of the tombstone, a similar study relating to the traces of pigment known to have been used in the Roman period may allow us to investigate its true origins, if further funding can be achieved.

---

[17] Verri, Opper, and Deviese 2010.

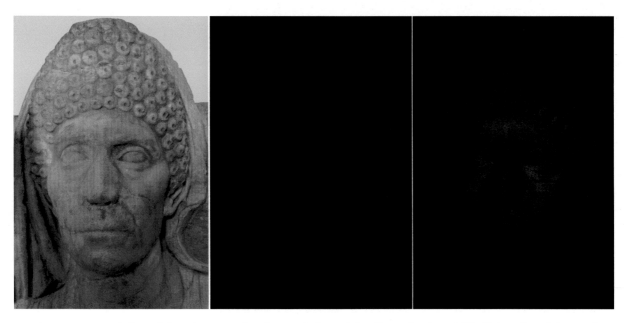

Figure 10. From left to right, photographs of Myrtale (ANMichaelis.155) using visible light, ultraviolet, and infrared filters © the author.

RTI

Although the application of RTI on faded or eroded stone inscriptions is well documented, its use on figural marble sculpture is a relatively new area of investigation.[18] A small number of objects from the collection were therefore selected for analysis based on their potential to reveal ancient and modern tool marks on the surface of the marble, with a view to investigating questions concerning their ancient and more recent biography. With this as the aim, the best results were garnered from the application of RTI to the Roman portrait head that bears damage in the form of a pock marked right cheek. With the light source directed from the right, as shown on the right of Figure 11, we can see that this was not damage inflicted from a tool held perpendicular to the marble but angled more obliquely to it, perhaps indicative of a chisel being struck down the surface of the cheek in a downwards, diagonal direction. Although tempting to think that this is directly related to the proposed changed identity of the subject, the lower cheek is not an obvious site for alteration since the original Caligulan sideburns would not have reached as far down as the indentations, and so may instead simply reflect accidental damage. Similar unexplained damage can also be seen on the left cheek.

---

[18] Several examples are documented as part of the University of Southampton and University of Oxford's RTISAD project - http://acrg.soton.ac.uk/tag/rtisad/.

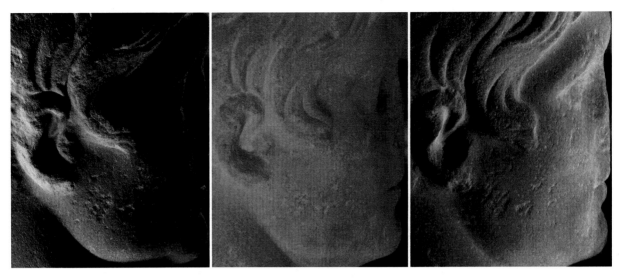

Figure 11. Still shots of the RTI on the Roman portrait head (ANMichaelis.69) with light source raking from left, centre and right © the author.

RTI was also undertaken on several inscriptions from the Arundel Collection that are now displayed throughout the antiquities galleries of the Ashmolean Museum. Since most are mounted and cannot easily be removed from their respective walls (and then, ideally, positioned under an RTI dome) the highlight-based method was employed wherein the objects are photographed in situ and a glossy sphere mounted on a tripod and positioned within the photographic frame.[19] Using this technique, the Greek and Latin funerary inscriptions from the newly-installed 'Garden of Antiquities' were captured and the results will soon be made available through an interactive RTI viewer built into the web resource, alongside translations and a guide to reading Roman tombstones. The Parian Marble (229 BC) had already undergone RTI investigation by the Institute for Digital Archaeology in 2013 and remains a key object for analysis because of the part it plays in the history of the collection and its importance as the earliest surviving chronological table from the Greek world.[20]

Photogrammetry and 3D laser scanning

Photogrammetry and 3D laser scanning were carried out on the sculptures with the aim of creating accurate models for manipulation and remotely-conducted research, and to widen access to the collection by displaying the models and ongoing research pertaining to them on the web resource.[21] Hand-held triangulation scanners proved ideal for recording objects mounted on walls or in constricted locations and did not encounter the same restrictions as the photogrammetry photography, which required the camera to be mounted on a tripod at a fixed distance from each object. The sheer size of the datasets created by the triangulated 3D scans, however, meant that viewing the files in their raw form on standard home or office computers would be problematic—44.5 million cloud points were captured for the funerary relief of the doctor and his wife, resulting in a file

---

[19] Mudge, Malzbender, Shroer and Lum 2006.

[20] It was probably acquired in Smyrna (modern-day Izmir, in Turkey) by William Petty in 1626, and formed part of the shipment of Greek and Latin inscriptions sent to London and subsequently published in John Selden's *Marmora Arundelliana*. The results of the RTI are eagerly anticipated.

[21] Barber and Mills 2011.

size of 2.74 GB. Manual re-work was needed therefore in the later stages of processing to increase efficiency and to help with content editing.

Processing the photogrammetry was similarly time-consuming, and masking the digital models, followed by aligning the photos with the 3D mesh (using Agisoft Photoscan version 1.2.0), and subsequent texturing took around two days per object.[22] Since photogrammetry offers a more affordable alternative to 3D laser scanning, it was selected as the most efficient means to create further digital models after the initial data-capturing day. The 'Oxford Bust' (a 17th-century composite of a Roman head, possibly based on Pheidias' statue of Aphrodite Urania at Elis, and a torso probably reworked from a different Roman bust) produced the most successful photogrammetry model, although it was affected by shadowing beneath the eyes and on the upper torso caused by the Randolph Sculpture Gallery's display lighting.[23] As the sculpture can be carefully rotated on its marble pillar mount, it was possible to capture the hollowed-out reverse of the bust and the back of the head and hair, creating a highly accurate 3D photogrammetry model for remote study and replication as required (Figure 12).

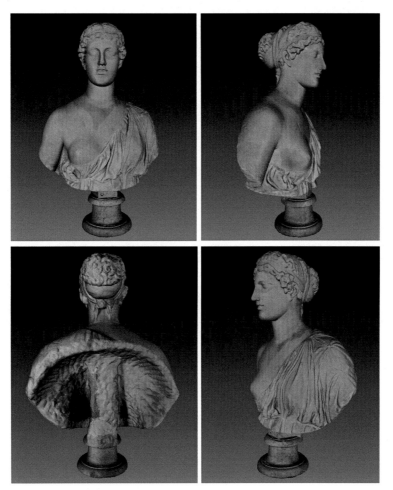

Figure 12. Still shots of the photogrammetry model of the Oxford Bust (ANMichaelis.59) © the author.

---

[22] The level of human intervention necessary in the processing of IBM (Image Based Modelling, in the form of photogrammetry) renders it a less accurate form of recording than 3D laser scanning, see Remondino and El-Hakim 2006.

[23] Vickers 1991; Haynes 1975, 21, pl.17.

Since one of project's objectives was to experiment with the emerging technology and to test its potential usage in the heritage sector, the Randolph Sculpture Gallery was cordoned off and the FARO Focus X330 scanner positioned in various locations around the room in an attempt to capture a full 3D model of the space and its sculpture. As time was limited because the gallery also serves as a connecting passageway between other museum displays, the scanner was unable to record all of the minute architectural and sculptural details in the allocated hour. Nevertheless, the results show how an accurate rendering of the gallery can be produced within a relatively short period of time, and will be converted into an mp4 video made available through the web resource.

Publishing the results: online resource

Since the primary aim of the project was to reinvigorate interest in the Arundel Collection and encourage further exploration into its story and sculpture, the results of the new research, as revealed and illustrated through the 3D models and the multispectral photography, will be made freely available by means of an interactive resource accessed through the Ashmolean Museum website. Developed by Grant Cox of Artas Media, a 3D representation of a 'virtual' section of the Randolph Sculpture Gallery forms the homepage and presents a display of the photogrammetry models of the sculptures created as part of the project. An early prototype of the design can be seen in Figure 13, which is being continually adapted and expanded as the photogrammetry models are processed and published.

Figure 13. Preliminary design of the front page of the web resource © Artas Media.

Using this format, research topics can be highlighted and discussed using relevant objects from the collection as an initial case study, leading on to more detailed pages explaining the technical processes of the analysis and the wider research themes. For example, clicking on the photogrammetry model of the colossal head of Dionysus/Apollo will first lead to a page describing its likely historical context and usage: probably a temple or sanctuary in the eastern Mediterranean in the late Hellenistic period. Visitors are then directed to pages describing ongoing research involving the head, including information about the results of the multispectral analysis and the early 20th-century plaster restorations revealed by the ultraviolet photography, as well as wider discussion of the sculpture's likely part in the shipwreck of 1625. In the same way, clicking on the photogrammetry model of the Parian Marble will reveal contextual information about the object itself and allow visitors to interact with the faded epigraphy through an inbuilt RTI viewer. Associated pages will provide historical information about Henry Howard's gift of 1667 and the display of the Greek and Latin inscriptions in Oxford throughout the late 17th century.

Perhaps the most exciting aspect of virtual modelling using photogrammetry and 3D laser scanning is its potential for the sculptural models to be reimagined in different settings and under varying conditions, allowing the viewer some sense of how they might have been displayed or interacted with over their two millennia or more of existence. Beale and Earl's commentary on the digitization of ancient artefacts plays a crucial role in this discussion:

> In order to develop insightful methods of considering the meanings which have shaped Roman statuary it is necessary to acknowledge our distance from the act of creation and to accept that we can only have a limited concept of the original meaning of statuary without an attempt to untangle the nexus of social, personal and inter-personal contexts that resulted in their creation and re-invention. Statues, then, are not miraculously preserved leftovers from a world which has long gone, but rather contemporary objects which have been subject to, and are records of, the interpretations and decisions of all who have come into contact with them. We argue that the creation of digital surrogates to these statues is therefore a further continuation in their life history.[24]

As the documentation relating to the history of the Arundel Marbles since the early 1600s is largely pictorial in form, it may be possible to reconstruct virtually a number of their display contexts over the centuries. For example, from the very earliest years of the collection is the portrait of Thomas Howard at Arundel House (Figure 2), which offers the potential for 3D reconstruction of the Jacobean sculpture gallery, particularly since all of the statues visible in the painting survive and can be identified in the Ashmolean Museum.[25] Pictorial and literary accounts record the statues and busts on display at Easton Neston in Northamptonshire in 1719; the Greek and Latin inscriptions mounted in bays surrounding the Sheldonian Theatre in Oxford in 1675 and outside the newly-constructed Ashmolean Museum building in 1684, now the Museum of the History of Science; and what were considered the unsaleable pieces from the collection (including two fragments from the Great Altar of Pergamum) adorning a pleasure garden at Lambeth known as Cupid's or Cuper's Gardens.[26]

---

[24] Beale and Earl 2010, 32.

[25] Mytens' representation of the gallery is probably a fanciful imagining of the how the Earl wished the space to look, thus more akin to an Italian palazzo than a Jacobean house. Arundel House itself was demolished in the 1680s. See Chamber 1869, entry for July 7: 'Thomas, Earl of Arundel – The Arundelian Marbles'.

[26] The Easton Neston drawings of Peter Tillemans in Bailey 1996. An engraving by David Loggan from 1675 showing the 'Garden of Antiquities' surrounding the Sheldonian Theatre, and a print by Michael Burghers dating to 1683 detailing an updated version of the 'garden', are currently being analysed by the author regarding their potential to reveal the layout of the inscriptions mounted in the niches. High resolution photography carried out by Anne Holly as part of the redevelopment of the Story of the Ashmolean Museum gallery has greatly facilitated this research and the results will be published in 2018/9. New research into the so-called Cupid's or Cuper's Gardens will be published in Peter Stewart's forthcoming *A Catalogue of the Sculpture Collection at Wilton House*.

The shipwreck

One area of investigation which still remains unresolved is the question of the shipwreck of 1625 which, it seems, almost led to the loss of a significant quantity of sculpture collected on the Aegean islands and in western Turkey by the most prolific of Arundel's agents, the Reverend William Petty. Until the imaging project, the only evidence for the shipwreck was a reference in the correspondence between the English ambassador in Constantinople, Sir Thomas Roe, and Thomas Howard himself, alongside the presence of unusual marble erosion on a number of the sculptures.[27] Roe's letter to Howard, dated to October 1625, documents the activities of Petty in the region:

> Mr Petty hath this while visited Pergamo, Samos, Ephesus, and some other places: where he hath made your Lordship greate provisions ... Mr Petty hath advised me, that returning from Samos, where he had gotten many things, going to Ephesus by sea, he made shipwreck in a great storm upon the coast of Asia; and saving his own life, lost both all his collection of that voidage, and his commands and letters by me procured; desiring me to send him others, or else, that he can proceed no further. He was put in prison for a spy, having lost in the sea all his testimonies; but was released by the witness of Turks that knew him. From thence he recovered Scio, where he furnished himself again; and is gone to the place where he left his boat to fish for the marbles, in hope to find them, and from thence to Ephesus; and this is the last news I heard from him.[28]

Roe's next letter (dated to March 1626) provides an update on the situation:

> My last letters brought your lordship the advice of Mr Petty's shipwreck, and losses upon the coast of Asia, returning from Samos: his commands and letters of recommendation, and his labours, together there perished. The first I presently renewed, and sent them to Smyrna; and the other, I think, he hath by great industry, since recovered. From that time, what adventures he hat passed his own enclosed will give best satisfaction; and it shall suffice me to say in gross, that, although he will not boast to me, yet I am informed he hath gotten many things, rare, and ancient.[29]

The timescale of the correspondence suggests that the ship carrying the sculpture was only 'submerged' for a few months in the summer of 1625, and then recovered by hired sponge divers. The straits of Ephesus were notoriously dangerous at this time of the year because of the strong Etesian wind, and so it seems that Petty was in something of a hurry in his endeavour, sailing at a particularly perilous time of year. This may have been prompted by competition in the form of the agent of the Duke of Buckingham, spurred on by a rivalry between Thomas Howard and the Duke, George Villiers, a keen favourite of James I, which ultimately saw the Earl banished from court until the assassination of Buckingham in 1628.[30]

The erosion visible on several of the Arundel sculptures at the Ashmolean is unusual, taking the form of pockmarks in the marble, but only present in bands and with a clear tidemark on many of the objects. Accounts by visitors to both Arundel House and Easton Neston in the 17th and 18th centuries

---

[27] I remain grateful to the former Sackler Keeper of Antiquities, Susan Walker, for bringing this to my attention.

[28] Letter from Thomas Roe to the Earl of Arundel, October 1625. Roe 1740, 444.

[29] Letter from Thomas Roe to the Earl of Arundel, March 1626. Roe 1740, 495.

[30] Hervey 1921, 279.

confirm that, for prolonged periods of time, much of the collection was displayed in the outdoors, and was therefore exposed to years of rain and wind damage. During the 3D laser scanning of the colossal head, however, a balanus barnacle was located in the hairline of the god, whose presence can only be explained by the object's submersion into seawater. Since balanus barnacles are rapid growing and prefer light and fast-flowing water, it seems likely that the ship carrying the sculptures in 1625 probably ran aground on hidden rocks, causing its hull to crack open and thus exposing the cargo to the current, rather than sinking to the bottom of the sea bed as we might have imagined. This would also explain the tidelines visible on many of the larger statues.[31]

Figure 16. Visualisation of the colossal head during the shipwreck © Artas Media.

A brief note by Adolf Michaelis tantalisingly suggests that further Arundel Marbles—those not in Oxford—might also contribute to this area of investigation. Michaelis cites a letter written by James Theobald to the president of the Society of Antiquaries of London describing excavation of a known burial site of the Arundel Marbles:

> When they were taken up, I was surprised to find sticking to some of them a small sort
> of conical Babani, which convinced me they must have formerly lain in the Sea, where
> those animals had fastened themselves to them as they do rocks and ship bottoms.[32]

If further funding can be achieved, this and other innovative areas of investigation and research into the Arundel Marbles and their fascinating story can finally be undertaken, with the results continually published online for the academic community and the general public. Virtual and interactive reconstructions of historical display contexts, as well as a recreation of the shipwreck itself, have the potential to add to our ongoing understanding of ancient sculpture and collecting in the 17th and 18th centuries, affording the Arundel Marbles the attention long overdue to them.

---

[31] I am indebted to Peter Campbell and Derek Smith for their advice on shipwrecks and sailing in the Aegean.

[32] Howard 1769, 104.

References

Bailey, B. A. (ed.) 1996. *Northamptonshire in the Early Eighteenth Century. The Drawings of Peter Tillemans and Others.* Northampton: Northamptonshire Record Society.

Barber, D. and J. Mills 2011. *3D Laser Scanning for Heritage.* 2nd ed. Swindon: English Heritage.

Beale, G. and G. Earl 2009. The Herculaneum Amazon: Sculptural polychromy, digital simulation and context, in A. Moore, G. Taylor, E. Harris, P. Girdwood and L. Shipley (eds) *TRAC 2009: Proceedings of the Nineteenth Annual Theoretical Roman Archaeology Conference, Michigan and Southampton 2009: 31-40.* Oxford: Oxbow Books.

Bray, W. 1901. *The Diary of John Evelyn. Edited from the original MSS by William Bray, Volume II.* New York: M. Walter Dunne.

Chamber, R. 1869. *The book of days. A miscellany of popular antiquities in connection with the calendar, including anecdote, biography and history, curiosities of literature, and oddities of human life and character.* London: W and R Chambers.

Giometti, C. 1999. Giovanni Battista Guelfi: New Discoveries. *The Sculpture Journal 3: 26–43.*

Goette, H.R. 1986. Antike Skulpturen im Herzog Anton Ulrich-Museum, Braunschweig. *Archäologischer Anzeiger*: 724–8.

Haynes, D. E. L. 1975. *The Arundel Marbles.* Oxford: University of Oxford, Ashmolean Museum.

Hervey, M. F. S. 1921. *The life, correspondence and collections of Thomas Howard, earl of Arundel.* Cambridge: Cambridge University Press.

Howard, C. 1769. *Historical Anecdotes of Some of the Howard Family.* London: Printed by G. Scott for J. Robson.

Hunt, J. D. 1986. *Gardens and grove: the Italian Renaissance garden and the English imagination 1600-1750.* London: Dent.

Johnson, G. W. 1835. *Memoirs of John Selden and notices of the political contest during his time.* London: Orr and Smith.

Kotoula, E. 2015. Virtualizing Conservation: Exploring and Developing Novel Digital Visualizations for Preventative and Remedial Conservation of Artefacts. Unpublished PhD Dissertation. University of Southampton.

Michaelis. A. 1882. *Ancient Marbles in Great Britain.* Cambridge: Cambridge University Press.

Mudge, M., T. Malzbender, C. Shroer and M. Lum. 2006. New Reflection Transformation Imaging methods for rock art and multiple-viewpoint display, in M. Ioannides et al. (eds) *The 37th CIPA International Workshop dedicated on e-Documentation and Standardisation in Cultural Heritage Incorporating: The 7th International Symposium on Virtual Reality, Archaeology and Intelligent Cultural Heritage, the EUROGRAPHICS Workshop on Graphics and Cultural Heritage, the 1st Euro-Med Conference on IT in Cultural Heritage, Nicosia, Cyprus, October 30 - November 4 2006: 195–202.* Airela-Ville: Eurographics Association.

Remondino, F. and S. El-Hakim. 2006. Image-based 3D modelling: A review. *The Photogrammetric Record 21/115: 269–91.* Oxford: Blackwell.

Roe, T. 1740. *The negotiations of Sir Thomas Roe, in his embassy to the Ottoman porte, from the year 1621 to 1628 inclusive: containing ... his correspondences ... And many useful and instructive particulars, ... Now first published from the originals.* London: S. Richardson.

Selden, J. 1679. *Marmora Arundelliana.* London: apud Ioannem Billium.

Varner, E. R. 2004. *Mutilation and Transformation.* Damnatio Memoriae *and Roman Imperial Portraiture.* Leiden: Brill.

Verhoeven, G. J. and K. D. Schmitt. 2010. An attempt to push back frontiers – digitial near-violet aerial archaeology. *Journal of Archaeological Science* 37: 833–45.

Verri, G., T. Opper, and T. Deviese 2010. The 'Treu Head': a case study in Roman sculptural polychromy. *The British Museum Technical Research Bulletin* 4: 39–54.

Vickers, M. 2006. *The Arundel and Pomfret Marbles in Oxford.* Oxford: University of Oxford, Ashmolean Museum.

Vickers, M. 1991. The Oxford Bust. *The Ashmolean* 20: 6–8. Oxford: Ashmolean Museum.

The Khosro Cup Replication Project: 3D imaging for a temporary exhibition[1]

Rachel K. L. Wood

Abstract

The Khosro Cup is an unparalleled 6th-century object from the Sasanian Persian Empire, now part of the collection of the Bibliothèque nationale de France, Paris. Within Sasanian studies, the Cup is arguably the most famous extant artefact, yet outside the field, even within ancient and classical studies, it is relatively unknown. As part of a temporary exhibition in the Ashmolean Museum, the unexpected opportunity arose to create a model of this artefact. Made of rock crystal, glass, garnet, and gold, its materials presented problems both for 3D scanning of the original artefact and for the 3D printing of a model. This chapter outlines the development of the Khosro Cup Replication Project and discusses the challenges in creating the model, the implications of the project, and reactions to its inclusion in a public exhibition. Creating a model for a temporary exhibition necessitated a particular set of priorities driving the process, in many ways unlike those required of other studies of artefacts using digital imaging. The project, however, represents a situation—particularly regarding resources of expertise, time, and money—that could be familiar to other museums and curators, and therefore provide certain insights into other aspects of the integration of digital imaging into our relationships with artefacts. The resulting digital image and physical model present an opportunity for a wider academic audience, students, and the general public to engage with a striking and extremely significant ancient artefact, thereby extending awareness of an important element in the Late Antique picture.

Introduction

In comparison to much research in digital humanities, and the majority of contributions to this volume, this paper outlines a 3D imaging project motivated by a different set of priorities. Those relationships with 3D imaging technologies often are driven by what research questions can be answered using the latest innovations in imaging techniques—usually involving ways to see or present more detailed information about the fabric and manufacture of the objects in question. Here, the desired result was to broaden public engagement with an object and with the cultural history surrounding its creation and biography, acting as an introduction to a side-lined field.

---

[1] This project would not have been possible without the involvement and support of many institutions and individuals: the Leverhulme Trust; Jaś Elsner and my colleagues on the *Empires of Faith* project; St John Simpson and Daniel Pett at The British Museum; Frédérique Duyrat and Mathilde Avisseau-Broustet at the Bibliothèque nationale de France; Trevor Proudfoot, Polly Westlake, Julia Gynn, and Anna Nestrup at Cliveden Conservation; Adam Bloomfield at IPF Ltd; Nicolas Berfini and Boris Lulac at Creaform Ltd; Steven Dey at ThinkSee3D Ltd; and Bert Smith and the Cast Gallery of the Ashmolean Museum. Particular thanks go to the directors of the Ancient World Cluster at Wolfson College, Oxford; and to the Lorne Thyssen Research Fund for Ancient World Topics at Wolfson College and the Soudavar Memorial Foundation for funding the endeavour. Also to Deryck Lamb of Measurement Solutions and Mona Hess, UCL, for initial consultation, and last, but not least, to all those involved in the *Imagining the Divine* exhibition at the Ashmolean Museum.

Made of transparent, translucent, and reflective materials (rock crystal, garnet, green glass, and gold), the Khosro Cup (Figure 1) had never before been the focus of a 3D copying process. For the most part, this was due to difficulties in scanning these materials, as well as obstacles to 3D printing the exact size and shape of the original in materials that could give a sense of the original appearance. This paper outlines the challenges that creating a model presented, how those challenges were tackled, and discusses public reactions to the model's inclusion in an exhibition. How should a copy be presented in a museum context? It was also evident that, to some, the question of *why* a copy should be exhibited alongside ancient artefacts needed to be addressed. What follows is therefore not a technical analysis of the imaging process, but an account from the point of view of a digital imaging newcomer thrust into a project management role, hoping to capitalize on a unique opportunity for public engagement.

The premise

The Khosro Cup Replication Project came about as part of a temporary exhibition in the Ashmolean Museum, Oxford, curated by the British Museum and Oxford University *Empires of Faith* research project, entitled *Imagining the Divine: art and the rise of world religions* (19th October 2017—18th February 2018).[2] The exhibition showed how visual identities that we recognise today as belonging to five distinct religious traditions—Buddhism, Christianity, Hinduism, Islam, and Judaism—were formed during the first millennium AD out of interactions with, and responses to, the artistic traditions of other religions and cultures. Within the section of the exhibition on art in lands under early Islamic rule, we presented a small display on how the earliest Muslim governors and caliphs adopted and adapted aspects of Sasanian Persian royal representation and court culture. Artists under the Umayyad and 'Abbāsid caliphs drew on visual elements popular in the time of their defeated predecessors, the Sasanians; these continuities between early Islamic and Sasanian art often included the patronage of motifs bearing Zoroastrian significance.

Likely made in the 6th century, the Khosro Cup is today part of the collection in the Département des Monnaies, Médailles et Antiques (also known as the Cabinet des Médailles) in the Bibliothèque nationale de France. It was desirable to include the Khosro Cup in the *Imagining the Divine* exhibition because it is an unparalleled representation of the sacred nature of Sasanian kingship. While Sasanian rulers feature frequently on gilded silver vessels, usually depicted hunting or enthroned, the Khosro Cup presents the image of the enthroned king carved into a large rock crystal medallion, inserted in a gold frame, and surrounded by garnet, glass, and rock crystal inserts. Not only is the object aesthetically impressive, contributing colour and intricacy to any display as well as demonstrating high levels of craftsmanship (see Morero et al., this volume), it also is perhaps the most famous piece of Sasanian art extant.

---

[2] Elsner and Lenk et al. 2017.

Figure 1. The original Khosro Cup. Rock crystal, garnet, glass and gold, c. 6ᵗʰ century AD, ?Iran. Bibliothèque nationale de France, inv.379. Image courtesy of the Bibliothèque nationale de France.

For the narrative of the exhibition, the Cup provides a visual representation of the Sasanian concept of universal and sacred kingship, a model of rule that was taken up by early Islamic caliphs after the fall of the Sasanian Empire in AD 651. Each of the three bands of circular inserts increases in size from the centre, as if emanating out from the central rock crystal medallion—emanating from the king. Images of Sasanian kings appear on vessels dating to the early Islamic period, suggesting the adoption of elements of the established Persian court culture and elite dining practices. Imagery of the king at the centre of all things was also key to the Sasanian rulers' self-presentation at the royal court, a mode of behaviour that seems to have been utilised by the early caliphs.[3] The particular Sasanian king most

---

[3] Wood 2017, 206.

likely depicted in the rock crystal relief on the Khosro Cup, Khosro I Anuširvān (r.531–79), was a figure celebrated in later Persian culture, especially epic poetry, as an ideal and just ruler: a quasi-mythical king to be emulated by the contemporary Muslim rulers.[4]

The Khosro Cup also provides a specifically Zoroastrian aspect to the presentation of the Persian *king*. The Sasanian *Shāhanshāh* (Kings of Kings) acted as a proxy for good/light against the forces of evil/dark in the material world (*getig*), as Ahura Mazda battles the evil spirit Angra Mainyu in the spiritual world (*menog*). By carving the central figure into rock crystal, the light shines through the king and suffuses him with light—the most sacred force in Zoroastrianism—creating a visual testament to the sacred nature of kingship. Rosettes, like those carved into each of the circular inserts surrounding the central medallion, are a solar symbol representing light, the most sacred force in Zoroastrianism, the religion of the Sasanian kings. As already mentioned, the rosettes on the circular inserts emanate out from the king in the centre, but, additionally, their arrangement in the alternating clear quartz and deep reddish-pink of the garnets creates a further floral shape of triangular red petals overlapping white with, once again, the king in the centre, emphasising the same message of the king at the centre of blossoming light.

Over the centuries, the arrival of the Khosro Cup in the treasury of the Abbey of Saint-Denis, Paris, was credited to its place among the ensemble of diplomatic gifts from the 'Abbāsid caliph Harun al-Rašid to Charlemagne in 801, bequeathed to the Abbey by Charles the Bald later in the 9th century. The earliest reference to the Cup's presence in the Abbey, however, is in the 13th-century *Grandes Chroniques de France,* which names it the Tasse de Salomon (Cup of Solomon)—how it is often referred to today. Since there is no reference to the Cup in earlier accounts of the Abbey and its treasures, such as in the detailed description by Abbé Suger, abbot of Saint-Denis from 1122–1151, it is more likely that the Cup came to Paris as loot from the sack of Constantinople in 1204 during the Fourth Crusade. How it got to Constantinople—perhaps as gift of Khosro I, one of his Sasanian successors, or an early Islamic ruler, to their contemporary Roman Emperor—remains a mystery.[5] It is likely the association with the Biblical king Solomon, also held up as a just and wise king like the Sasanian Khosro I, developed after the Cup's arrival in a Christian setting, whether Paris or Constantinople.[6]

In light of all these factors, a loan request to the Bibliothèque nationale de France was drawn up. The Khosro Cup is, however, one of the main treasures of the collection, as well as being fragile, and therefore is not available for international loans. To our surprise and delight, however, we were offered the opportunity at the suggestion of the Director of the Département des Monnaies, médailles et antiques, Dr Frédérique Duyrat, to make a 3D scan of the Cup that could be used to create a model for inclusion in *Imagining the Divine*.

---

[4] The king on the Khosro Cup wears a mural crown bearing a crescent on the front. His corymbos (ball of hair on top of the head) is framed by another crescent tied with ribbons that fly out on either side. Above a plain rim, the crown is decorated with a band of small vertical lozenges. The king's hairstyle - clipped beard, long thin moustache, and large bunches of curling hair either side of his head - is typical of many kings. From their portraits on coins, Khosro's father Kavadh I (488–496 and 498–531, the usurper Zamasp (494-499), Khosro I's son Hormizd IV (r.579–590) and great-grandson Kavadh II (r.628) are alternative possibilities. Khosro I usually is the favoured identification because of the longevity, stability, and prosperity of his reign. See Curtis, Askari, and Pendleton 2010.

[5] Shalem 1994.

[6] Fischer 2014, xii, however, notes that Solomon is an ideal and wise ruler in Islamic tradition, also, and therefore the identification could have been made at the caliphal court, or at least the commonality may have contributed to its appropriate nature as a gift to contemporary ruler of another empire.

Why make a copy?

While there is no doubt that displaying the original Khosro Cup would have been the ideal, with that option impossible the new question became whether it was worth attempting to make a copy—especially bearing in mind the absence of experience and knowledge in digital humanities among the curatorial team—or moving on and telling the narrative using different objects. It was decided that the presence of a precise copy of the artefact in the exhibition conveyed the narrative strands mentioned above and provided additional benefits, outlined below. An alternative object, such as a gilded silver plate showing a Sasanian ruler, would not have told such an interesting story, nor attracted the eye in the same way. A replica, therefore, was deemed strong enough to carry these narrative strands and merit a place in the exhibition.

A copy of the Khosro Cup was desirable because it would be able to convey the shape, size, colours, and the translucency of the original artefact. A 2D image would not have the same impact since the Cup is a particularly difficult object to photograph well; the hidden foot, the curvature, the relief carving only on the outside, and, of course, the light passing through it, would all be obscured if presented as a photograph on a gallery wall panel. Several features of the original artefact would, however, over the course of the replication project, ultimately need to be sacrificed. These included primarily, of course, the original materials (rock crystal, gold, garnet, and glass), and therefore the surface texture and the weight. During the exhibition itself, however, a 3D model would provide the additional advantage of an unusual mode of presentation that could engage visitors in a different manner to traditional displays of ancient artefacts. Variety in the modes of presentation of information in exhibitions, whether touch screens, VR displays, projections, or other forms of interactivity, helps to engage viewers in the historical subjects—and maintain that engagement during their visit to the galleries, providing a more memorable experience.

Beyond the physical copy of the Khosro Cup, online access to the digital scan would engage people online, widening access to an aspect of *Imagining the Divine* beyond Oxford in the four month duration of the exhibition, and contributing to the longevity of the project beyond the exhibition's opening. It was also hoped that online content surrounding the creation of the model—whether social media entries, blog posts, or documentary videos—would increase awareness of the exhibition and encourage potential visitors. While advertising the exhibition was an advantage to the specific circumstances of our exhibition, widening access to and awareness of the Khosro Cup to an audience beyond those who visit the Bibliothèque nationale de France, and indeed *Imagining the Divine,* was also a priority. From the commencement of the project in March 2016 to the time of writing, the Bibliothèque nationale de France is undergoing extensive renovations, only likely to re-open to the public after 2020. Therefore it has not been and will not be possible for the general public to view the original Khosro Cup over several years, other than via photographs.

While we came across some curatorial anxiety over what the inclusion of a 3D print might mean for a museum's reputation, it is worth pointing out that the Khosro Cup replica was not the only copy of an artefact to be displayed in the exhibition. The earliest is a large 17th-century oil-painting by Peter Paul Rubens of the first-century Roman Grand Camée de France (another star object in the Cabinet des Médailles, Bibliothèque nationale de France) that triples the scale of the original cameo, allowing for details of the carving to be more easily seen by the naked eye.[7] The other three 'copied' objects in the exhibit replicate the exact size and form of their respective originals. The first is a plaster cast of the second-century Kushan Kanishka Casket, found in the 19th century in what is now Pakistan, one of

---

[7] Ashmolean WA1989.74.

several copies made before the original was returned to Peshawar. The smallest copy of an artefact in the exhibition was made in the 1990s and is a gold electrotype of a so-called Standing Caliph coin of the Umayyad caliph 'Abd al-Malik that was minted in Damascus at the end of the 7th century. The final copy in the *Imagining the Divine* exhibition comes from the British Museum's collection: a resin copy made in 1996 of the whalebone Franks Casket, which was possibly made in Northumbria in the early 8th century. These last two examples also imitate the medium of the originals. This array places the Khosro Cup model as the latest in a line of different media and techniques used to create copies of artefacts for study and the dissemination of historical awareness and knowledge.

Contextualising the Khosro Cup model in a longer-term scheme of cast and copy-making of artefacts will be accentuated after the close of *Imagining the Divine* in February 2018, when the copy joins the collection of the Ashmolean's Cast Gallery. The Cast Gallery, begun in 1884, numbers over 900 casts of mostly Greek and Roman sculpture. There, the Khosro Cup model will be accessible to the general public, free to access, beyond the few months' opening of the temporary *Imagining the Divine* exhibition. It will also be a rather unusual addition, being the only Sasanian artefact in the collection, and representing a very different type of object— a ceremonial bowl—as well as adding a vibrant splash of colour to the collection.

Fortuitously, the production of the Khosro Cup model coincided with the expansion of Oxford University's teaching of the Late Antique Middle East, since two new relevant posts—the Bahari Associate Professor of Sasanian Studies and the I.M. Pei Professor of Islamic Art and Architecture— were established in autumn of 2017. It is hoped the model Khosro Cup will be used in teaching students of Classical and Byzantine art and archaeology, as well as relevant topics in the History Faculty, Oriental Institute, and the History of Art Department. These additional benefits—of the 'legacy' of the exhibition and the *Empires of Faith* research project, of widening interest in Sasanian studies, and access to the resource for the general public as well as students—were strong contributing factors in the motivation to proceed with investigating whether the replication project was feasible.

It is rarely suggested that Rubens' study of the Grand Camée or the plaster versions of sculptures in the Cast Gallery invalidate the authenticity of the Ashmolean's collection. These objects augment the collection and the visitor experience, and are invaluable in raising awareness of the ancient cultures and artistic productions that they represent. As Fiona Cameron argues, the selection of an object to digitize accentuates the artefact's importance rather than diluting its significance and the 'cultural capital' of its home institution.[8] Not only that, but while the post-Enlightenment 19th-century concern with civilization being bound up in, and demonstrated by, material progress remains, the absence of representation of a culture within a museum whose collection implies a world-encompassing view seriously imbalances the projected image of history. In short, while acknowledging that comprehensiveness is unrealistic, if a culture is not represented in material form then that culture is excluded from the institution's story of civilization.[9]

---

[8] Cameron 2006, 57.

[9] Witcomb 2003, 105.

Method

The imperative factor for this project was time. It was necessary to identify early on whether the method could be identified and costed, the funds secured, and model completed in time for the final deadline to confirm the exhibition layout and the publication of the accompanying catalogue. From the initial conception, this allowed a timeframe of approximately 15 months.

Within these firm time constraints, it was necessary to find a method that would cost an amount reasonable to request from funding bodies, as well as the obvious essential task of finding those interested and willing funding bodies, yet would make a copy of high enough standard for our requirements. The priorities among those requirements were to give a viewer an understanding of the visual qualities of the object, namely the precise size and shape of the Cup, including traces of damage, and an effective indication of the materials, transparency, colours, rather than to produce a precise copy that could pass as the original. Weight and surface texture, for example, were secondary features for our purposes.

These priorities meant certain methods and options for 3D printing were discounted, such as a 3D printer that could create an object in multiple colours of clear polymer but only up to a certain size, requiring the model to be printed with a slightly different curvature, to a smaller scale, or printed in separate coloured pieces subsequently fitted together afterwards–the latter being prohibitively expensive. Similarly, while it is possible to 3D print in solid gold, this was hardly an option for our budget. One proposed method would 'restore' the Cup to an idea of its original appearance, such as by replacing the missing inserts, but for our requirements, imitating the precise shape and size was most important, including indicating the imperfections, damage, and ravages of time. This approach no doubt was influenced by the history of cast-making of antiquities, which frequently are missing the colour information or original texture, prioritising the scale and form of the original artefact for the viewer.

The process also needed to be practicable in situ, in a small, controlled environment, since the original Khosro Cup could not leave its place in storage in Paris. It almost goes without saying that in order to be a viable option the process also had to be non-invasive and require little handling and movement of the artefact, leaving no trace. The available route, outlined in detail below, was laser scanning after application of cyclododecane spray powder, followed by printing the model in a clear polymer that could then be painted and gilded by hand.

Scanning

Photogrammetry of gold artefacts has advanced significantly in recent years, but the rock crystal, garnets, and glass of the Khosro Cup made this process untenable and so the available option was laser scanning. Due to the transparent nature of the rock crystal and translucency of the garnets and glass, however, it was necessary to cover the Khosro Cup with a powder that could form a surface for the scanner to identify. Usually for a process such as this, chalk powder would be applied to the surface of the object. Chalk, however, needs to be removed from the surface with water afterwards, which was not an option for the Khosro Cup. Cyclododecane powder, however, presented a viable alternative. Cyclododecane is a neutral substance that when sprayed onto an object forms a water-tight surface, and after a period of time sublimates entirely, leaving no residue. It is used in conservation processes and also in excavations to protect delicate artefacts from the weather or wear during transport.[10]

Although we were warned that cyclododecane might capture less detail than chalk powder, since chalk was not an option this was a gamble we had to take. Due to the layer of cyclododecane, the STL file (Figure 2) would also, of course, be without the colour and texture information from the surface of the original, including the fine detail of the delicate Middle Persian inscription scratched inside the gold foot. One unforeseen aspect to the process concerned the sublimation of the cyclododecane. Articles attesting to the advantages of using cyclododecane powder suggested the sublimation process would take 24–48 hours, but since the Khosro Cup is kept in a conditioned environment at a low temperature and with limited air circulation, the sublimation process instead took several weeks. While not kind to our heart rates, patience was rewarded with the eventual complete sublimation of the cyclododecane.

As one of the most precious artefacts in the Cabinet des Médailles, the Khosro Cup was understandably unable to leave its storage facility and could only be handled by its curator. To resolve this difficulty, we employed Creaform Ltd who have portable handheld scanners that could be taken to the Cabinet des Médailles' storerooms, with the additional advantage that these scanners require no special lighting or significant amount of space in which to operate.[11]

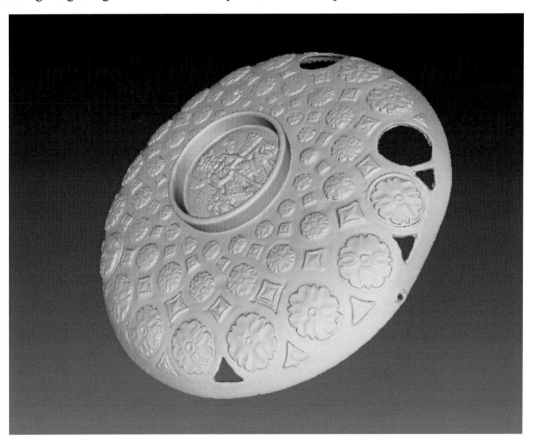

Figure 2. The result of the scanning process. Creaform/Bibliothèque nationale de France.

---

[10] Bruhin 2010; Díaz-Marína et al. 2016.

[11] Go!SCAN 20 was used for this task, but Go!SCAN 50 has a higher resolution and would have been more effective.

Printing

In an effort to combat certain areas of noise created by the compromises to the scanning process, the STL file resulting from the scanning was sent to a 3D imaging company–ThinkSee3D–to tidy and clean for the printing process, thereby counteracting some of the obstruction from the cyclododecane. Since the driving purpose of the model, both physical and digital, was for visual impact rather than, say, precise analysis of the surface, smoothing out the surface of the model by eye was an advantage rather than a problematic issue in this instance. The improvements were marked, and included removing overall noise and sharpening the details of the central figure (see Figure 3). It is clear, however, that this stage is one that, if there had been more time, we would have liked to take further, and a stage that could be returned to for full digital restoration if another model were to be made from the scan. Impending deadlines for other elements of the exhibition that required confirmation of the model's inclusion in the show–such as the catalogue manuscript, label text, and the gallery design itself–cut this process short.

Figure 3. Details from digital cleaning the STL file, showing the original in grey and the processed result in red.
Steven Dey, ThinkSee3D Ltd.

Industrial Plastic Fabrications Ltd printed the model in a transparent polymer resin, Object VeroClear, using a Stratasys Polyjet 3D printer (Figure 4). The Stratasys printer was able to create a model without altering the size or shape of the Cup, and also to maintain the imperfections of the object's structure such as the missing inserts and the holes in the rim.

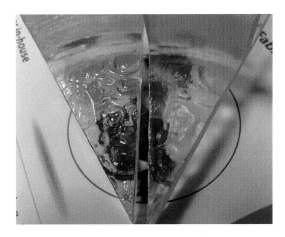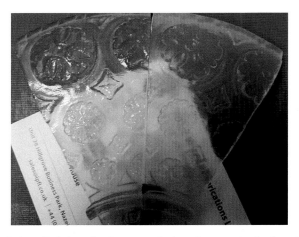

Figure 4. Objet VeroClear test pieces for comparison of gloss (left-hand side examples) and matte (right-hand side examples) finish. Adam Bloomfield, IPF Ltd.

The model was printed with a layer thickness of 16 microns for the highest level of detail to convey the surface carving. A gloss finish was chosen for the upper, outer side of the Cup in order to convey the sheen of the original material as far as possible, but matte finish was necessary for the inner surface of the Cup due to that surface's contact with the support structure during printing. Each layer of the Objet VeroClear was cured in UV light, which creates the structural integrity necessary for the overhangs, holes, and undercuts. Once the model was printed and the support structure removed, a layer of clear lacquer was added to the inner, concave matte surface of the Cup in order to add shine.

We were warned that beyond a certain thickness the material could have a yellowish tinge, but that did not affect our model as the structure is roughly 4 mm thick, which is too thin for any discolouration to be noticeable. The clarity of the polymer improved as the model matured in UV light (daylight) after printing (Figure 5). Another warning was that the model must then be kept out of daylight to prevent it maturing to a yellow tint; a side effect that is not a problem for an object destined to be kept in a museum.[12]

---

[12] With thanks to Steven Dey of ThinkSee3D for this information.

Figure 5a, above. Detail of the central medallion immediately after printing. Adam Bloomfield, IPF Ltd.

Figure 5b, below. The printed model of the Khosro Cup during UV curing (exposure to sunlight). R. Wood.

Colouring

The colouring process was conducted by working from high-resolution photographs at the Cliveden Conservation workshops at Taplow in Buckinghamshire. First, the model was sanded to remove the rough surface created by the cyclododecane and increase the transparency of the Objet VeroClear. After applying masking fluid around the targeted area, water-based airbrush paint was applied to the model to replicate the original colours. During trials, it was found that an airbrush did not enable control of the amount of paint applied, so instead the paint was applied using a pipette. Reducer was added to the paint in order to suggest the translucency of the original. The paint was applied to both sides in order to create depth to the colour. Yellow ochre paint was added to the areas to be gilded in order to create a richness of colour similar to the antique state of the original Cup (Figure 6). Also in preparation for the gilding, Vaseline was added to the painted areas to prevent the gold leaf from straying. Then, on top of the yellow ochre, small pieces of gold leaf were pressed into glue, and, once dry, the excess was brushed off.

In addition to precisely copying details of the Cup's extant state, such as the number and placement of remaining garnet inserts in the rim, it was possible also to imitate the solitary piece of glass in the original that is a slightly different shade from the other green inserts, presumably due to its repair in antiquity (see Figure 7). It was also possible to restore the effect of a broken large garnet circular insert that had been 'fixed' during the scanning process. The Middle Persian inscription scratched into the gold inside the foot of the original Cup, too thin to be observed by the laser scanner–especially after the application of cyclododecane–was imitated by hand. Once finished, several layers of clear lacquer were added to the model in order to imitate the shine of the original materials, as well as to protect the model from UV (Figure 8; Figure 11).

Figure 6. Anna Nestrup of Cliveden Conservation painting and gilding the model. R. Wood.

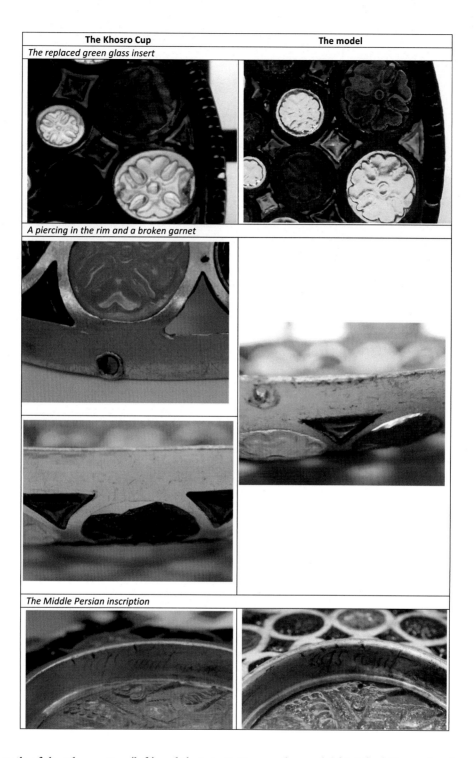

Figure 7. Details of the Khosro Cup (left) and their imitation on the model (right): a) the replaced green glass insert; b) one of four piercings in the gold rim, and a broken large garnet insert; c) the Middle Persian inscription. R. Wood, images of the original by permission of the Bibliothèque nationale de France.

Figure 8. The original Khosro Cup, and the finished model. R. Wood, the former courtesy of the Bibliothèque nationale de France.

In addition to colouring the physical model, we were able to create a coloured 3D digital image, courtesy of ThinkSee3D, by adding the colours, transparency, and surface texture of the original from photographs to the colourless STL file. It was also possible to re-establish some of the holes in the original that were filled in during the scanning process. The coloured 3D image is accessible to the general public on Sketchfab (Figure 9) at:

https://sketchfab.com/models/fe5a660d7abd41b99e9c51c1668c166b

The Khosro Cup

Empires of Faith
+ FOLLOW

+ Add To   Embed   Share

Description   **Model information**

Sasanian gold, garnet, glass, and rock crystal dish.
Département des monnaies, médailles et antiques, Bibliothèque nationale de France, Paris, inv. 379.
6th century? H. 5cm; Diam. 28.2cm; Wgt. 2110g

Figure 9. Screenshot of the 3D model on Sketchfab. By permission of the Bibliothèque nationale de France.

Public feedback[13]

A short questionnaire was given to visitors to the *Imagining the Divine* exhibition in order to gauge responses to the inclusion of a 3D print in a display on the ancient world, and to assess the impact the Khosro Cup model had made on a non-academic audience. While from a brief survey it was difficult to extract too much detail about people's opinions on the matter of displaying a 3D print in an exhibition (Figure 10), the overwhelming response, however, to the inclusion of a replica in situations where the original was not able to leave its collection was positive. The majority of those questioned preferred a physical copy of the object to a photograph in order to get a sense of the depth, size, and, for this object, the luminosity and aesthetic impact of the dramatic colours.[14]

Only two of the 26 people surveyed (8%) viewed the inclusion of any copies in an exhibition as always negative. From this brief snapshot, familiarity with digital technology or museums, or the age of the participant, did not seem to determine their opinion: both people considered themselves comfortable using digital technology, they spanned different age groups, and they occasionally or often frequent museums. The first of these two said they would rather see the original artefact (which, of course, we all would), while the second said that although the model of the Khosro Cup did help their understanding of the issues at hand, they would still prefer not to have copies in museums and that the message could be conveyed by text.

Generally, there were a few concerns raised about authenticity—that any copies should be clearly labelled so as not to deceive the viewer—and the role of museums: that visitors come to a museum to see original artefacts. This latter view plays into that described (and argued against) by Andrea Witcomb, of the museum as a treasury or 'store-house, a centre for the accumulation of material objects, separating them from the life-forces which gave them their original social and political meanings'.[15] There was also on occasion a clear tension visible between differing views among members of the public, with some visitors taking the archaeological approach, wary of added interpretation and restoration, while one visitor was firmly of the opposite view: copies should tell more than the original can (i.e. through informed but imaginative reconstruction).

These points aside, the majority of opinions conveyed agreed that visitors come to museums to learn, and that widening access to knowledge can only be a positive endeavour. Those surveyed engaged particularly with ideas surrounding filling gaps in collections or exhibitions; of broadening exposure to ancient artefacts and culture; of using new methods to engage with people who might not usually be the target audience or who might have become disaffected with traditional display methods (particularly attracting the attention of and inspiring children); and finally, an appreciation of having an additional legacy beyond the opening of a temporary exhibition, and one that can add a new perspective to the Cast Gallery's collection of plaster casts of Greek and Roman sculpture.

---

[13] Feedback gathered from members of the general public from a survey conducted over four hours on a Saturday afternoon, December 2017.

[14] In an ideal situation, the model Cup would have been lit from underneath to accentuate the transparency and luminosity of the object, but, while in the end it was not possible in this exhibition's layout, it was at least a relief to hear that many visitors could appreciate those characteristics from the light falling through the model and onto the case.

[15] Witcomb 2003, 104.

Figure 10. The model Khosro Cup on display in *Imagining the Divine: art and the rise of world religions*, Ashmolean Museum. R. Wood.

A few visitors suggested that they would have liked to have a more detailed presentation of the 3D printing process, such as an information panel or video presentation about the scanning and printing processes. We had also wanted this but were constrained by limitations of space in the gallery, and so a link to three short documentaries and the 3D digital model were provided on the label. One participant suggested they would like to touch the model Khosro Cup, which, although not possible in this exhibition instance, does attest to the tactility suggested by the inclusion of a model rather than a photograph of the original. The sensory aspect of 3D modelling, which can reinforce a point or make it more memorable, is commented upon in numerous studies.[16]

Almost all of the participants in the survey said that the inclusion of the Khosro Cup model had changed their attitudes to the uses of 3D printing for cultural heritage projects and made them aware of the possibilities in new digital imaging technologies for a museum context. This feedback suggests there is an appetite for further inclusion of modern technologies and methods of display that surprise the visitor. Specifically for the narrative of the *Imagining the Divine* exhibition, the majority of participants felt that the inclusion of the model Khosro Cup made them aware of art and culture in the Sasanian Persian Empire, as well as drawing their attention to early Islamic period uses of Sasanian ruler representation and interactions between different religious communities.

---

[16] Cameron 2006, 62; Lakovic 2015; Dey, this volume.

Conclusion

One of the certainties of digital imaging is that the techniques and methods employed for this project will soon be, or are already, out-dated. No doubt, also, that with unpressured time constraints, funding, or prior specialist knowledge and experience, a closer copy of the original object could have been rendered. It is hoped, however, that the details of this endeavour will prove useful to other projects that address similar issues, and demonstrate the accessibility of 3D imaging methods for public engagement projects. The project illustrates how we worked with the available resources of time, money, and specialist knowledge to grasp the window of opportunity resulting in physical and digital additions to the *Imagining the Divine* exhibition, to the Ashmolean's Cast Gallery, and to the online presence of the Khosro Cup. The overwhelming response from academics and the general public has been one of enthusiasm, demonstrating that augmenting a traditional exhibition display with some visual surprises helps to stimulate and engage the viewer in the broader subject matter at hand, as well as completing the primary aim of bringing the original Khosro Cup into wider awareness.

Figure 11. The Khosro Cup model. Ashmolean Museum, University of Oxford.

References

Bruhin, S. 2010. *Le processus de sublimation du cyclododécane.* European Graduated Generation 1. Accessed http://journals.openedition.org/ceroart/1593

Cameron, F. 2006. Beyond the cult of the replicant: museums and historical digital objects-traditional concerns, new discourses, in F. Cameron and S. Kenderdine (eds) *Theorizing Digital Cultural Heritage: A Critical Discourse.* Cambridge, MA: 49–75.

Curtis, V. S., M. E. Askari, and E. J. Pendleton 2010. *Sasanian Coins. A Sylloge of the Sasanian Coins in the National Museum of Iran (Muzeh Melli Iran), Tehran, Volume 1 Ardashir I - Hormizd IV.* Royal Numismatic Society in association with the British Institute of Persian Studies.

Díaz-Marína, C., E. Aura-Castroa, C. Sánchez-Belenguer, and E. Vendrell-Vidal 2016. Cyclododecane as opacifier for digitalization of archaeological glass. *Journal of Cultural Heritage* 17: 131–40.

Elsner, J., S. Lenk, P. Adrych, N. Ali, R. Bracey, K. Cross, D. Dalglish, M. Frenkel, M. Lidova, Y. Sharma, and R. Wood 2017. *Imagining the Divine: art and the rise of world religions* (Ashmolean Press).

Fischer, A. 2014. Introduction, in A. Fischer and I. Wood (eds), *Western perspectives on the Mediterranean: cultural transfer in late antiquity and the early middle ages, 400-800 AD*: ix–xxiv. London: Bloomsbury.

Hess, M. and S. Robson 2013. Re-engineering Watt: a case study and best practice recommendations for 3D colour laser scans and 3D printing in museum artefact documentation, in D. Saunders et al. (eds) *Lasers in the Conservation of Artworks* IX: 154–62. London: Archetype.

Lakovic, N. 2015. 3D printing in education: a framework for learning with 3D artefacts, in *The Fourteenth Conference on Rapid Design, Prototyping and Manufacturing*: 109–118.

Shalem, A. 1994. The Fall of al-Madā'in: Some Literary References concerning Sasanian Spoils of War in Mediaeval Islamic Treasuries. *Iran*: 77–81.

Witcomb, A. 2003. *Reimagining the Museum: beyond the mausoleum.* London: Routledge.

Wood, R. 2017. The Khosro Cup, in J. Elsner S. Lenk, P. Adrych, N. Ali, R. Bracey, K. Cross, D. Dalglish, M. Frenkel, M. Lidova, Y. Sharma, and R. Wood, *Imagining the Divine: art and the rise of world religions*: 206–9. Oxford: Ashmolean Press.